THE VERNE CODE

The secret of the Anunnaki,
Atlantis and the true shape of the
Earth unveiled

Jesús Cediel Monasterio

© Jesús Cediel Monasterio

Madrid 2017

ISBN-13: 978-8461791262

vernecode.com

"Don't believe in anything without question... stay always alert to the possibility that what you believe to be true may not be true and that what you don't believe to be true may be ... but take care that this attitude does not leave you without direction and prevent you from taking decisions and actions throughout your life"

J Cediel

"Tell your mind: I am watching, I am you and not you; I can change you, so you lose your shadows, and find the light."

J. Cediel

To my father and my mother

CONTENTS

PREFACE

IN THE NEWS

On Monday April 26, 2010, *Europa Press* reported on a press conference at the University of Potsdam attended by the British astrophysicist, Stephen Hawking. At the conference, the renowned scientist presented a new series for the *Discovery Channel* called *Into the Universe with Stephen Hawking*.

In this series, Hawking said that "*aliens surely exist*", but advised humanity to avoid contact with them. He claimed that it is perfectly rational to assume the existence of intelligent life in other parts of the Universe, but he warned that aliens would be unlikely to visit Earth with altruistic motives. Instead, he believes that, if aliens visited Earth, the result would be similar to the events which followed Christopher Columbus' arrival in the New World – an encounter from which the indigenous peoples of the Americas most certainly did not benefit.

The professor believes that humans should do everything possible to avoid contact with aliens, rather than actively attempt to communicate with them. In his view, humans only need look at themselves and their own history to understand that contact with another intelligent organism might not be all we hope and desire.

Stephen Hawking is raising these future possibilities on the basis of his mathematical and scientific knowledge, but what would you think if someone told you that the possible future Hawking cautions us against has already happened in the deep history of mankind? That this incursion of aliens on Earth, to extract resources and then leave – with an outcome similar to the fate of the indigenous American societies after Columbus' momentous discovery – was exactly what came about in remote antiquity.

Welcome to THE VERNE CODE...

AN EXTRACT FROM MY DIARY

For several days I have missed what is a regular nightly appointment with my dairy; however, I have to say that this is more than justified given the events that have occurred in the last few days and which I am going to narrate.

On Wednesday morning I woke up a little earlier than usual because I had before me a very important journey. I packed quickly, a small hand bag in which I included sportswear and spare underwear, as well as personal hygiene items. At 8 in the morning I was already behind the wheel of my car, heading in a north-easterly direction.

A landscape of scarce vegetation accompanied me during almost all of the journey. As time went on, even that scarce vegetation gave way to a total absence of greenery. For more than an hour I drove through lonely roads in the desert landscape on the southern slope of the Alto Rey Range.

Finally I arrived at a place where the paved road ceased to exist. This rural landscape was peppered with buildings in ruins, remains of the old mining facilities which in their heyday made the region a prosperous area. I recognized the tool shed that marked the beginning of my journey on foot. I parked the car under an improvised portico, next to a small, rusty old wagon, a memory of earlier times. I took my kit bag and headed off on a sandy trail, and after just a few hundred meters, took another trail that came out toward the right and descended to the river gorge. I went through the gorge, walking alongside beautiful fences made of stone slabs, intended for livestock. Here, the road became a path and required appropriate footwear. Thankfully I had my mountain boots.

For approximately three quarters of an hour I walked up through tiny paths which, in some places, became non-existent. As I ascended, I could see the landscape of the valley, with the picturesque backdrop in the distance, in all its beauty. This eagle eye's view increased the sublime feeling that the experience I was approaching was going to be a very special one.

Suddenly, camouflaged in the rocky landscape, appeared a construction of average size. It was the place where I had agreed to meet don Joaquín. I headed to the door of the eighteenth-century building, a farmhouse made of stone walls, and using the rounded bronze door knocker, I announced my arrival. Not more than fifteen seconds went by before a lady of a certain age, whom I shall call Ofelia, opened the door; her gaze inscrutable, she indicated with a gesture of her hand that I should go in .

- Wait a moment, don Joaquín will soon be with you.

We could describe don Joaquín as a very special being who alternated his work in the fields with his skill as a healer and as an initiating spiritual master. The contact had been provided by the Marquis of Braciel, the last time I visited his office, at the *Plaza de los Cubos* in Madrid. The *Marques* is a spiritualist and recognized psychic within the esoteric community of Madrid, who is said to cooperate with the police in some cases of disappearances. It was he who proposed to me that I should have this experience. His words still echoed in my mind: "Everyone has a mission to fulfill in this existence. I can see in your feline eyes what is to come for you, but I am not going to tell you. Some people have the potential to see for themselves, and that includes you. When this happens we should not interfere in their visions. I will give you a phone number. Call this person and meet him. He knows what has to be done. Trust him."

Suddenly, my thoughts were interrupted; a little man, with sharp looks and an aquiline nose had appeared. With kindness in his eyes, he turned to me:

- Hello, Jesus. Diego told me that you would come today. The others are already inside. Follow me, please.

He made a hand gesture to show I should follow him. We went through a corridor and then down some stairs that led to a kind of chamber whose walls were formed by the rocks of the mountain range.

There I could see two people sitting; they stood up to greet me.

Devi, a woman in her thirties, with a fascinating appearance and Venusian traits; one could divine winding and sensual forms under that large pleated skirt. She greeted me with two kisses on the cheek, as is usual in Spain, which allowed me to appreciate her exquisite taste in fragrances.

Miguel, a man of a certain age but with buzzing energy, was the other person; he greeted me with a handshake, and at the same time mumbled an inaudible:

- how are you?

Once introductions were made, don Joaquín addressed all three of us, adopting a tone of a certain solemnity:

- All of you are here because have been recommended by someone. It is not easy to be here. You have been chosen for some reason that you still don´t know…but during the coming days it will be revealed to you.

- There are some rules that you must respect as if your life depended on it. From this very moment until you leave this house, you will not be able to talk among yourselves under any circumstances; nor with me, unless I tell you. Nor with Ofelia, the lady who welcomed you. You have to understand this as a silent retreat.

- In your room there is a bell. When it rings you must come, at once, to this place where we are now. You will wake up with the sun and will carry out a ritual especially designed to absorb its energy. Each day you will walk around 20 km through these mountains, by a route on which I will personally lead you. You should also, three times a day, perform some breathing exercises that I will teach you. Similarly, you will practice, every day, three periods of psychic centering. You will also have to perform the solar healing ritual every day during its sunset. And I repeat, all of this in the most absolute silence. If someone breaks the silence, even once, he or she will be invited to leave this place. There will be no return.

- Today you will receive some special foods. Tomorrow and the day after tomorrow you will fast. You will be able to drink all the water you need. On Saturday you will get in touch with the mediator.

- And now Ofelia will show you your rooms. We will meet here, in one hour's time. I hope that your stay will be fruitful.

He gestured toward the stairs and we walked back up to the house. The rooms were comfortable but not luxurious, as was expected in a quiet and rustic place. After an hour we returned and don Joaquin spoke to us in more detail about what we were going to do. He demonstrated the breathing exercises and then we went for lunch. In the afternoon we made the first of the walks that we had to do every day. It lasted more than five hours and made us all ready for a good night s sleep.

The following two days continued very much as don Joaquin had indicated to us at our arrival. Physical activity was mixed with adequate resting periods, breathing, meditation and other exercises that would be tedious to describe. The prohibition to speak, rather than isolate us, actually increased our levels of non-verbal communication. The repeated and intense meeting of glances with Devi had a profound meaning which we both understood. I was thinking some quite naughty thoughts. Don Joaquín had forbidden us to talk, but would it be considered breaking the rules to have sex in the most absolute silence?

When Saturday came, the lack of food had not weakened me; on contrary I felt stronger and more energetic, with a greatly increased perception of things. The colors appeared more intense and I appreciated their nuances with more clarity. My senses of hearing and smell also seemed to be waking up from a long lethargy. I could smell the perfume of Devi from my room with the door closed, while she was in her room at the other end of the aisle. From the second night I felt that my sleep was much lighter. Something was changing.

That Saturday afternoon we had to take a bath with purifying plants. The steam began to flood the room and I could feel the deep fragrance of the aromatic herbs. Don Joaquin hung a plastic tarp above the steam, placed some wooden stools in the enclosure he had made and asked us to take our clothes off. Finally he closed the top opening with a kind of gate. We found ourselves in something between a cleansing steam bath and a sweat lodge. While we made the psychic centering, we sweated and sweated. Don Joaquin told us when we needed to come out for a while and when to return to the bath. The minutes became hours. I believe that five hours went by when, finall , don Joaquín addressed us:

- Now you are going to get in touch with the mediator. The mediator is both a plant root and a nature spirit, which will help you to contact the highest levels of cosmic consciousness. As contradictory as it may seem, it will help you to make a journey through your own unconscious. Make conscious the unconscious; that is the secret. Each one of you will receive appropriate answers to questions that have never been asked; that is the law.

- The potion that you will take is bitter but heady and you will remember its effects with great joy, in the years to come. No one knows what experience or vision the mediator will decide to put you through. Whatever it may be, it is just what you need, although at first you may not understand. Allow the soul of the mediator to take hold of you because its power is great; to resist would only obscure the experience. If you feel that you have to vomit, feel free to use the buckets that are placed in your rooms.

- Now drink what I offer you and then go to your rooms, leaving the door open; lie down on the bed, relax and do the breathing exercises I have shown you. The rest is yet to come. I will look after your dreams.

The enigmatic words of don Joaquin were wrapped in tenderness and kindness, so that we all felt very safe.

After having drunk the potion we turned to our rooms. The three of us said goodbye to each other with a look. The sweetness of the gaze of Devi contrasted with the bitterness of the potion that we had just drunk.

The night promised very warm. I lay down on the bed, completely naked. I could hear my heartbeat, so I start building the respiratory rate that don Joaquin had taught us. Breathe in, hold, breathe out ... again and again. The perception of my heartbeat was very present, but at some point that I do not remember, this ceased to be the center of attention and I began to see circles and geometric shapes, in black and white, gleaming; then vivid colors moving from left to right, up and down, turning. After that, faces coming toward me... and then darkness and silence.

Suddenly, a spiral of colored light began to dance around me. It opened me up to a vision without limits; everything was light, peaceful and joyful. And having seen it, I fell in love with it. I felt that everything was revealed instantly before me. I saw my deceased mother looking at me with a sweet smile. I was overwhelmed by a feeling of great joy.

Once again, unknown faces coming and going.

Faces that came and went...but all of them seemed to be equal...

Unexpectedly, I saw a human figure in front of me. It had a welcoming countenance with wide brows and unkempt white hair, gray beard and moustache. The expression was fatherly and friendly, which transmitted calmness and serenity. He looked at me with an enigmatic smile.

"Don´t you know who I am?" He said without moving his lips; he spoke only with his eyes.

I could hear him… although he did not speak.

"Who are you?" I thought. And then I felt that the enigmatic expression said: "You know who I am but do not remember. Let me come closer. And think of your fifteenth birthda ."

He could read my thoughts. Or maybe I should say that we had established telepathic communication.

My fifteenth birthday? A warm swirl of images began to hover around me. My dearest friends from that time, laughing and singing. Gifts. Poems. Songs. And a book…

Suddenly I knew who I was seeing. I knew who I was talking with. Yes, it was him …unmistakable, dressed in his nineteenth-century costume. I had before my eyes the master of science fiction of the nineteenth century: Jules Verne.

"Are you truly Verne?" I thought. And he, guessing my thoughts, simply made an affirmative gesture with his head

It was then that he approached closer and with a gesture of his hand, indicated me to follow him.

What happened after that is still confusing to me. I heard a sound similar to that made by an aircraft landing at an airport, strong and intense. And then I felt as if I was filled with light. At the same time, I experienced a state of great inner peace, love and appreciation. It seemed as if time had stopped. The colors were becoming increasingly intense, louder sounds and there was lots of light, lots of light….

I began to see images of planets moving through space. Images of the beginning of time. Everything was so clear, like on a huge, four-dimensional film-screen. I was within the movie, could touch it, could see it and I could smell it… but I have to say that I did not feel any fear. I felt protected by my mysterious companion.

So I was able to see incredible visions. I saw living planets talking among themselves. They smiled, shouted at each other... and fought. I saw a violent collision between two of them, while the rest cheered. It was a moving experience, and very real, colorful... and noisy. And in spite of the violence that followed, it curiously brought me peace and tranquility.

Then I began to see many spacecraft traveling at impossible speeds.

I heard a great explosion.

Terrified men running away. Women shouting. And behind them winged giants with beastly expressions.

And a huge wave which invaded and crushed everything.

And after the storm, the calm. The sun came out.

I also saw a ship docking in a port as I have never ever seen. Crossing a sort of giant waterfall, which drew a rainbow formed of unknown colors. And then the boat was sailing a channel that went through beautiful gardens and circles of water. I counted up to seven gates in the channel.

At that time I realized that the mysterious character, who guided me through this journey, was smiling with complicity. I was beginning to understand...without a word.

"The time has come for certain hidden knowledge to be revealed to humanity. You have been chosen to begin its dissemination. The incoming Aquarian Age will bring revolutionary changes for society as a whole. To achieve this change in the near future it is necessary for society to know what really happened in the past, so they can stop living in an illusory world. People, today, have created a golden calf with two heads: science and the internet. They believe that science has progressed so far that everything is known and they do not doubt that what they are offered is the authentic truth. They do not realize that they have been deceived. They are like the children of Hamelin, hypnotized by the trickster sound of the strange music that comes from the charmed flute which brings them walking and singing with joy, without suspecting that they are heading for the cliff over the waters of the river Weser, where they will drown."

Again I was invaded by a whirlwind of colors and light that penetrated my body.

I was able to observe strange beings manipulating simian forms. A snake fighting against a ram. And tremendous explosions. And screams…

"Go back and reread the book that was given to you on your fifteenth birthday. Read the dedications written by your friends at the time. The book will inspire you and I will be behind you to guide your pen."

"You know me as Jules Verne, although I have also been known by other names in other times and places. In Ancient Greece I was a beacon of light for humanity."

Then, I saw how the image of the mysterious character that had accompanied me until that moment was faltering and transformed. The beard grew in length, at the same time as the brow narrowed and the hair was shortened. The gray suit gave way to a broad white tunic. And I saw him speaking in a courtyard surrounded by Doric columns, while a group of people listened to him with rapt attention.

Then his image began to fade between the columns and the crowd. So I searched for him around the whole square. There was a large crowd. I was looking for him in each group of people but could not find him. I was shaken because I did not want to lose him, but he appeared to have vanished, never to return.

Suddenly I felt a breath of fresh air on my forehead and heard a voice that whispered:

- Calm, everything has gone well.

I saw don Joaquin at my side. I knew that I had just returned from the trip.

- You have been unconscious for more than 12 hours, he said, at the same time placing a damp cloth on my forehead.

- The bowl, as you can see, is completely clean. You have not vomited even once. This happens only on very rare occasions. Congratulations, you are clean. Drink this tea that I have prepared and rest a little.

A couple of hours later, don Joaquín gathered all of us together, this time in the porch of the house. There he spoke to us his last words and made his farewell:

- What has been unveiled to you might not find meaning now, but I can assure you that it will, in time. Once you have come in contact with the mediator, it never leaves you. I wish you a pleasant trip back to your worldly obligations; may the light be with you.

I have just returned home. It is late in the night but I am completely awake, and a multitude of images assault my mind. Had all these so vivid images been simply the result of my imagination?

Something had happened that had changed my relationship with life and the Universe. I could feel now how I formed a part of the whole. I understood without using my analytic mind. I felt I was real in all those times and in all those places. I experienced unity with everything that surrounds me.

And now, most importantly, I know that I have something to do. Tomorrow I will begin to reread the book that my friends gave me for my fifteenth birthday

CHAPTER I

ON MYTHS AND SCIENCE

The scientists of today think deeply instead of clearly. One must be sane to think clearly, but one can think deeply and be quite insane.

Nikola Tesla, Serbian Physicist (1856-1943)

T he dictionary of the *Royal Academy of the Spanish Language* defines "myth" as a wonderful narrative located outside historical time and featuring divine or heroic characters. The myths of ancient civilizations and cultures are, in general, despised by scientists. Using a well-known example, they reject the existence of a Universal Deluge, seeing it as a mere fable, while they ignore the large number of stories from many cultures around the world, all sharing a common subject: a prehistoric cataclysm that virtually eliminated humanity from the surface of the Earth. We must ask the question: was the Universal Deluge a real event? If so, was there a civilization which predated those that are historically recognized?

The thesis of the Universal Deluge is not considered intellectually respectable by the scientific establishment. However, is the scientific community impartial and objective on this subject? Are they rigorously following their own scientific principles and methodologies?

Throughout the history of mankind, science has given more weight to theories than to the facts required to validate them. However, theories should be derived from facts and not vice versa, as the emergence of new data has the potential to change or to disprove theories which had been considered certainties. This is where the problem arises, as this new information is often ignored by the academics. Science labels data that does not corroborate the official theory, "anomalous facts", or "evidence that does not fit". Michael Cremo and Richard Thompson, in their book, *Forbidden Archaeology*, argue that this is exactly what has happened with some of the archaeological findings of the last 150 years, which contradict the theories officially accepted by the global scientific community.

This phenomenon is characterized by a "filtering of knowledge", which results in the researcher paying attention, exclusively, to the data which is favorable to his thesis and, as a result, drawing conclusions that are consistent with that thesis; in doing so, he ignores any data which is opposed to the idea or theory that he seeks to validate. This is a fundamental characteristic of human nature, and we must not forget that scientists are human beings. The consequence is that the majority of scientists tend to eliminate the data that does not agree with the dominant paradigm in their moment of history. Archaeologists see a coherent picture in the analysis of their findings, but this consistency is due to the fact that they discard the evidence which does not fit their predetermined model.

> *The experimenter who does not know what he is looking for will not understand what he finds.*
> Claude Bernard, French Physiologist (1813-1878)

This tendency becomes easily identifiable if we consider the history of science retrospectively. Scientists have always followed this practice and it has been repeated on a cyclical basis. First, there is a scientific paradigm or dominant theory that is accepted by the overwhelming majority of scientists or thinkers. Suddenly, one or several researchers or thinkers appear who contradict the widely accepted orthodoxy. This, in turn, provokes a reactionary movement against them from the wider scientific community, which may do considerable harm to the newcomers. With the passage of time, the proponents of the new theory grow in number, until a critical mass is achieved sufficient to overthrow the dominant theory, thus altering the scientific paradigm. A new scientific truth does not usually succeed through convincing its opponents with reasoned argument, but rather because those aligned to the previously dominant theory are replaced by a new generation of scientists who are sympathetic to the new theory. Once this process is complete, the new theory will become the new scientific paradigm.

History will tell if these pioneers were ahead of their time but, in the end, it all comes down to simple arithmetic, the number of people in favor of a theory or not, as if knowledge and truth could be reduced to a mere majority vote. In essence, it does not seem that the bulk of scientists act in a very scientific way; rather, they are subject to continuous, generational struggles of power and influence

A scientific truth does not triumph by convincing its opponents, but rather because its opponents eventually die and a new generation grows up that is familiar with it.
                    Max Planck, German Physicist (1858-1947)

An illustration of this, one of many examples, is the state of physics at the end of the nineteenth century. At that time, physics was proud to be a stable and mature scientific discipline, with only some details left to be refined. As Lord Kelvin confidently asserted in 1900, *"There is nothing new to be discovered in physics now. All that remains is more and more precise measurement."* Five years later, Albert Einstein published his research on special relativity, establishing a simple set of physical laws that revolutionized the Newtonian mechanics which had governed force and movement for the preceding two centuries.

At the beginning of the twenty-first century, the culture of academic circles has not changed. There is no debate about facts which contradict the dominant paradigm. Such data are not openly discussed in the scientific community. Those best qualified to assess new data are far more likely to ignore them because they are not taught in the centers of learning. What is more, the researchers who persist in approaches contrary to the official line, even when presenting incontrovertible data, are stigmatized and marginalized by the community, in which the dominant paradigm prevails. In many cases, this can ruin their careers.

> *How is that little children are so intelligent and men so stupid?*
> *It must be education that does it.*
> > Alexandre Dumas, *fils*, French writer and dramatist
> > (1824-1895)

However, nobody should think that I am suggesting a deliberate conspiracy, in the sense that a group of people gather in a boardroom and decide on a plan to deceive people. Rather it is something unpremeditated and unconscious that happens automatically, in society in general, and in the academic community in particular. This impersonal network relies on a human means of transmission, those with an academic background who might qualify as "hypnotized hypnotists"; as well as the media, whose unconscious mission is to maintain the intellect of the community in restful sleep, allowing the transmission of only those ideas considered truths, without encouraging the awakening of the free thinker (see appendix A and C).

To this condition of collective hypnotic trance must be added the current trend of increasing specialization by scientists and scholars and, as a result, the significant shortage of researchers capable of integrating different specialties in a multidisciplinary initiative that might make it possible to achieve a truly global vision. For this reason, there are many scientists who, despite possessing a formidable level of knowledge in their chosen specialty, are unable to comprehend the situation as a whole. To paraphrase Danny Kaye, the US singer and comedian, you might say that "there are researchers who know more about less, until they end up knowing everything about nothing and nothing about everything."

> *It is better to know something about everything than everything about something.*
> > Blaise Pascal, French scientist and philosopher
> > (1623-1662)

The official version of history, taken as fact in academic circles, is based on the belief that civilization has achieved continuously higher levels of organization, harmony and knowledge over time; thus, according to this assumption, the further we go back in time, the greater should be the disorganization that we find. However, what I have found in my research is precisely the opposite; the more I immersed myself in remote antiquity the greater was the harmony and knowledge I found, something which seemed to go against all logic.

Let's look at a few examples to illustrate this. In our time, Nicolaus Copernicus is characterized in academic textbooks as being ahead of his time for his discovery, in the sixteenth century, that the Earth is a planet that rotates on its axis while orbiting the Sun. What is not reported is that he based his work on millennia of astronomical works which postulated that the Earth was not flat but spherical. These were the same sources that Christopher Columbus had studied and used in his journey to the Americas, and were based on ancient Greek and Roman traditions. Copernicus studied in detail the work of the Greek astronomers Hipparchus of Nicaea and Aristarchus of Samos. The latter, in the third century BC, explained the movements of the planets by positioning the Sun at the center and not the Earth. Hipparchus of Nicaea, director of the Library of Alexandria in the second century BC, had a perfect understanding of the astronomical phenomenon known today as the "precession of the equinoxes", something that can only be explained with the knowledge that the Earth is spherical. The astronomers of the third century BC had a better technical understanding than the astronomers of the year 400 or even 1500. Therefore, Copernicus only rediscovered the heliocentric concept that was already known to the Greeks. Now the question is, were the Greeks the first to reach this conclusion or were they also inspired by older sources?

In a further example, in 1996, the British scientific journal *Nature* astonished the world with the publication of an article describing a method to clone an unlimited number of sheep from a single fertilized egg. Dolly the sheep became an instant star and cloning went from a science-fiction fantasy to a very real scientific possibility. A week later, the publishers wrote an editorial in which they predicted an imminent revolution in genetics and reproductive biology technologies, and discussed the impact this would have on society. Amongst other things they said:

The growing power of molecular genetics confronts us with the future possibility of being able to change the nature of our species.

Today, the annals of science describe how, for the first time in the history of mankind, a team of scientists led by Ian Wilmut and Keith Campbell made a momentous scientific advance, with the cloning of Dolly the sheep at the Roslin Institute. It is considered a turning point because scientists now had absolute control over what they were creating; the technique was applicable to other mammals, and had therefore brought us to the brink of human cloning; although this final step would only be achieved, according to them, in combination with advances in genetic engineering. This breakthrough would allow us to alter genes to the extent that humanity would enter the era of animal design; with the result that tailor-made organisms might be designed and engineered in the laboratory. What if, however, as was the case with Copernicus, these scientists were not the first in history to understand and to use these techniques of cloning and assisted reproduction?

For the last five hundred years, science has been rediscovering and reinventing ancient concepts. In this book I will discuss the truth behind these great scientific advances: penicillin before Fleming, air travel before the Wright brothers, accurate ancient maps of parts of the Earth only 'discovered' in the twentieth century, a detailed understanding of the human genome before Craig Venter, cloning before Dolly, nuclear explosions before Hiroshima and Nagasaki, the quest for immortality before the Geron Corporation and an endless, yet hitherto unknown, deep past, just shocking and inconceivable enough to be true.

There are many questions to pose and enigmas to consider but, until now, there has never been the weight of evidence to justifiably reach unconventional answers. Regrettably, very few scientists are able to consider this subject without prejudice, leaving only those with a genuinely scientific approach in that they do not exclude any possibility, however strange or contradictory it might seem. The alternative is to allow oneself to be guided by belief, something which may be respectable but is certainly not scientific

Writing this book could be said to be daring on my part, but it is no less daring to read it. Dear reader, if you are comfortable with the orthodox belief that the human species evolved slowly from ignorant cave man to the sophisticated modern citizen of the great metropolises of the twenty-first century, this book is not for you; but if, despite this warning, you decide to continue reading, you should consider the possibility that the world and history as we know it are not all that they seem, and you should prepare to be amazed by what you are about to discover.

In the origins of every legend, tradition or myth there is a grain of truth, a foundation upon which the popular imagination has constructed a fantastical edifice while deforming, embellishing and sublimating the truth through the slow process of transmission over generations. To study ancient traditions and popular folklore is the easiest path to knowledge; one that is reserved for those with sufficient respect and courage to examine them without prejudice. If you possess these qualities, I have no doubt that you will enjoy what follows. If, on the other hand, you do not have the strength to cast aside old ways of thinking and to open your mind to new possibilities, I suggest you read no further.

CHAPTER II

SIZE REALLY MATTERS

Even if you are in a minority of one, the truth is still the truth
Gandhi, Hindu thinker (1869-1948)

Throughout its existence, humanity has possessed an innate sense of spiritual transcendence, an inner strength that impels us to search for lost knowledge, to recover our original unity with the intrinsic spiritual essence of the Universe. Man has tried, through several means such as religion, yoga, philosophy and modern science, to find a sense of meaning in his life and his place in the Cosmos.

Although these are different systems of knowledge, their essential purpose is always the same, as can be seen if we analyze their etymological origins. The word religion comes from the Latin *religare*, meaning "to bind, to join". The Sanskrit word yoga means "union, tying together". The discipline of philosophy, translated from the Greek *philosophia*, means "love of wisdom; pursuit of knowledge", while the term science derives from the Latin *scire* or "to know". From a broader perspective, we can identify a common denominator in all these systems and, if we transcend language and its semantic connotations, we may discern that man is, ultimately, a seeker of lost knowledge.

At this point, well into the twenty-first century, a new form of religion has emerged in force across the globe, and in western societies in particular.

This new form of religion, called "science" or "scientific knowledge", has led to the retreat of ancestral religions. Man may feel proud because, for the first time, knowledge does not come by the hand and grace of God, but as a result of our own efforts and our seeking after knowledge. There is no longer a central place for the revealed knowledge once universally respected and venerated. Objective and rational systems of thought have instead been imposed. Certainly, much progress has been made in this area in recent times.

When reflect ng on the scientific advances achieved by mankind, one of the things of which modern *Homo sapiens* may be most proud is, without doubt, our system of measurement: an accurate and reliable system carried to infinitesimal extremes. We can now measure distance and time with a precision that is close to perfect and, at the same time, the system can be understood and used by everybody, with all the benefits that flow from thi

This was not always the case. Until little more than two centuries ago, systems of measurement were not at all as precise as they are today. Each country, each region and, sometimes, even each village, had their own system of measures. There were no exact and universal methods; in fact, a hypothetical traveler crossing Europe from north to south had to change not only language and coins, but also measures, as, at that time, a unit of measurement in London was not the same as it was in Paris, Berlin or Madrid. The inevitable confusion was brought to the extreme by the fact that different measures even shared the same name. Coins were minted with different weights and sizes in each place; so when traveling to a different region or country, the first thing that a traveler had to do on his arrival was to weigh the amount of gold he carried to know what exactly the value of that currency was. As a result of these disjointed systems, the money changers made a killing, determining the value of coins and providing foreign exchange for the trader.

The French did not escape this chaotic situation. France is one of the oldest states in Europe although it only acquired this name during the Middle Ages; the exact date is difficult to determine. It had already become an administrative unit under the Roman Empire, with a slightly larger area than its current borders, under the name of "Gaul". The fall of the Roman Empire and the subsequent mass migrations of nomadic tribes from the east led to the fragmentation of the territory into small states which, as a result of conquest and dynastic marriage in the Middle Ages, were reunited in the form we know today as France.

The result of this fragmentation, as in the rest of Europe, was a real mishmash of units of length, weight and volume, coexisting across the new state. An example of the chaos and arbitrariness of the French system of measures at that time is the *toise*, the main unit of length. It was equal to six *pied du rois* (the king's foot), which originated in the Middle Ages as the distance between the big toe of the monarch and his heel. By the early eighteenth century this measurement was defined as *four palms*, or the width of the four longer fingers of the right hand, placed together flat on a table. You can imagine astute merchants measuring with the skinniest hand they could find to maximize their profits. For the measurement of volume, the situation was even more confused. The *bichet*, a measurement used for grain, ranged from 20 to 40 liters depending on the region. One can imagine the fortunes that some unscrupulous traders amassed at that time.

The problem of translating measures from one country (or region) to another was commonplace and prevented efficient communication between researchers of different nationalities, which had a pernicious effect on scientific progress. Some scientists had long attempted to solve this thorny problem, but they were often ignored. In 1670, Jean Picard, a French priest, who had, for the first time, measured the distance between two meridians, proposed that the Academy of Sciences adopt a measurement called the *virga*, which corresponded to a defined fraction of the terrestrial meridian. The following year, he proposed they adopt a new unit of measurement defined by the distance traveled by a pendulum in a second. In this way, a race began between the two systems to define a universal unit of measurement.

The first to define the concept of the "pendulum of seconds" was Galileo. Isaac Newton later calculated that a pendulum located at 45° latitude, swinging freely from one end to the other, would travel a distance of

39.14912 inches. By Picard's time, it was already understood that the force of gravity, which affected the result, was not equal in every location but depended on the latitude at which the pendulum was placed; as such, different locations were considered, although French astronomers, in a display of chauvinism, were inclined to place the so-called "pendulum of seconds" in Paris.

In the eighteenth century, with the emergence of more precise astronomical equipment, new ideas in the field began to multiply. Meanwhile, the Academy of Sciences had not yet decided which system to use for the creation of the new unit of measurement; that based on fractions of the terrestrial meridian or on the movement of the pendulum. The storming of the Bastille on July 14, 1789, was the moment that would change history forever. The system of measurement also benefited from the revolutionary effect. The Constituent Assembly in France created a commission composed of brilliant scientists, with the purpose of studying the viability of a new metric system. The commission decided (though not unanimously) to abandon the concept of the "pendulum of seconds" as the foundation of a new linear measurement, because there was no stopwatch capable of measuring a second of time with total accuracy. With that, the "pendulum of seconds" was relegated to the proverbial back of the cupboard to await its time.

With this matter decided, a system based on the measurement of a terrestrial meridian was adopted. Clearly the method's proponents did not think that it would be possible to measure a terrestrial meridian in its entirety, at a time when reaching the poles was the stuff of fiction. The distance between the cities of Dunkirk, north of Paris, and Barcelona in Spain (a precise measurement of only nine and a half degrees) was used to calculate the total length of the meridian. The new unit of measurement was named the "meter" and was defined as a ten-millionth of the quadrant of a meridian or, in other words, a forty-millionth of the Earth's polar circumference.

The commission's report showed only a tiny difference between the two competing systems: the "pendulum of seconds" and the measurement of meridian. In fact the meter, corrected using the pendulum system of seconds, began its official existence on December 10, 1799. Once the length of the meter had been officially determined, the largest linear unit, of 1000 meters, was defined as the "kilometer", and a thousandth of the meter as a "millimeter". The units for volume and mass were derived from these linear metrics. A cubic receptacle of the dimensions 10 cm x 10 cm x 10 cm filled with distilled water was used to define the "liter" as a unit of volume, and the "kilogram" was derived from the weight of its contents. The commission ordered the creation of an official template of the meter, crafted in platinum, as well as a cylinder to be the template of a kilogram. These were preserved in the archives of the Republic until they were replaced in 1889 by others created with greater precision, in platinum and iridium, which served as the international standard until displaced by new scientific methods

Today, the meter is defined as the distance that light travels in 1/299,792,458 of a second. We now have instrumentation of sufficient sensitivity to measure such tiny events, but the reality is that, behind this sophisticated definition, the primitive pendulum of seconds remains. It would seem that we are witnessing the latest and greatest advances in human society and civilization; but what if things are not as they appear? What if this knowledge was already known to earlier civilizations?

To answer these questions, I invite you on a voyage back through time to the end of the nineteenth century. Ernest de Sarzec, official of the French consulate, had a consuming interest in oriental art and had visited many archaeological sites during his stay in the land of the Nile, Egypt, but he lacked experience as a digger. When, in 1877, he was posted to Basra on the Persian Gulf, a sleepy place at the time, he spent his time buying clay tablets in the local antique shops until, finall , he decided to excavate in the area of the ancient city of Lagash. His excavations soon resulted in the discovery of bricks, walls, temples, clay tablets and statues. Sarzec quickly realized that he had discovered a Mesopotamian civilization older even than the already well-known Babylonian and Assyrian kingdoms, located further to the north. Although he was not a professional archaeologist, we owe to him the definitive discovery of the Sumerian civilization, until then known only by vague references in Babylonian cuneiform tablets.

**Figure 2.1 One of the diorite statues of King Gudea found in
Sarzec's excavations**

Among the objects found by Sarzec were two diorite statues of
King Gudea, holding a tablet on his knees on which is depicted the
architectural diagram of a temple; while on the side there is a carefully
graduated rule that defines the measurement "medium *Kush*" with a
value of 24.97 cm. The general consensus is that the *Kush* or "barley
cubit" (which corresponds to two "medium Kush") was the main unit of
linear measurement during the Sumerian period. Although there are not
sufficient archaeological findings available for definitive study, we can
say that the "double *Kush*" is significantly close to the modern meter.
The data found reveal that the *Kush* had a value of 49.94 cm and that the
widely used "double *Kush*" had, according to Professor Livio Stecchini,
a value of 99.88 cm. All this supports the thesis that the Sumerians,
six thousand years ago, already knew and used the meter as a unit of
measurement. Pure coincidence? Or, on the contrary, might there be
another explanation?

The *Kush* or "barley cubit" was composed of 180 *se* or "barley seeds".
It was also split into 30 *shu-si* or "hands" of 6 *se* each. Researchers
Christopher Knight and Alan Butler decided to look deeper, to see if

there was some truth in this uncanny similarity between the modern meter and the Sumerian system, or if it was mere fantasy. Since the barley seed did not seem to have changed since the height of the Sumerian civilization, they decided to carry out a very simple experiment, as they explain in their book *The First Civilization*. They placed a number of barley seeds in rows next to one another on a transparent, graduated tape and noted that, if they placed the grains touching end to end, the barley cubit had less than 180 grains but, if they placed them side by side, it was evident that, on average, about 180 grains measured the same as a *Kush*. It seems that the knowledge of the Sumerians should be taken seriously after all.

With this discovery as a starting point, I decided to go further, to see if this odd confluence between the meter and the measurement used by the Sumerians was coincidental, or was in fact due to a deeper level of knowledge. Based on the results achieved by Knight and Butler, I observed that, if the *Kush* was composed of 180 barley seeds, the double *Kush*, a measurement that is very close to the meter, would be composed of 360 barley seeds; as everyone knows, this is the number of degrees in the Earth's circumference. It is also known that, in spite of the fact that there are 360 degrees of terrestrial circumference, the Earth takes 365 days to complete its orbit around the Sun. I then decided to extrapolate the number of days in a year to the corresponding number of barley seeds defining the value of the double *Kush*, which yielded the following values.

Double Kush (360 grains)	99.88 cm
Double Kush (365.25 grains)	100.01 cm

Surprisingly, the result was impressively close to the modern meter. Is this just a coincidence?

Returning to the discoveries of Knight and Butler: they applied the principles of the pendulum of seconds to the double *Kush* in order to find how long it would take for a pendulum of the same length as a double *Kush* to complete a single movement.

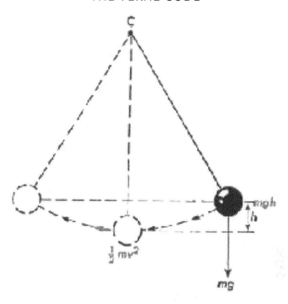

Figure 2.2 A diagram of the pendulum mechanism.

Let's take a moment to understand the importance of experimentation with the pendulum of seconds. When we observe a traditional clock, the most important aspect of its mechanism is the pendulum in motion; the rope or the electric motor is nothing more than the energy source which makes the pendulum swing from left to right. However, the time the pendulum takes to swing is determined by two factors. The first is the mass of the Earth, hence the variations mentioned previously, depending on the latitude where the experiment is performed. The second factor is the length of the pendulum. Here is the surprise; the experiments of Knight and Butler, to measure the double *Kush* with a pendulum of seconds, gave a result of 1.003 seconds. Only 3 thousandths of a second away from the modern second; this is more than a coincidence.

It follows that the linear unit of measure used by the Sumerians, the *Kush*, and the second, are two sides of the same coin. We now know that there is a measurement of time incredibly similar to the one we use today and a measurement of length that, for practical purposes, is identical to the modern meter. Understanding this phenomenon is of vital importance, since physicists accept that the concepts of time and space are different expressions of the same thing. Something that, according to what we have seen here, the Sumerians already knew…six thousand years ago.

If we go deeper, we must ask whether, in remote antiquity, one of the fundamental properties of the Universe, the speed at which light travels, was already known. Light travels in a vacuum at 299,792,458 meters per second, or 600,305,283 *Kush* per second, a figure that is almost too neat for a sexagesimal system, such as that used by the Sumerians. Let's consider the speed at which the Earth orbits around the Sun. The circumference of the orbit followed by our planet is 938,900,000,000 meters and takes 365.2596425 days to complete. This makes the speed of Earth's travel 59,573 *Kush* per second, another suspiciously round figure in the context of a sexagesimal system, almost 60,000 *Kush* per second. In addition, this amount is exactly ten thousandth of the speed of light, which suggests a combination of decimal/sexagesimal relationships was used by the Sumerians. This demonstrates an incredible degree of harmony with modern measurements.

More than that, the light of the Sun takes 8 minutes and 19 seconds to reach Earth, 499 seconds. The Earth revolves around the Sun at a speed of 59,537.8 *Kush* per second, almost 60,000 *Kush*. If we multiply the two figures, we have a result of 29,709,362 or 29,940,000 *Kush* (depending if we take 59,537.8 or 60,000 *Kush*), a figure that coincides curiously with a tenth of the speed of light expressed in meters.

Of course, we cannot be completely sure if the second used by the Sumerians was exactly the same one we use today, but given a difference of only three thousandths it would certainly be some coincidence. In fact, there really are too many coincidences. Perhaps we can now dimly perceive that the second and the *Kush* are something more than mere mathematical conceptualizations; that they are, in truth, grounded in understanding of deeper realities about the Earth, the solar system and the Universe. Therefore, it is reasonable to assume that the Sumerians were well acquainted with the mass of the Earth, its orbital speed around the Sun and even the speed of light, which led them to design units of measurement relating these variables to one another.

How was it possible that this mysterious people, fresh from the Paleolithic period, used concepts as modern as the meter, the second or even the speed of light? This simply did not fit the official version of history and human development. There were too many coincidences not to suspect a hidden truth. The key to my research appeared to be a people of unknown origin that burst suddenly into history.

CHAPTER III

HISTORY BEGINS AT SUMER:
THE ORIGIN OF CIVILIZATION

The science that humankind has in a given time depends on what humanity is in that moment.

Georg Simmel, German sociologist
and philosopher (1858-1918)

In Spain, although we have esteemed specialists like Professor Federico Lara Peinado, there is a limited understanding of the Mesopotamian world; to such an extent that it could be considered almost non-existent. In the Anglo-Saxon nations, more experienced in this field of research and with a longer tradition of exploring the ancient history of the Near East, the civilizations which flourished in the lands between the Tigris and the Euphrates, and particularly the Sumerian people, occupy an honored place in history.

In spite of all the discoveries made over the last two centuries, most educated people, and even many historians, consider Egypt to be the origin of civilization. This vision is widespread and Egypt is in fashion but, as with all fashions, that vision is only as strong as the half-truths repeated *ad nauseam* by the media.

To maintain this point of view is anachronistic and, from the point of view of historical science, it lacks intellectual rigor and is, importantly, incorrect. Such fashions are carved indelibly on the collective memory of society by events of tremendous cultural import; the great discoveries made in the Nile valley by the iconic Napoleon Bonaparte and his *savants*, the sensational finds of Howard Carter and Lord Carnarvon that, through the popular "curse of Tutankhamun", inspired so many headline writers and filmmakers, succeeded in dazzling western society. When attempting to establish the point at which humanity made the decisive step from prehistory to civilization, everything seemed to lead us toward Egypt.

Few people are aware of the advances made in the study of ancient history in the last hundred years. There have been discoveries, less spectacular than the news from Egypt, but certainly more important for understanding our origins. At the beginning of the twentieth century, the name of Sumer had been all but forgotten. Even a celebrated scholar like Gaston Maspero, in his *History of Egypt, Chaldea, Syria, Babylonia and Assyria*, did not say a single word about the Sumerians.

It was not until 1956, when Samuel Noah Kramer published *History begins at Sumer*, that the dominant narrative began to be challenged. The book had a considerable impact and should be recognized for its great contribution to this field of study but, unfortunately, although Sumer and its historical importance is now much better understood in academic circles, public opinion continues to be mesmerized by the glamorous world of pharaonic Egypt. Even half a century later it is not an easy task to find people who are aware of the discoveries relating to Sumerian civilization and their essential message: that civilization and history begins in Sumer.

The term civilization refers to an advanced level of development and organization of human society. Civilizations are distinguished from tribal societies by the predominance of a model of urban life; the development of agriculture, leading to a sedentary lifestyle; and a complex economic system based on the marketing of surplus produce, the division of labor and well defined political institutions, among other features. From a historicist point of view, man becomes civilized when he leaves the nomadic life and begins to live in cities. Enter *homo urbanites*.

The Bible records the beginning of civilization in the following verses of Genesis, in which *Shinar* is the Hebrew name for Sumer. In this passage, the term city appears for the first time and its Mesopotamian residents are clearly identified through descriptions of the methods they used to manufacture bricks and construct their buildings.

> *And it came to pass, as they journeyed from the east,*
> *that they found a plain in the land of Shinar,*
> *and they dwelt there.*
> *And they said one to another,*
> *Go to, let us make brick, and burn them thoroughly.*
> *And they had brick for stone,*
> *and slime they had for mortar.*
> *And they said, Go to, let us build us a city ...*
>
> (Genesis 11:2-4)

When speaking of Sumer, we are talking about the first known civilization on Earth, prior to Egypt and to the proto-Indian cultures of the Indus valley; older even than the earliest civilizations of China and the Aztec, Maya and Inca in the Americas. With Sumer we are presented with no simple prehistoric culture, but civilization at its maximum expression, with the richness and complexity that entails: social and political organization, urban life and states, institutions, codes of obligations and rights, an organized system of production of food and clothing, a trading system and means of payment for exchange, the development of higher forms of art and scientific knowledge and, most importantly, the creation of a system of communication that would mark a turning point in human history, a system of graphical representation of language, the cuneiform script, which allowed for the dissemination of knowledge. All these systems of human organization, only distinguishable from the modern age by a matter of degree, could be found in the fourth millennium before our era in Sumer, Mesopotamia, in the plain between the Tigris and Euphrates Rivers, in modern-day Iraq.

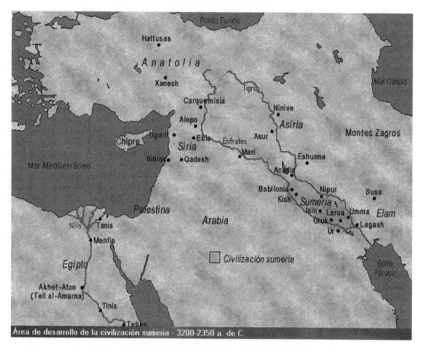

Figure 3.1 Map of Mesopotamia

Sumer was the first civilization on our planet and, as a result, was the source of all, or almost all, the essential concepts and inventions of modern civilization. We cannot understand what happened in Sumer if we do not appreciate, in all its grandeur, the incredible change that mankind experienced. Overnight, man was transformed from a survivor, only concerned with satisfying his basic needs, to a master of advanced mathematics, metallurgy, astronomy and astrology, the higher forms of art, medicine and more.

In Sumer the first written language was born at the end of the fourth millennium before the present. The Sumerian scribes printed pictographs on wet clay tablets with a punch, creating characters in wedge-shaped cuneiform, the origin of the term "cuneiform writing". The tablets were then dried and hardened in kilns. The only things that have changed since that time are the materials used, but the qualitative and revolutionary leap that the creation of a written language represented has not been seen again in human history. It represents the decisive step from prehistory to history. It is imperative to recognize the role played by writing in the development of historical knowledge. When an ancient civilization disappears and the line of living tradition between them and us is broken, all we know of them is what they have passed down through their written testimony. The number of clay tablets that archaeologists have found in ancient Mesopotamia is so enormous that many remain stacked and waiting for translation, so, although we now know many things about them, the future will bring even more surprises.

It is through what is written in these clay tablets that Samuel Noah Kramer frames his study of the Sumerian people, listing a series of historical firsts including: the first schools, the first parliament, the first historian, the first reduction in taxes (and indeed the first taxes), the first sentence of a court, the first pharmacopeia, the first farmer's almanac, the first cosmology, the first literary debates, the first literary plagiarism, the first library catalogs, the first irrigation system, and many mor

The wheel, a seemingly simple invention, is essential for transportation and the evolution of machinery of all kinds, from primitive carriages, mills and potter's wheels to modern automobiles, airplanes and gears. It also had its origin in ancient Sumer. They also possessed a legal system very similar to ours, with laws that protected the weak and the unemployed, penalties for offenders, and judges with powers very like our own.

Sumerians enjoyed developed and highly scientific medicine from very early, as can be seen by the manner in which it was organized and through the enormous number of tablets found in the medical section of the library of Ashurbanipal in Nineveh. There are books that deal with issues of hygiene, the use of alcohol as a disinfectant, and advanced surgical procedures which include those used for the removal of cataracts. A curious find was a Steatite vessel belonging to Gudea, ruler of the city of Lagash, on which are depicted two snakes coiled around a staff, a symbol of medical knowledge which, much later in Greece, was known as the caduceus of Mercury, and is still used today to represent pharmacology and medicine.

Sumerian construction techniques were also very advanced from the earliest period of their civilization. They built houses, palaces, temples, ziggurats and walls using bricks made of adobe or clay and, during the later period, incorporated glazed bricks, rich in lime and iron oxide, baked until vitrified.

The Sumerians became great experts in foundry technology. They reached temperatures in excess of 800 degrees in the kiln, but even more amazing was their proficiency in creating metal alloys, a process of combining different metals within a furnace, producing bronze – an alloy of copper and tin – for the first time in history, despite the fact that Mesopotamia does not contain any significant sources of tin. This adds a twist to the mystery.

The first ships and naval technology also originated from this mysterious people. Beer also appears to be a Sumerian invention, although the Egyptians were the first to adapt it to a form similar to that we currently enjoy.

Sumerian advances in mathematics and astronomy deserve a separate chapter. It is obvious that they already knew the Earth revolved around the Sun, despite the fact that this knowledge was lost in subsequent periods of history. We owe to the Sumerians the division of the firmament into three bands: northern or "the path of Enlil", central or "the path of Anu" and southern or "the path of Ea". The concept of spherical astronomy, the circle of 360 degrees, the celestial axis as an extension of the land, the poles, the ecliptic, the equinoxes, solstices, the zenith, horizon and other astronomical terms emerged almost overnight in Sumer.

The Sumerians created the first known mathematical system that, unlike our current decimal system, a system in base 10, was a sexagesimal system, in base 6. The sexagesimal system is, in many ways, superior to the decimal system used today, and is perfect for calculation and geometrical astronomy, an important science for the Sumerians. In fact, the influence of this system may still be seen today. For example, the mathematical system created in Sumer is the origin of our modern measurements of time, that one hour is divided into 60 minutes, one minute into 60 seconds, a day into 24 hours and a year into 12 months.

Sumerian mathematics and astronomy were not childish pseudo-sciences. Hundreds of books could be written on the knowledge that this people acquired, seemingly overnight. Anecdotal evidence of this is the so-called *series of Khorsabad*, which included two sculptures of Gudea: *the Architect of the Plane* and *the Architect with the Rule*, in which anthropomorphic proportions are applied. These proportions are related to the so-called "golden ratio" attributed, subsequently, to Euclid in the first century BC

The mathematics developed in Sumer was a science corresponding with the celestial order, an arithmetic designed to understand the Cosmos as a living being. For the Sumerians, math, and the complicated astronomical calculations it allowed, was the basis of one of their most important branches of knowledge, astrology, a science reviled today for the simple reason that the essential knowledge on which it is based has been lost. There is a tablet written by an astrologer dated to the year 2,300 BC, which contains an omen concerning the founder of the dynasty of Akkad, based on the position of the planet Venus and a lunar eclipse.

The king of Akkad dies and his subjects are safe. The power of the king of Akkad will weaken, his subjects will prosper.

It seems that this eclipse coincided with the death of Naram-Sin, grandson of King Sargon of Akkad. It's important to note that even the oldest astrological inscriptions yet discovered frequently referred to texts dating back to an even more distant antiquity. Sumerian astrologers made their predictions on the basis of tablets that no longer exist, which means that the Sumerian period should not be considered the birth of astrology, but simply the most ancient historical footprint that we possess.

The Sumerians already knew the zodiac, which was created by dividing the 360 degree circle that the Earth makes in its orbit around the Sun during a year into twelve equal parts of 30 degrees, the twelve signs of the zodiac. The original Sumerian names are similar to the modern ones and leave no doubt about their origins. It is surprising that they already understood the great precessional cycle of 25,920 years, divided into twelve astrological ages of 2,160 years. This astronomical knowledge was later adapted in India, leading to the Hindu puranic model of time, split into *Yugas*, *Manvantaras* and *Kalpas*.

The earliest known calendar is the one from Nippur. It connected the solar year division (two solstices and two equinoxes) and the phases of the Moon. This calendar was used subsequently by the Akkadians, Babylonians, Assyrians and other peoples, and we know the start date, in the year 3,760 BC, due to the fact that it is still used today by the Jews.

However, the influence of this first civilization goes much further. The fervent believer who reads the biblical *Genesis*, which lists the names of the first men from Adam to Noah, does not imagine that this sacred story is the blurred recollection of an original source, from a thousand years before: the Sumerian tale. He does not know that its real subject is the ten kings who reigned from the arrival of the gods until the Flood, a period that lasted for 432,000 years, or 120 *sares*. Like the Noah of the Bible, the last of these kings was the hero of the diluvian epic; he was known as Ziusudra in Sumerian, the Babylonians called him Utnapishtim, the Akkadians knew him as Atrahasis, and Berossus, the Chaldean priest-astrologer, hellenized the Sumerian name to Xisuthros. From all of this, a single and indisputable conclusion can be reached: the story of the biblical flood is a Sumerian myth embedded by the Hebrews in their sacred book.

As we have seen, the scientific and cultural refinement achieved by the Sumerian civilization was of the highest standard, which obliges us to ask some questions about the origin of those advances and knowledge. There are no historical records that demonstrate a slow evolution of this knowledge; on the contrary, there is evidence that it appeared suddenly and in an unexpected way, from an unknown source, as if it had fallen from the sky...

CHAPTER IV

EVERYTHING CAME FROM THE SKY

In the beginning, Earth, Heaven and sea were confounded in common mass together; then, as a result of grievous strife, they were separated one from another.
Argonautica, Apollonius of Rhodes, 3rd Century BC

In 1931, the controversial French anthropologist Marcel Griaule, thanks to the approval of a new law that allowed government funding, organized an expedition from Dakar to Djibouti, with the purpose of collecting African tribal masks for the *Musée d'Ethnographie* (Ethnographic Museum) of Paris. The journey lasted 22 months and he visited 15 countries across the continent. During this trip, he was lucky enough to meet Ogotemmeli, an elderly hunter of the Dogon ethnic group, blinded by a backfiring rifle. Ogotemmeli passed on to him a series of startling revelations, of which Griaule would later write in the book *Dieu d'eau* (God of water). The Dogon are an ethnic group who live in the present day Republic of Mali, near the River Niger and the Bandiagara escarpment. Their religious and cultural traditions are ancient. It might even be said that they are living fossils, as their customs and rituals date back hundreds of years into the past.

Griaule was surprised because these primitive people worshiped the star Sirius and spoke in their ancient traditions of the existence of a companion star to Sirius (what we now know as Sirius B), which was called *Po Tolo*. When he returned to France, the anthropologist set out to investigate what was known about Sirius B but was left puzzled as, in fact, very little was known.

Sirius was recognized in antiquity and the Egyptians marked the beginning of the Nile flood by its first visible appearance on the eastern horizon before sunrise (its heliacal rise). In 1844, the German astronomer Friedrich Bessel suggested Sirius could be a binary system with two stars, attributing the irregularities in its movements to the presence of a less bright companion invisible to telescopes of the time. It was not until 1862 that the American astronomer Alvan Graham Clark confirmed Bessel's theory by using a refractor telescope with a 47 cm lens; Sirius B had just been born. In fact, Sirius B is not invisible, but it is 10,000 times less bright than Sirius A, hence the reason it had not previously been detected. In 1970, Irving Lindenblad, from the US Naval Observatory in Washington, captured the first image of Sirius B. Today we know that it is a white dwarf, a tiny stellar remnant. However, the Dogon already knew it when Griaule visited them in the first half of the twentieth century.

In 1943, Griaule was appointed professor at the Sorbonne, where he established the first chair of Ethnology in the history of France, but he was still captivated by the Dogon so, in 1946, he returned to Mali, accompanied by Germaine Dieterlen, also an ethnologist and secretary of the *Societé des Africanistes-Musee de l'Homme* (Africanist Society of the Museum of Man) in Paris. Four years later, they published their research in an article entitled *A Sudanese Sirius system*, currently held at the *Musee de l'Homme* (Museum of Man) in Paris. In this work, which went virtually unnoticed, the researchers discussed the information supplied by Ogotemmeli and their observations of the simple but impressive drawings made by the Dogon of the Sirius system. They acknowledged the fact that there was no explanation for this knowledge, as the Dogon lacked telescopes or other optical instruments. However, they knew of the existence of a star that cannot be seen with the naked eye and that science had not discovered until the middle of the nineteenth century.

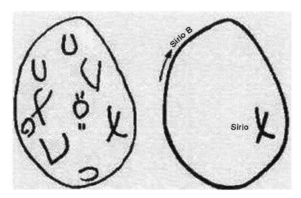

Figure 4.1 Dogon illustration of the Sirius system.

Dieterlen and Griaule noted that the Dogon were aware Sirius B took 50 years to orbit Sirius A. This was the reason they celebrated a festival called *sigui* every 50 years. Today we know that Sirius B has an orbital period coinciding with that contained in the Dogon traditions.

As if this were not enough, the Dogon described a third companion which they called *Emme Ya* which, according to them, also takes 50 years to complete an orbit of Sirius A. We would be talking at this point about Sirius C. This has not been borne out by official science despite continuous inquiries although, according to some astronomers, its existence could reasonably be suspected at a mathematical level. Time will tell if the Dogon are proved correct but, if the discovery of Sirius B was complicated, what difficulties might there be in locating Sirius C

The indisputably amazing fact is that this small African tribe's rich mythology includes incredible astronomical knowledge for a culture which does not even have a codified system of writing. Even before any astronomer speculated on the possible existence of Sirius C, they already believed it to be a triple star system. How did the Dogon know, according to a tradition lost in the mists of time, of the existence of Sirius B and its invisibility to the naked eye? The answer is disturbing because, according to their own ancestral tradition, the knowledge had been given to them by the *Nommos*, amphibian gods who came from the sky in a flying boat

According to Robert Temple, in his book, *The Sirius Mystery*, if the astronomical knowledge of the Dogon did not come from modern astronomers, it is likely that such knowledge was transmitted in ancestral times, before they migrated to their current territory, Mali, in sub-Saharan Africa. Temple's hypothesis is that the knowledge was transmitted to the Dogon by the Egyptians, for whom Sirius was the most important star in the firmament and identified with the goddess Isis. Temple writes:

> *The Dogon were in possession of information concerning the system of the star Sirius which was so incredible that I felt impelled to research the material. The results, in 1974, seven years later, are that I have been able to show that the information which the Dogon possess is really more than five thousand years old and was possessed by the ancient Egyptians in the pre-dynastic times before 3200 BC.*

It is very possible that the Dogon acquired their knowledge of Sirius from the Egyptians, but from whom did the Egyptians obtain such knowledge? Through my research, I have come to the conclusion that the Egyptian knowledge of science came from the peoples of the Mesopotamian Fertile Crescent which had, in turn, originated from the Sumerians.

In the previous chapter, I described the achievements of the first historic civilization. There is no fiction in the long list of inventions that the Sumerians were already using six thousand years ago. Anyone who takes the time to read about them will have access to the same information. All this is taught in academic institutions. However, the academics do not reflect on this information in sufficient depth or even ask the questions such reflection should surely suggest. Instead, they formulate the most bizarre explanations and hypotheses so that the facts fit the current ruling paradigm of histor .

The Dogon say that their knowledge was given to them by the *Nommos*, but what do the Sumerians say about all this in their writings? Although official science interprets these texts as myths and legends, despite having any scientific reason for doing so, they are very interesting if read with an open mind. The Sumerians are, in fact, very clear on this subject; all the knowledge and expertise they enjoyed was given to them by the grace of the gods, the *Anunnaki*, a term which literally means "the followers of Anu" or "those who from Heaven to Earth came". In the book of *Genesis* in the Bible, they are referred to by various names including "*the Anakim*", "*the Elohim*" or "*the Nephilim*".

Who were the Anunnaki? Where did they come from?

Thousands of Mesopotamian texts and illustrations deal with astronomy: lists of stars and constellations and their relative locations, as well as manuals instructing the reader how to observe their movements. In fact, Sirius was known in the Babylonian cuneiform texts as *Kak-Si-Di* (bright as copper), the arrow star, the one which shows the way.

Let's pause for a moment for a small exercise in phonetics. Which modern country's name is directly related to the star Sirius? Which ancient empire's name sounds similar as well? Of course, you know that the country we are talking about is the current Syrian Arab Republic and the empire is that of Assyria. Syria is derived from *Assyria* which itself was most likely derived from the Akkadian word *assur*. Syria is located on the eastern shore of the Mediterranean Sea and shares borders with Turkey, Iraq, Lebanon, Jordan and Israel. In the past, Syria was a Semitic center of great importance, particularly around the cities of Ebla and Ugarit, the first being famous for its more than 20,000 cuneiform tablets in Sumerian and Eblaite, a variant of the East Semitic language. In antiquity, it was a battleground and trade emporium for the great empires: the Sumerians, Assyrians, Babylonians, Hittites and Egyptians, among others.

As a result of war and migration, a great variety of peoples inhabited the area. We, however, are particularly interested in one of them. The Arameans, also known as Syriac (note the similarity to the names we discussed above), were a nomadic Semitic tribe who inhabited the region of *Aram-Naharaim*, a Hebrew name translated as "Aram of two rivers". These two rivers are not explicitly named in the Bible, although it is thought that the first was the upper course of the Euphrates. The Ancient Greek Bible or *Septuagint* gives a more accurate translation of the term as "Mesopotamia of Syria" or "rivers of Syria". The historian Josephus refers to the subjects of King Chushan-Rishathaim of *Aram-Naharaim* as "Assyrians". Therefore, the historical sources indicate that the Arameans lived in some areas of Syria, particularly in the region dominated by the Assyrians (in Arabic, the star Sirius is known as *Ash-Shira*).

So, what do the Arameans have to do with all this?

The answer is concise and enlightening. To the Arameans, the term *Nephila* referred to the constellation of Orion, suggesting that the Nephilim came from that constellation. Next to Orion is Sirius in the constellation *Canis Major* (the Greater Dog) and it is the brightest star visible from the Earth. Sirius has been known since ancient times by several names such as the Dog Star or the mysterious denomination the Arrow Star, "that which indicates the path to follow".

On the one hand, we have very significant phonetic matches, unique across the entire planet, that link Syria and Assyria with the star Sirius. On the other, we have the Aramean peoples, who lived in the same area, and whose language associates the Nephilim with Orion and Sirius. To all this we must add that the Assyrians were contemporaries of the Sumerians and heirs to their knowledge, so there is a clear relationship between Sirius, Orion and ancient Mesopotamia.

Once again, the direction of my research pointed me toward the fertile ground of the Arameans and Assyrians who, as parts of a linguistic game of unpredictable outcome, formed the base of a magic triangle whose apex pointed squarely to the first civilization in the area: the Sumerians. It is unquestionable that Sirius was well known to the peoples who inhabited ancient Mesopotamia. However, did they know, as did the Dogon, of the existence of Sirius A, B and C?

It is revealing that the name for Sirius in ancient Iranian is *Tishtrya*, a word that originates in the Sanskrit word *tri-stri* (three stars). From where did these peoples acquire the idea, in common with the Dogon, that the Sirius system is formed of three stars, something that, even today, science has not confirmed

Adding to this mystery is the so-called *Stele of Naram-Sin* (pictured on page 54). A stele is a monument, usually monolithic, bearing inscriptions which may have a commemorative, religious, funerary or geographical purpose. In the middle of the 24th century BC, another Semitic people, the Akkadians, unified all Mesopotamia to create an empire that reached as far as the Mediterranean Sea. Their expansion began during the reign of Sargon the Great, reaching its peak under his grandson Naram-Sin (2254-2218 BC). The conquests of this monarch have left an interesting relic that bears his name, the *Stele of Naram-Sin*, currently in the Louvre Museum in Paris. This stele, erected in the city of Sippar in commemoration of a victory over the Lullubi, is a block of sandstone around two meters high, and represents the apogee of Akkadian art.

Naram-Sin is shown climbing a hill, accompanied by some of his warriors, who bear the royal standards; his enemies are depicted falling from the mountain, crushed underfoot or begging for mercy. The most striking aspect, however, are two stars that appear at the top of the stele, and in fact we can just make out a third star, somewhat deteriorated. What is the meaning of these three stars at the top of the relief? It seems obvious that this is not a representation of the Sun, to show that the tableau takes place during the day; on the contrary, I believe it carries a hidden astronomical message.

As an astrologer, when I first saw the relief and the figure of this monarch wearing a horned helmet, I thought immediately of the sign of Taurus and, in particular, the astrological age of Taurus. The possibility occurred to me that the three stars depicted were Sirius A, B and C and that the artist was pointing to their location in the sign of Taurus in the year that the stele was carved. To astrologers, Sirius is considered a fixed star. Zodiacal signs move due to the precession of the equinoxes, the reason why fixed stars seem to move in the zodiac. I knew that, currently, Sirius was in the 12th degree in the sign of Cancer. So I consulted an ephemeris, which gives the positions of astronomical objects in the sky at a given time, to calculate the exact position of Sirius in the years 2,254-2,218 BC, Naram-Sin's lifetime. Imagine my surprise…

Sirius, during that period, was in the 12th degree of Taurus. This could not be a mere coincidence, it was a bullseye. The possibility that the three stars pictured at the top of the relief were related to Sirius A, B and C seemed more and more likely.

On the other hand, I discovered a revealing mathematical relationship between the distances from Sirius to the solar system and the distance from the Earth to the Sun. Sirius is located 8.6 light-years from the solar system or 4,520,160 light-minutes. The Earth is 8 light-minutes and 19 light-seconds from the Sun. If we divide the distance from Sirius to the solar system by the distance from the Earth to the Sun, the result is approximately 542,636 light-minutes or approximately 376 light-days, bearing a significant numerical relationship to the time the Earth takes to orbit the Sun (365.25 days). There are simply too many mysterious synchronicities that, if seen separately, are not conclusive but, once seen together, made me feel I was at the gates of an enigma of transcendence. I felt the same emotion that you feel when you put together the first pieces of a jigsaw puzzle and begin to perceive the picture behind it.

Now that we have reached to this point, we must raise the question: what is the relationship between Sirius and Orion?

The ancient Egyptians showed a great veneration for Sirius, "the Dog Star", which is situated in the constellation *Canis Major*, the Greater Dog. However, it was not the only star they adored. According to Egyptian mythology, the gods descended from Orion and Sirius, the brightest star in the Earth's night sky. The Ancient Egyptians believed that Isis and Osiris were beings with human form that came from Sirius (Isis) and Orion (Osiris) and who had led to the formation of humanity.

Figure 4.2 Stele of Naram-Sin

As observed from Earth, the Orion constellation is one of the most outstanding in the night sky. Ancient cultures spread throughout the world venerated it. For the Greeks, Orion was one of their demigods, represented as a man. According to Greek Mythology, Orion was a giant with superhuman powers. He was an astute hunter who, accompanied by his faithful dog, Sirius, killed animals with an unbreakable club of solid bronze. The most recognizable of the constellation are its three major stars: Alnitak, Alnilam and Mintaka, that make up "Orion´s belt."

In the desert of Nubia researchers have found what could be one of the earliest stone megalithic-aligned structures of mankind's ancient past, which points in the direction of Orion. Located approximately 800 km south of modern day Cairo, on an inhospitable plain in the eastern region of the Sahara Desert, is a mysterious archaeological site called Nabta Playa, which is about 1,000 years older than Stonehenge. The ancient remains of Nabta Playa were first discovered in 1974 by a group of scientists led by anthropology Professor Fred Wendorf. The scientists believe that the megalithic stones spread around the area formed, in its day, part of a ritual center belonging to a civilization, between 6400 and 3400 BC, just before the rise of Egyptian civilization. It was not a settlement but a ceremonial center. One of the central parts is a circle that has been called the "Mini-Stonehenge" of the desert.

The builders of Nabta Playa possessed a thorough understanding of astrophysics and mathematics, as well as advanced knowledge of constellations. Robert Bauval and the astrophysicist Thomas Brophy have studied the configuration of this megalithic monument for more than ten years. In their book, *Black Genesis,* they suggest that this was a sort of astronomical observatory, a prehistoric calendar with four pairs of stones as doors, faced two to two: a couple oriented in a north-south direction and the second heading northeast-southwest, in which the stone circles formed a star map to scale. The six central stones and their different inclinations would also be a part of the observatory. Brophy hypothesized that the southerly line of three stones inside the Calendar Circle represented the three stars of Orion's Belt, and the other three stones inside the calendar circle represented the shoulders and head stars of Orion as they appeared in the sky. He proposed that in 4900 BC these three central stones lined up perfectly with the three brightest stars in the Orion constellation that make up the belt. Is it true that these stones were aligned so perfectly at the summer solstice in those days? In that case, how could our ancestors build such an advanced chart of that constellation? The inhabitants of Nabta Playa mysteriously disappeared around the year 3400 BC, and there are those who believe that they migrated to the area of the Nile valley, where the Egyptian civilization arose in the 4th millennium BC.

The astronomical knowledge used in Nabta Playa is the same that was employed in the Egyptian pyramids. Why was the location of Orion so important for the Egyptians? The legend of Isis and Osiris is one of the most important in Egyptian mythology, although there is no single encompassing account of it. Osiris is god and sovereign of the Earth, who introduces civilization to primitive men and expands it beyond the borders of the Egyptian Empire. Seth, his brother, is full of envy and conceives the thought of killing him, Egyptian mythology tells how Osiris (Orion) is betrayed and murdered by his brother Seth, whom he holds in a sarcophagus and throws into the Nile. After the murder of Osiris, Isis (associated with Sirius) rescues his body and then copulates with him; the goddess becomes pregnant with the god Horus. When Seth hears about this, he is full of anger. He finds Osiris and tears his body into fourteen pieces, which he once again drops into the sacred river of the Egyptians. Seth's aim is to hinder the ritual of mummification of Osiris's body, and prevent the spirit of Osiris from returning to his mummified body. Isis retrieves from the Nile thirteen pieces of the remains of her beloved god, but she never finds the fourteenth piece, the phallus, a symbol of procreation and a suggestive allegory to our condition of "children of Orion".

The *Pyramid Texts*, written on the walls of funeral cells in the pyramids, dating back to 2400 BC, speak of Unas, an Egyptian pharaoh and the last king of the Vth Dynasty, who ruled for 30 years before making his final voyage to the star system Orion. Did pharaoh Unas really travel to space, as argued by the *Pyramid Texts*?

At this point we must consider "the Orion correlation theory" that Robert Bauval and Adrian Gilbert proposed in their book, *The Orion Mystery*. Robert and Adrian advocate that that the three pyramids of Giza are an accurate replica of the stars Alnilam, Alnitak and Mintaka of Orion's belt (the Three Marys). The truth is that the link between Sirius and Orion, at least from an astronomical point of view, is undeniable. The Egyptians knew that Orion disappeared into the horizon before Sirius, (known as *Sothis* by the Egyptians) which followed about one hour later. Sirius is also ancient Egypt's inspiration for one of its first Calendars. In the Egyptian Sirius calendar, the year began with the heliacal rising of Sirius. The heliacal rising of a star occurs annually when it first becomes visible above the eastern horizon for a brief moment just before sunrise, after a period of time when it had not been visible

Teotihuacan (The City of the gods) is found in Mexico, 56 km from Mexico City. The construction of the city was attributed to the Quinametzin Giants, a race of giants who, legend says, populated the world during a previous era. It is said that in 3114 BC, the gods came from the heavens to Earth for a convention, and this meeting occurred in *Teotihuacan*. As in the pyramids of Giza, the pyramids that stand in Teotihuacan also seem to be aligned with the belt of Orion.

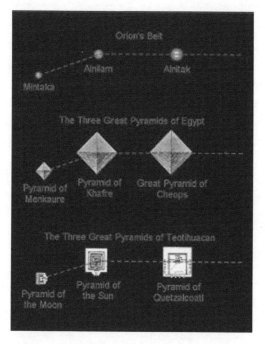

Figure 4.3 The Orion correlation theory

The Maya called Orion the "Star Tortoise", and it is represented in the *Codice de Madrid* as a turtle with the glyph three tun ("stone") on his back. In the *Popol Vuh*, the Maya book of creation, Orion is seen as the first father, Hun Hunahpú, the god of the Corn.

Was it a mere coincidence that Egyptians, Aztecs, Mayas and Greeks worshiped the same constellation? Were these monuments made to commemorate some extraordinary event for mankind?

Let us go where it all began, toward the original source of the mystery, the cradle of civilization. All that we know from the history of Babylon is thanks to excavation and the fact that we were able to decrypt a large number of cuneiform texts. For this reason, we know they viewed life from a very religious perspective. They worshipped the gods of the planets and different constellations. It was a cosmic religion. In 1840, in the north of Iraq in Mosul, a team of archaeologists from the British Museum discovered thousands of clay tablets written during the seventh century BC. Between the tablets there were two mysterious relics which are now known to be Babylonian star catalogs. The cuneiform tablets clearly showed that the Babylonian astronomers knew the precise movements of various celestial bodies, constellations of stars that originated what now are known as the signs of the zodiac. The Babylonian star catalogs are a compilation of information with extremely accurate mathematical equations. The most surprising data are the estimates of the huge distances between the planets, which produces confusion between archaeologists and researchers, who are not able to respond to the question of how a civilization in the past could have had access to this kind of knowledge. Was it provided by some outer space beings whom they called "gods"?

The Babylonians, as well as many other cultures and civilizations of antiquity, already knew Orion. They referred to Orion as *Sipazi Anu*, the "Loyal Shepherd of Heaven". Were the Babylonian star catalogs interstellar guides?

In this regard, there is a bas-relief where Orion is represented in the shape of a bird and referred to as a messenger. In the rock, we see the image of a bird behind the guide and its position could indicate that he carried messages from Earth to Orion. So the real questions are: how did they do it? Do we have to understand everything in a symbolic form? Was it an interstellar communication device? Were the Babylonian star catalogs maps of interstellar communication? Is it possible that the Babylonian gods were actually extraterrestrials messengers from Orion?

Mesopotamia was the first place where these beings arrived and brought about the first civilization on the planet: the Sumerian. If we look at the

Sumerian and Egyptian hieroglyphs and the Mayan legends, what we see is the same story told in different ways in different languages: beings from the stars came to our planet and generated our civilization.

Ancient civilizations described Orion's Belt as the door to life. When the Mayas, the Egyptians and all these cultures make reference to the beginning and end of life, they always relate it to the belt of Orion. Modern astronomers referred to Orion as M42, but ancient humanity knew about this constellation thousands of years before modern day astronomy, without telescopes such as the Hubble. The question is: how and why? Orion is a place where stars are born and astronomers refer to it as a "Stellar Nursery." Does it have anything to do with the origin of life on Earth? Our ancestors had the feeling that Orion was at the heart of the galaxy; it was the source of the answers to many questions. Do the stars of Orion represent the origin and final destination of mankind? A place where we come from and where we are going...

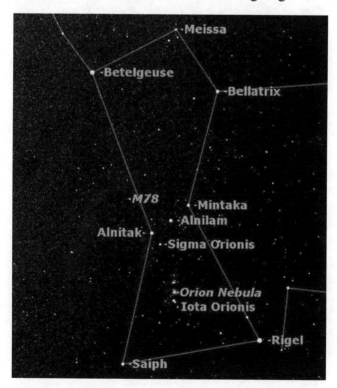

Figure 4.4 The Orion constellation

Figure 4.5 Nabta Playa

The idea that advanced extraterrestrial civilizations visited the ancient Earth and that they interacted to a greater or lesser extent with certain cultures, helping them to perform great works and so influencing human progress, is not new and has been propsed in certain circles at least since the Victorian era. Nevertheless, the concept did not enter popular culture until the 1960s, through the work of authors like Erich von Däniken, who brought the study of this subject to a new level. Von Däniken was the great popularizer of the hypothesis that, in the remote past, we were visited by alien beings from another planet. Later, many other authors, with greater or lesser success, have taken advantage of the momentum generated by the Swiss hotelier. However, we owe a particular debt to Zecharia Sitchin, brilliant scholar and tireless writer; in his first book, *The Twelfth Planet*, he developed this thesis to a hitherto unexpected depth.

To return to the mysterious first civilization, how did the Sumerians explain the origin of their knowledge? The Sumerians, as well as the Dogon, say in their writings that all they knew was taught to them by beings who came from the stars and who they called gods, a term that had no religious connotations at the time in which it was coined. Although it is currently fashionable to deride the ancient myths as children's fairy tales, this is the most plausible explanation of all. This would explain why, without leaving a single trace of intellectual evolution, fully developed sciences such as astronomy, medicine and math emerged overnight. In the same way that children go to school and are taught trigonometry or second degree equations, this knowledge was taught and not discovered over time. This is what the protagonists of this story say in their texts, although critics insist on disparaging it. Why should we accuse the Sumerians of writing nonsense? Were any of those critics there when these texts were written? Who are they to say that the Sumerians meant something diametrically opposed to what they said?

Modern man is skeptical about anything outside the limits of the current scientific paradigm. In contrast, the Sumerian thinker was convinced that his conception of the Universe was correct, because he knew how the Universe had been brought into being and how it worked. We know why they were so confident in their knowledge. The reason was that it had been given to them by the gods, superhuman and immortal beings. In Sumerian, they were referred to as *Dingir* (gods from Heaven), beings with whom humans had a special and cordial relationship. However, it is curious that the Anunnaki gods were represented in human form and that their feelings, thoughts and actions were also reduced to a human scale. Gods, like humans, ate, drank, got married, had a family and were subject to all sorts of weaknesses and human passions. They were the same as humans except for superhuman powers and immortality. The Sumerians saw no contradiction in the gods' similarity to humans and their immortality, or in the fact that, in spite of their immortality, the gods could consume food, fall ill, be wounded or even die (in reality, gods were not immortals but enjoyed great longevity). This was considered natural in the context of what they described as a relationship of everyday coexistence with the gods, a view that, today, seems entirely lacking in logic and sense.

To illustrate this last point, I will quote one of the tales translated by Samuel Noah Kramer in his book, *Sumerian Mythology* (1944), later corrected and enhanced by Thorkild Jacobsen. The story tells that, in a time before man was created, the city of Nippur was inhabited by the gods. There lived the young goddess Ninlil with her mother Nunbarsegunu. She saw that the supreme god Enlil was a good match to marry her daughter, so decided to set a simple and ancient trap, one that often works. She advised her daughter to follow these instructions.

In the pure stream, woman, bathe in the pure stream.
Ninlil, walk along the bank of the stream Nunbirdu,
The bright-eyed, the lord, the bright-eyed,
The Great Mountain, Father Enlil, the bright-eyed, will see you,
The shepherd who decrees the fates, the bright-eyed will see you,
Will forthwith embrace you, kiss you.

Ninlil followed her mother's instructions; she went to the stream where Enlil walked so that, when he saw her bathing, his desire would awaken.

The Great Mountain, Father Enlil, the bright-eyed, saw her,
The shepherd who decrees the fates, the bright-eyed saw her,

The Lord speaks to her of intercourse, but she is unwilling,
Enlil speaks to her of intercourse, but she is unwilling;
My vagina is too little, it knows not to copulate,
My lips are too small, they know not to kiss...

Enlil and Ninlil. *The Begetting*

The end result of this is that Enlil forced himself upon Ninlil, thus conceiving the lunar god, Sin. The gods, dismayed by this immoral offense, seized Enlil and banished him from Nippur to the nether world; he was followed by Ninlil, who now carried his child.

No tales or stories of gods have ever been found of greater antiquity than those of Sumer. There were hundreds of gods in the Sumerian pantheon but each had their role. Not all were of equal importance, nor did they have the same responsibilities. There were gods of farming, of brickmaking, of canals and dikes; and there were great gods who governed Heaven and Earth. There was a structured hierarchy in which each god played a role with certain attributes and responsibilities, comparable to the political and social organization of Sumerian society.

There was a supreme god, recognized by all the others as their sovereign or king, leading a system of government, monarchy, which was the system used on their planet, and one that, from the time it was brought to Earth in the most remote antiquity, has survived to this day. The government of the Anunnaki gods met in an assembly chaired by the monarch. The Assembly, similar to some modern senates, was composed of fifty great gods and seven supreme gods, as well as the four royal gods. This system of parliamentary monarchy was subsequently adopted by the first King of the Sumerian civilization.

It may be surprising to know that, as early as the year 3,000 BC, the first recorded Parliament met in the city of Uruk, in a solemn session, to discuss whether to go to war against the city of Kish, or to submit to them and recognize their sovereignty. The Parliament was composed, as in most modern democratic systems, of two chambers: a Senate or Assembly of Elders, and a Lower Chamber formed of young able-bodied citizens with the capacity to bear arms.

Gilgamesh presented the issue before the elders of his city,
carefully choosing his words:
'There are wells to be finished, many wells of the Land yet to be
finished;
We should not submit to the house of Kish!
Should we not smite it with weapons?'
In the convened assembly, his city's elders answered
Gilgamesh:
'There are indeed wells to be finished.
So we should submit to the house of Kish.
We should not smite it with weapons!'
Gilgamesh, the lord of Kulaba, placing his trust in Inanna, did
not take seriously the advice of his city's elders.
Gilgamesh presented the issue again, this time before
the able-bodied men of his city, carefully choosing his words:
'There are wells to be finished.
Never before have you submitted to the house of Kish.
Should you not smite it with weapons?'
In the convened assembly, his city's able-bodied men answered
Gilgamesh:
You old men should not submit to the house of Kish! Should we
young men not smite it with weapons?
When Aga comes, what terror he will experience!
That army is small, and scattered at the rear. Its men will be
incapable of confronting us.'
Then Gilgamesh, the lord of Kulaba, rejoiced at the advice of
his city's able-bodied men and his spirit brightened...
"Do not put you down to the house of Kish, let's attack them
with our arms!
The combatants of the city gathered in assembly,
Responded to Gilgamesh: do Not put you down to the house of Kish
Let's attack them with our arms!
Then, Gilgamesh, the lord of Kullab,
In front of this council of the combatants of the city,
He felt his heart with happiness, his soul clarified."

Gilgamesh and Aga

At the top of this family of gods was An (Anu in Babylonian and Assyrian texts), the god of Heaven, the sovereign of the planet where the Anunnaki (literally the 'followers of Anu') originated. The city where An had his temple or residence when he visited Earth was Uruk. After Anu, there were his children, Ea (Enki), Enlil and his daughter Ninhursag (Ninmah or Nintu), forming the four royal gods.

Ea, also known as Enki, was the Lord (En) of the Earth (Ki), a title which he received as he commanded the first Anunnaki expedition to Earth and built their first settlement, the city of Eridu, on his arrival. Enki was the God who held the technology of the mysterious *me* (powerful weapons in the form of objects such as jewelry or ornaments), the bearer of wisdom, the arts, the knowledge of civilization, which allowed the colonization of Earth and the creation of man. Enki was the eldest son of Anu but, due to the laws of succession of his planet, Enlil, his half-brother, became the "Prince of Heaven", the heir and successor to the crown, as well as the "Lord of the Command", the highest authority in the Anunnaki expedition to Earth, senior to Enki. The texts describe Enlil as the king of all the countries and sovereigns boasted that they received their royal status from him. It was Enlil who declared the name of the king and who gave him the scepter which denoted his authority.

In the Heavens, Enlil is the Prince;
On Earth, he is the Chief;
Enlil, whose command is far reaching;
Enlil, whose pronouncement is unchangeable:
The gods of Earth bow down willingly before him;
The Heavenly gods who are on Earth humble themselves before him;
They stand by faithfully, according to instructions.

Hymn to Enlil

Enki was the first son of Anu, the fruit of a relationship with a concubine, not with his official consort, his half-sister Antu. Enlil had been born later but was the son of the king and queen. For that reason, he was the legal heir to the throne. The Anunnaki gave priority to dynastic succession based on blood lineage, a sophisticated system, the purpose of which was to maintain their genetic purity. For that reason, there was a distinction between nuclear DNA, contributed by both parents, and mitochondrial DNA which is only passed from the mother to her children. This is why the role of the mother was so important and, although the succession passed only through the male line, it was customary for a firstborn son to be next in the line of succession unless a son was born subsequently with a half-sister (a daughter of the same father but different mothers), who became heir and legal successor, as in the case of Enlil. Enki did not take kindly to the loss of the crown or the loss of influence on Earth, colonized by him through considerable effort.

Enki professed a deep sympathy for the human race; they were his creations after all. Enlil, however, tolerated humans only as a necessary evil for the welfare of the gods, disliking them to such an extent that he contemplated a plan to exterminate humanity. Enki was responsible for the affairs of the Earth, while Enlil had overall control of strategy. Enki, with his considerable talents, and with the optimal combination of wisdom and boldness, dealt with the finer details of its execution.

The disagreements between Enki and Enlil, as well as the rivalries of their family clans, is the key which will allow us to understand the events that occurred on Earth and that determined the destiny of the human race. This is a history that the biblical texts have completely erased in favor of the Judeo-Christian monotheistic doctrine, but one that the original Mesopotamian texts describe in great detail and that will be analyzed in the following chapters.

Ninhursag appears, depending on the time and place, under different names, among which are Nintu (lady of birth), Ninmah, Belet-Ili, Dingir Mah, Aruru or Damkina. She was a fertility goddess, who knew the secrets of biology and assisted Enki in the creation of the human race.

The Sumerians possessed texts which included a great deal of information about the solar system, a detailed list of the planets, their order, their relative distances and even their appearance. I have already mentioned that the Sumerians knew the Earth revolved around the Sun and was part of a planetary system. They also knew that the solar system was formed of a series of planets: Mercury, Mars, Venus, Jupiter and Saturn; they knew of the existence of planets that official science did not discover until relatively recently like Uranus, Neptune and Pluto. They even spoke of a planet not yet discovered by modern day science. They named it Nibiru, the planet of the crossing, and it will play a decisive role in this story.

It was Sitchin who first published the following illustration of a cylinder seal, held under reference VA/243 in the *Vorderasiatische Museum* (West Asian Museum) in Berlin, the image on which represents the solar system and which is at least 4,500 years old. The cylinder seal was used to impress an image onto a surface. The artist engraved the inverted negative of the desired image on the stone, in order to print the true image when it was rolled on wet clay.

Figure 4.6 Zecharia Sitchin

Figure 4.7 VA/243 Cylinder seal representing the solar system

In the upper left of the relief is a detail that represents the solar system. Clearly recognizable is the Sun at the center, surrounded by the planets of the solar system. Here we must note that the Sun is located in the center, not the Earth, which tells us that, even in remote antiquity, they possessed an accurate understanding of the solar system and how the Earth and the other planets revolved around the Sun. This knowledge was lost over the passing of the centuries until 1543, when Nicolaus Copernicus died and his followers published his heliocentric theory, considered revolutionary and heretical in equal measure. If we analyze the low relief in detail, we see a representation of our solar system, including all the planets we know today, their relative sizes and their distances from the Sun. This is consistent with modern science.

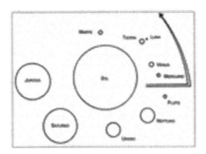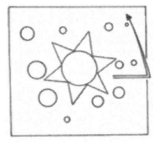

Figure 4.8 Diagrams comparing the representation of the solar system on the cylinder seal to that established by modern science

There are some differences between the seal and the prevailing scientific doctrine of today. The first is to do with Pluto and the controversy that has followed it since its discovery in 1930. Since that time, many astronomers have speculated that Pluto might have originated as the satellite of another planet, perhaps Neptune. More recently we have seen the dispute over whether Pluto should be considered a planet, an asteroid belonging to the Kuiper belt or simply a dwarf planet. In 2006, the International Astronomical Union (IAU), arguing that Pluto cannot be classified as a planet; it is too small to be able to plot its own orbit (crossing, in fact, that of Neptune), so they announced that Pluto would be reclassified as a dwarf planet, in the same category as Ceres or Eris. The solar system would now be composed of 8 planets and several officially recognized dwarf planets (According to the IAU definition, more dwarf planets will be added in the future). The dwarf planet Pluto is recognized as an important prototype of a new class of trans-Neptunian objects. However, although the IAU voted to re-designate Pluto as a dwarf planet, only 424 of the 10,000 professional astronomers around the world were able to vote. The controversy was magnified by the fact that there is very little agreement between astronomers on the criteria which define a planet

According to RESOLUTION 5A of the IAU General Assembly there are 3 conditions that an astronomical body must meet in order to be defined as a planet

1. It must orbit a star (in this case, the Sun);
2. It must have sufficient mass for its self-gravity to overcome rigid body forces so that it assumes a hydrostatic equilibrium (nearly round) shape, and
3. It must have cleared the neighborhood around its orbit.

A dwarf planet, in the same resolution is defined as

1. It must orbit a star (in this case, the Sun);
2. It must have sufficient mass for its self-gravity to overcome rigid body forces so that it assumes a hydrostatic equilibrium (nearly round) shape, and

3. It has not cleared the neighborhood around its orbit, and
4. It is not a satellite

For some astronomers it is not clear if Pluto meets the second condition, i.e. sufficient mass (although it has a nearly rounded shape), or the third in that it is too small to become gravitationally dominant in its own orbit. In fact, Pluto's orbit is not clear and contains a swarm of icy objects, one of which, Eris, is more massive than Pluto. Nothing seems to be certain with regard to Pluto; indeed, it is striking that Pluto's place in the relief carving of VA/243, differs markedly from the accepted astronomical model of the composition of our solar system.

In the VA/243 image, Pluto is not depicted after Neptune, but between Saturn and Uranus. This is because, according to Sumerian cosmology, Pluto had been a satellite of Saturn, only to gradually free itself and reach its destiny to independently orbit the Sun. This conception of Pluto and its origins, already understood in this ancient period, reveals extremely precise astronomical knowledge that required a sophisticated understanding of the processes which led to the formation of the solar system. It also reveals the existence of some very advanced astrophysical theories postulating that a satellite can become a planet or that a planet can become a moon; something that modern astronomers have since speculated thanks to the observations made by the Pioneer and Voyager space probes.

It is truly exciting to see how many modern discoveries in cosmology and astrophysics are merely rediscoveries of knowledge that already existed in ancient times; and not only that, we may observe how the knowledge of the mythic past can provide coherent explanations for many of the phenomena that modern science has yet to solve, as we shall see.

The second difference that we see in the relief representing the solar system, according to the Sumerians, when compared to the hypothetical diagram representing the modern scientific paradigm, is to do with the representation of an unknown planet, larger than the Earth, but smaller than Jupiter. This will provide the answer to many questions about the origins of our planet. This unknown planet is located in the empty space between Mars and Jupiter. Modern scientists do not have any evidence to corroborate the existence of a planet in that orbit but the ancient Sumerian texts insist on this point. They call it Nibiru, the planet of the crossing. What mysteries are contained in this planet and its name?

CHAPTER V

THE ORIGIN OF THE SOLAR SYSTEM

How many things have been denied one day, only to become realities the next.

Jules Verne, French writer (1828-1905)

We owe the discovery of the fascinating history of Mesopotamian civilizations to the vigorous competition between French and British archaeologists during the mid-nineteenth century that, on one hand, gave birth to assyriology as a science and, on the other, enriched many museums with the valuable artifacts they found. Among many others, and worth a special mention, is the large collection of clay tablets from the Royal Library of Nineveh, otherwise known as the Library of Ashurbanipal, preserved today in the British Museum in London. What follows is a story that illustrates this very well: the setting was the British Museum and the protagonist a man almost unknown today outside archaeological circles, George Smith. Who was George Smith?

George Smith was apprenticed at age 14 to a publishing house, where he learned to engrave banknotes. His consuming interest, however, was the Bible and Assyrian culture, encouraged by the amazing discoveries being made in Mesopotamia at the time. Smith spent much of his spare time at the museum on Great Russell Street, studying the cuneiform tablets, and was eventually employed to catalogue the mass of fragmentary texts. In 1872, Smith, who had learned to read cuneiform and was now an accomplished assyriologist, made probably his greatest and most transcendent discovery. In one of the fragments found at Nineveh, he translated an Assyrian version of the Universal Deluge. The announcement of his discovery was greeted with great interest in British society and the London newspaper, *The Daily Telegraph*, stepped in with an offer of 1,000 guineas to finance a new archaeological expedition, led by Smith, with the intent of finding the remaining fragments of the story.

The following year, his great adventure began at Nineveh, the realization of his long-awaited dream: just one week later, he unearthed a fragment that completed the story of the Assyrian Deluge, part of the *Epic of Atra-Hasis*. Later, he found further tablets that dealt with the subject of creation, known as the *Epic of Creation*. In 1876, Smith published his masterpiece, *The Chaldean Account of Genesis*, in which he presented evidence of the parallels between Babylonian history and the biblical *Genesis*.

In 1902, L. W. King expanded on Smith's work in *The Seven Tablets of Creation*. He established with great clarity the similarities between the so-called seven days of creation in the biblical *Genesis* and the Babylonian text, divided into seven clay tablets. While the Babylonian *Epic of Creation* is divided into seven fragments or tablets, in which the first six recount the process of creation and the seventh is entirely devoted to exaltation of the national god Marduk, the biblical *Genesis* divides the creation into seven days, six of which tell of the divine work, leaving the seventh day for rest and glorification of the Supreme Creator.

Any expert in ancient history knows that Assyria owed its cultural heritage to Babylon, and that the latter, in turn, owed its culture and knowledge to the Sumerian civilization. As such, when we speak of the *Epic of Creation*, although it focused on exaltation of the Babylonian god Marduk, the text itself was undoubtedly based on a Sumerian source. The same process seems to have inspired the biblical account. Abraham belonged to a family from the Sumerian city of Ur, connected to royalty and the priesthood; he was, therefore, in possession of certain secrets. His descendants compiled and shortened the story, later adding a monotheistic slant although, as we shall see, they did not remove all of the original details from the story.

The *Enuma Elish*, another name for the story, derived from its opening words: "*When on High*", was required reading for priests and scholars of the time as it was recited annually at the celebration of the New Year, at the beginning of spring, as well as on other ceremonial occasions. It consists of seven separate narratives on seven clay tablets, with lengths ranging from the 139 verses of the third tablet to the 167 verses of the sixth, a total of approximately 1,100 verses.

In my research I have assumed that neither the original Mesopotamian text, nor the later biblical tale, is an allegorical myth with no basis in reality. On the contrary, these texts, written by initiates for fellow initiates, conceal an extremely advanced scientific cosmogony that describes the formation of our solar system using a poetic metaphor that tells of a battle among the "gods", a word that, in this case, carries the additional meaning of "planet" or "satellite".

Official science perceives these texts as nothing more than primitive myths, based on the false premise that those who wrote it possessed only a primitive level of knowledge and cultural development; despite the fact that this position is itself unscientific. In this book, I will present proven facts that point to precisely the opposite position. The non-scientific paradigm, currently dominant in academia, is based on the theory that the evolution of the history of mankind and, therefore, of human knowledge, is a linear progression. For that reason, scientists conclude that it is simply impossible for the Sumerians, 6,000 years ago, to have known of stars, planets and concepts that have only recently been discovered by science. If they chose to carefully assess the available information with a critical and scientific spirit, they would realize that there are many pieces which do not fit the house of cards they have constructed, the official version of histor .

For example, the word "gods" often induces fear and aversion among researchers, but this is nothing more than a simple problem of terminology, a conditioned reflex originating in the subconscious mind, a Pavlovian response that, rather like the famous canine salivation triggered by a bell, is itself inspired by a religious-cultural background. The seeker of truth, the bearer of the true scientific spirit, must transcend the semantics of the words, the illusory "veil of maya" that conceals true knowledge. Now let's return to the subject we were discussing.

The discovery of fragments of the oldest version of the Sumerian *Enuma Elish* has convinced many scholars that the *Epic of Creation* was originally a Sumerian text in which the name Nibiru was later replaced by the name of the Babylonian god Marduk. The text explains how the solar system was formed and the origin of each planet, with special reference to the formation of the Earth and the Moon. It also clarifies how the asteroid belt and comets were created and finishes with the story of our blue planet, the genesis of humanity and the emergence of human civilization.

When on high Heaven was not named,
And the Earth beneath did not yet bear a name

Enuma Elish

Thus begins the poem, in which the expression "was not named" or "did not yet bear a name", means that it did not yet exist; so the story begins long before the creation of our planet. The gods (the planets) did not yet exist, nor did they possess destinies (fixed orbits)

When of the gods none had been called into being,
And none bore a name, their destinies undetermined.

Enuma Elish

The story describes the youth of the solar system. At the beginning was only the Sun (Apsu, "the one who exists from the beginning"), which was joined by Mercury (Mummu, "the one who was born") and Tiamat ("Maiden of life"), a planet that will play an important role in the future of the Earth and the human race.

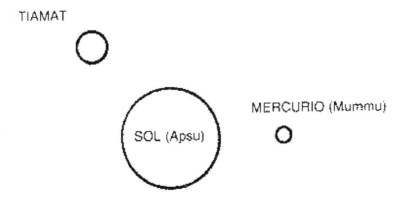

Later, the group expanded with the birth of the inner planets, Mars (Lahmu) and Venus (Lahamu).

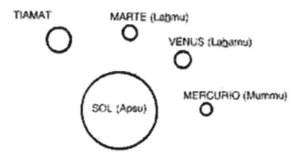

The pair of giant planets Jupiter (Kishar) and Saturn (Anshar) then appeared.

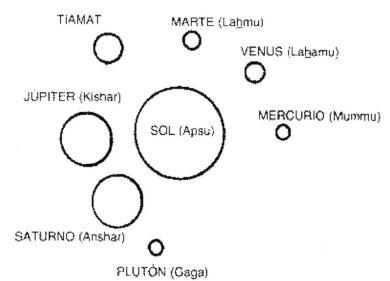

Finally, Uranus (Anu) and Neptune (Ea) made their appearance in more distant orbits.

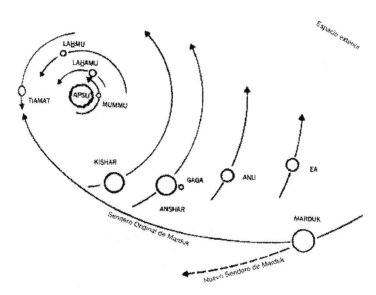

As I have pointed out, in this very young solar system, the orbits (destinies) of the planets (the gods) were highly unstable. Tiamat, which was orbited by eleven satellites, exercised and was subject to many gravitational influences, including from the two planets closest to the Sun, Mars and Venus; as well as the two distant giant planets, Jupiter and Saturn, which caused many problems and tensions between all the members of the solar system.

> *The divine brothers banded together,*
> *They disturbed Tiamat as they surged back and forth,*
> *They troubled the mood of Tiamat,*
> *By their hilarity in the Abode of Heaven.*
>
> Enuma Elish

At some point, according to the story, an invader planet appeared. The Sumerians called it Nibiru, the Babylonians Marduk, in honor of their national god. This planet came from outer space but, due to its proximity to the solar system, it began to be attracted by the gravitational forces of the planets most distant from the Sun, in particular by Neptune (Ea), the outermost.

> *Ea, the all-wise, saw through their scheme*
> *And He traced a master design*
>
> Enuma Elish

The planet of the crossing, Nibiru/Marduk, is described as possessing an impressively majestic appearance, wonderful to contemplate. Orbited by four satellites, it later acquired a further three due to its gravitational force when passing the outer planets of the solar system. The following verses recount these events, using expressions such as "eyes" and "ears" to describe "satellites".

> *Greatly exalted was He above them, exceeding throughout,*
> *Perfect were his members beyond comprehension,*
> *Impossible to imagine, unbearable to see*
> *Four were his eyes, four were his ears.*
> *Four were his ears, and his eyes in the same number.*
>
> Enuma Elish

In this way, Nibiru was attracted to the Solar System. It went through the orbits of Neptune and, later, Uranus, causing astrophysical phenomena that shaped both planets, and leaving them with their current satellites. During this process, Nibiru acquired three new satellites from Neptune and Uranus, making a total of seven.

The planet then traveled deeper into the planetary system, attracted by the massive gravitational fields generated by Saturn and Jupiter. On approaching Saturn, the planet of the crossing experienced two decisive events: firstl , Nibiru's orbital trajectory changed forever while, at the same time, the primary satellite of Saturn, Gaga, later to be known as Pluto, broke away from the orbit of Saturn to end up in the rather peculiar orbit it currently occupies.

The new orbit (supreme destiny) of Nibiru directed it inevitably toward Tiamat

If I, your avenger,
conquer Tiamat,
and save your lives,
set up the Assembly,
and proclaim supreme my destiny!

The planet of the crossing, a prisoner of this new orbital trajectory, protected by its seven satellites (Winds) like an imperial guard, was preparing to fulfill its destin .

Then He sent forth the winds He had created,
the seven of them.
To disturb the inside of Tiamat,
they followed after him.

The next act of the *Epic of Creation* leads to the inevitable moment when Nibiru/Marduk veers so close to Tiamat that the forces of gravity and magnetism come into action, producing collisions between their respective satellites (Winds), and impacting those belonging to Nibiru into Tiamat, causing great damage to the latter.

Then they faced,
Tiamat and Marduk, the wisest of gods.
They swayed in single combat,
locked in battle.
The Lord spread out his net
and caught her.
And the Evil Wind, which followed behind,
He let loose in her face.

This was the end of Tiamat, and of its eleven satellites, which were driven out of its orbit, some of them being caught in the gravitational field (the net) of Nibiru. Only Kingu remained in orbit around Tiamat, a dead satellite.

When He had slain Tiamat, the leader,
Her might was broken,
Her host was scattered
And the gods her helpers, who marched by her side,
Trembled and were afraid, and turned back.
They took to flight to save their lives;
But they were surrounded, so that they could not escape.
He took them captive, he broke their weapons;
In the net they were caught and in the snare they sat down.
They... of the world they filled with cries of grief.
They received punishment from him, they were held in bondage.
And on the eleven creatures which were filled with the power of
striking terror.

According to Sitchin, after this collision, and once Nibiru had been captured in its orbit around the Sun, it returned to collide with Tiamat, inflicting the fina *coup de grace*.

These events, narrated in the Chaldean *Epic of Creation*, have their correlation in the first verses of the creation account in the Hebrew

Genesis, where "Heaven" refers to a specific location in the solar system in the vicinity of the asteroid belt.

*"Veha'arets hayetah tohu vavohu vechoshech al-peney **Tehom** veruach **Elohim** merachefet al-peney hamayim"*
(Genesis 1, 2 in transliterated Hebrew)

In the translation from Hebrew to English, important words have been omitted or silenced. For that reason, I have included the original words while keeping the rest so you can see what the real meaning is.

In the beginning,
*The **Elohim** created the Heaven and the earth.*
And the earth was without form and void,
*And the darkness was upon the face of **Tehom***
(Genesis 1, 1-2)

Here, *Elohim* means the planetary gods while *Tehom*, translated by official compilers as the Deep, in reality refers to Tiamat, taking the Mesopotamian cosmogony up to the time when the Earth was separated from Heaven (the asteroid belt). The Sumerian myths corroborate what is said in the first chapter of *Genesis*: that, at some time prior to this separation, Earth and Heaven were united.

When the Heaven was away from the earth,
When the Earth was separated from the sky.
Gilgamesh, Enkidu, and the Netherworld

The story narrates, in an epic manner, as if speaking of flesh and blood people, the movements of the planets of the solar system from its birth until the final act, the collision of Tiamat and Nibiru, the point at which the solar system acquired its current configuration. This collision caused Tiamat to split into two parts, one that retained its spherical and planetary nature, today known as the Earth, and the other, which was completely fragmented and shattered, that would become the firmament (Heaven), full of comets and leading to the formation of the asteroid belt.

I will digress from the ancient myths for a while and look at the subject from a different point of view. The asteroid belt is a region of the solar system that is located between the orbits of Mars and Jupiter. It occupies an area of approximately 550 million square kilometers and hosts over 600,000 asteroids. Similar to the discovery of Neptune and Pluto, the asteroids were initially perceived on a theoretical basis. As early as 1776, the German astronomer Johann Daniel Titius was convinced of the existence of a planet located between the orbits of Mars and Jupiter. Johann Elert Bode then refined Titius' hypothesis, giving rise to the well-known Titius-Bode law.

Later, in 1801, Giuseppe Piazzi discovered a celestial body which he named Ceres, but it could not be the hypothesized missing planet as it was too small (only 952 km in diameter). An interesting aside is that, after Ceres was discovered, it was then lost (or unobservable) for a year until the German astronomer Heinrich Olbers finally located it again, in the position predicted by the great mathematician Carl Friedrich Gauss. In addition to this, Olbers discovered and named the second-largest asteroid, Pallas, with a diameter of 532 kilometers. Olbers formulated the theory that the asteroids were fragments of an ancient planet that had exploded. The planet was given the name *Phaeton*, in honor of the Greek myth.

The Titius-Bode law predicts the existence of a planetary body in the area occupied by the asteroid belt. It provides empirical calculations of the distances between the planets and the Sun, based on an observed pattern related to the structure of the solar system. The modern reformulation of the law is much more accurate and you can see the similarities between the calculated distances and the real distances in the following table (the distances are given in Astronomical Units, AU).

Planet	n	Titius-Bode distance (AU)	Real distance (AU)
Mercury	-	0.4	0.39
Venus	0	0.7	0.72
Earth	1	1.0	1.0
Mars	2	1.6	1.52
Asteroids	3	2.8	2.8
Jupiter	4	5.2	5.2
Saturn	5	10.0	9.54
Uranus	6	19.6	19.2
Neptune	-	-	30.1
Pluto	7	38.8	39.4

The similarity between the calculated distance of the planets to the Sun and the real distance is amazing, including the area occupied by the asteroids. The exception, however, is Neptune. A careful look shows that Neptune is located in an orbit in which the Titius-Bode law predicts there should be nothing, and that, instead, Pluto is located in the orbit that the law predicts for Neptune (almost precisely: 39.4 AU compared to 38.8 AU). How is it possible that the Titius-Bode law predicts planetary orbits perfectly up to Uranus (including the non-existent fifth planet and its asteroids) and thereafter begins to fail? Why is Pluto located in the position that Neptune should occupy?

Since the nineteenth century, astronomers around the world have detected disturbances in the orbits of the outer planets (Uranus, Neptune and Pluto). Some astronomers are certain that only the existence of another large celestial body that was once part of our solar system could cause and explain these discrepancies. This suggests the existence of a tenth planet, not the asteroid Sedna, but a huge planet that seems to be causing fluctuations in the orbit of Pluto. The next number in the Titius-Bode series is 77.2 AU. According to the Titius-Bode law, the celestial body in question – sometimes called Planet X – would be located at the enormous distance of 77 AU. Once again, the development of modern astronomy seems to be providing evidence for the Sumerian's legacy.

Their clay tablets mentioned the mysterious Planet X and the key role that it played in the formation of the Earth, born from the ashes of Tiamat.

Comets are another of the unfathomable mysteries that remain unsolved, despite the large amount of existing data. These planetesimals, the diameters of which can reach tens of kilometers, are composed of water, methane, ammonia, iron, magnesium and silicates. These molecules are often frozen solid due to the low temperatures caused by their relative distances from the Sun. They are mainly located in the Oort Cloud, situated between 50,000 and 100,000 AU from the Sun, and the Kuiper Belt, located beyond the orbit of Neptune. Most of these celestial bodies describe highly elliptical orbits, which cause them to travel inexorably closer to the Sun and, as a result, they must withstand the higher temperatures produced by their increased exposure to photons from the Sun, the so-called solar wind. One effect of this is that the materials from which the comet is composed are heated and sublimated, passing directly from solid to gas, that is to say, from ice to gas. The resulting gases are projected backwards, forming the tail of the comet, which can be millions of kilometers long. When the Earth crosses the orbit of a comet, fragments penetrate the atmosphere and cause spectacular displays of shooting stars. During the passage of Halley's Comet in 1910, its tail reached almost 30 million kilometers in length. During its life, a comet, on average, passes close to the Sun approximately two thousand times before completely sublimating and disappearing.

A very curious aspect of the orbits of comets, one that has still not been explained, is that they move in the opposite direction to the orbital motion of the planets in the solar system. The comets move in a clockwise direction, while the planets describe a counter-clockwise movement. It should be added here that their orbits around the Sun also have different planes or angles.

Most astronomers believe that the solar system has remained essentially unchanged since its formation. However, Tom Van Flandern, an American astronomer (recently deceased), was clearly in favor of the hypothesis that a planet had exploded in the area where the asteroid belt is located, explaining the formation of the comets and their orbital movement contrary to that of the planets.

This begins to sound rather like the story of the Mesopotamian creation. Zecharia Sitchin postulated that it was the orbital movement of Nibiru, contrary to that of the rest of the planets, which caused comets to orbit in the same manner. When Nibiru passed by, the satellites of Tiamat were shattered, causing them to break into small planetary bodies (gods), which were pushed into new orbits (destinies), with a motion that was contrary to that of the other planets in the solar system (turned back).

When he had slain Tiamat, the leader,
Her might was broken, her host was scattered.
And the gods her helpers, who marched by her side,
Trembled, and were afraid, and turned back.

Enuma Elish

In addition to providing a new perspective, Van Flandern's theory is notable by his prediction that many asteroids and comets could possess satellites, something that seems to have been verified by recent discoveries. On July 23, 1995, the comet Hale–Bopp was discovered by two amateur astronomers. On September 26, 1995, NASA took a photograph of the comet with the Hubble Space Telescope. On December 15, 1995, a press release was issued by Meta Research, who had analyzed the image, stating that "the so-called body ejected from the comet's nucleus", was in all likelihood a satellite of the kernel in a stable orbit.

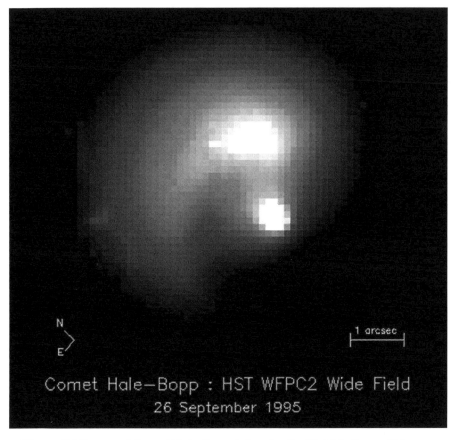

Figure 5.1 Image of Comet Hale-Bopp taken by the Hubble Space Telescope

A similar case is that of the asteroid Eros; after photographic analysis undertaken in 2000, the astronomer Andrew Cheng presented evidence that the asteroid originated from the destruction of a planetary body. At a press conference held by NASA, Cheng explained that too little is currently known to be able to determine the size of the planetary body that gave rise to the asteroid, but he provided information which lends credibility to the exploded planet theory, including the existence of geological layers in the asteroid that could not have developed in its current form as its escape velocity is very low. There is also a marked differentiation in its chemical composition with the consequent separation of heavy and light elements, something usually associated only with planets. Now let's return to the myths of antiquity...

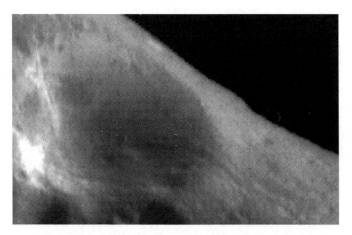

Figure 5.2 Image of crater on the surface of Eros

To understand the nature of the Earth it is essential to understand the structure of Tiamat, known as Nammu in the Sumerian version of the story. His nature was watery. It was the planet of waters.

> *In the beginning, before Heaven and the Earth were named, it was Nammu, the water, the infinite ocean, the goddess who gives life.*

The former Tiamat/Nammu, transformed into the Earth and with a smaller size as a result of the impact, changed its orbit and retained only one of its satellites: the Moon (Kingu). The Earth retained much of the original water of Tiamat/Nammu (the watery monster), while the remaining water went to the firmament, where various phenomena of condensation were produced. This process is clearly described in the verses of *Genesis* in which a distinction is made between the waters above and the waters below, separated by the *Raki'a* which is usually translated as "firmament" but whose literal transcription is "the hammered-out bracelet"; this differentiates the water which remained on the new planet from the water that was ejected as a consequence of the collision. Currently, it is known that many asteroids have frozen water. It is also known that there is abundant frozen water on planets such as Jupiter and its satellites, Saturn, Uranus and Neptune; the moons of the outer planets also contain large reserves of water.

And God made the firmament, and divided the waters which were under the firmament from the waters which were above the firmament: and it was so.
And God called the firmament Heaven.

Genesis 1, 7-8

Some scientists wonder if the water on Earth has always been here or it came from space. Astronomer Humberto Campins, chief investigator of the Planetary Sciences Group at the University of Central Florida, USA, explains that evidence in favor of the Earth's water originating in space is that "the molecular composition of terrestrial water is similar to the water found in asteroids and comets". This molecular similarity between terrestrial water and frozen water in comets and asteroids further reaffirms the hypothesis of a common past for the Earth and the asteroids scattered throughout the belt.

What astronomers should ask themselves, is: could some of the water on Earth have moved to the asteroids and comets rather than vice versa? The reason why astronomers think that Earth was originally a very dry place and that water came from outside is based on the empirical observation that, the further asteroids and planets are from the Sun, the greater their water composition. Therefore, given the distance from the Earth to the Sun, water should not be so abundant. What they don´t contemplate is the possibility that the body from which the Earth was formed (Tiamat/Nammu), was located at a greater distance from the Sun than the current orbit of the Earth, exactly in the area of the asteroid belt. This would allow it to possess a greater amount of water, although in a frozen state, as is the case for the asteroids that now occupy that position and contain water of the same molecular composition as that found on Earth. The Earth, as it is told in the Mesopotamian texts, abandoned its former orbit for its current position, which would explain why the primordial frozen waters were melted by the higher temperatures caused by its greater proximity to the Sun.

The Earth, after the violent shock of the collision, remodeled its form and regained a spherical shape through the action of kinetic and gravitational forces. At the same time, there began a process of change in its primary elements, in particular, the waters and the land.

And God said,
Let the waters under the Heaven be gathered together unto one place,
And let the dry land appear:
And it was so.
And God called the dry land Earth;
and the gathering together of the waters He called Seas.

Genesis 1, 9-10

According to the Bible verses, on Earth there was a process of separation between the waters and the land; between the seas and of the continental shelf which, until then, had not been differentiated. In fact, thanks to research conducted by space probes on the structure of the planets of the solar system, we know that the Earth is the only planet on which there is a distinction between oceans and continents.

From a geological point of view, the Earth is divided into a series of layers. The Earth's crust is the most superficial layer and is formed of tectonic plates that float on the mantle, a layer of hot and viscous materials that sometimes well up to the surface through a fault or volcano. Another puzzle becomes evident when we note that the Earth's crust varies in thickness from as thin as 5 km at the bottom of the sea, up to 65 km in the mountainous areas of the continental shelf. In addition, each has a different age: the oceanic crust dates back about 200 million years, while the continental crust is at least 4 billion years old. At the same time, it should be noted that the Earth's crust is much thinner than it should be in relation to its mass, as shown by studies conducted on other planets. How can the existence of a crust formed by parts of different thicknesses and ages be explained?

If we understand that planets are living entities, an idea already understood in past ages and one partially adopted by environmentalists, we can make a comparative analogy between a planet and a human being. A human being is made up of an outer layer, the skin, which is the point at which physical contact is made with the external environment, protecting and regulating the exchanges between the internal and external environments. In the same way, a planet has a planetary crust that performs, on a geological level, similar functions to those performed by the skin for the human body. If we continue with this analogy, the question arises: how can we explain the skin of a person formed by parts with different molecular structures and biological ages? The most obvious explanation would be that something traumatic had happened in the past, leading to healing and the growth of new tissues, involving cellular restructuring.

The part of the Earth's crust beneath the oceans seems to have been broken at some point in the geological history of the planet, only to grow again in the form of a thin layer of solid material and sediment, following a process similar to the healing of a wound, the clotting of blood and the growth of new skin. This idea is consistent with the hypothesis that the Earth experienced a catastrophic collision which fractured the planetary crust at the site of the impact, leading the oceans to flow into the area. In turn, the land emerged from the opposite side, producing a separation of the land and waters, as *Genesis* explains.

The idea that land emerged on one side of the globe, separated from the waters on the other side, is in line with the theory of "continental drift" postulated at the beginning of the twentieth century by the German geophysicist, Alfred Wegener. In 1915, he published *The Origin of Continents and Oceans*, in which he suggested that, in the beginning, there was a single, huge continent that later fragmented, giving rise to the present continents, which slowly drifted into their present positions. In subsequent editions, he called this primitive continent *Pangaea*, which means "all lands", and the vast ocean that surrounded it *Panthalassa*, which means "all oceans"; expressions strangely similar to those used in the ancient texts. Now the verses of *Genesis* seem neither so enigmatic nor so inconsistent.

Over the following years, Wegener drew his evidence from different fields, but the scientific community, as usual, rejected and ridiculed his daring theories. It was not until the 1950s that, due to a series of scientific developments, the theory was resurrected in the form of its direct descendant, "plate tectonics", now the prevailing thesis in science.

It is thought that *Pangaea* was formed at the end of the Permian period, roughly 250 million years ago, a date that is rooted in the 200-million-year age attributed to the oceanic crust, and demonstrating a temporary link between the formation of land and seas. Whatever happened, roughly 250 million years ago, something occurred that violently transformed the structure of the Earth, according to the analysis of the scars were left behind.

During the Mesozoic period, *Pangaea* was fragmented. First it was divided into two continental landmasses: *Laurasia* to the north and *Gondwana* to the south. Then, about 135 million years ago, America began to separate from Eurasia and Africa, resulting in the formation of the Atlantic Ocean. In this way, different seas and oceans connected to each other emerged from the original continent.

What becomes apparent from all this research, as well as from a careful reading of the myths of antiquity, is a common denominator between all of them: water. In early traditions, it is always from the primordial waters, the chaos, that life flows. Something not at all surprising when we note that the primeval Earth (Tiamat/Nammu) was primarily composed of water, according to the Sumerians.

The Maya, on the other side of the planet, describe in a very similar way the composition of the Earth in its early stages. *The Popol Vuh* or *Book of Counsel* is a compilation of several legends of the Quiche people, a Mayan kingdom which controlled large areas of southern Guatemala. It has come to be called "the bible of the Quiche Maya", and explains the origins of the world and civilization. It comes from an ancient oral tradition; an original written version has never been found.

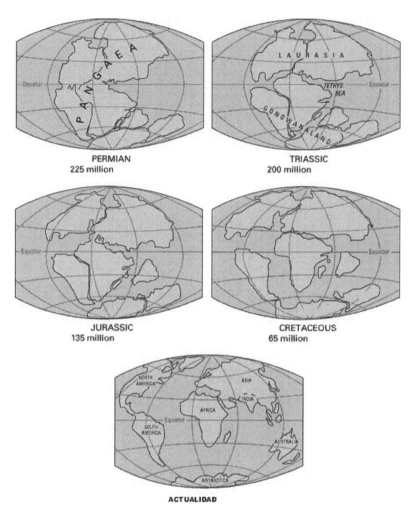

It was intended as a book of paintings and hieroglyphics to be used by priests to convey knowledge to the people of the origins of their race and religion. The first written compilation dates to the mid-sixteenth century. Let's take a look at what it says in the opening lines.

This is the account of how all was in suspense, all calm, in silence;
All motionless, quiet, and empty was the expanse of the sky.
This is the first account, the first narrative. There was neither
man, nor animal, birds, fishes, crabs, trees, stones, caves, ravines,
grasses, nor forests; there was only the sky.

The surface of the earth had not appeared. There was only the calm sea and the great expanse of the sky.
There was nothing brought together, nothing which could make a noise, nor anything which might move, or tremble, or could make noise in the sky.
There was nothing standing; only the calm water, the placid sea, alone and tranquil. Nothing existed .
There was only immobility and silence in the darkness.
All alone are the Framer and the Shaper, Sovereign and Quetzal Serpent,they who have borne Children and they who have Begotten Sons.
They are in the water surrounded with light, wrapped in quetzal feathers and cotinga feathers.

Popol Vuh

It continues, with a description of great simplicity but, also, great expressive power.

When the mountains appeared from the water;
and instantly the mountains grew.

Popol Vuh

All the mythologies of the planet agree on these aspects of the formation of the Earth. This is not by chance, since all these traditions come directly or indirectly from the original Sumerian myths. As has already been said, they received all this knowledge, in many cases subsequently rediscovered by modern science, from travelers from another world. Something that official science, despite the extensive evidence, will not admit in any way.

Why is it that someone willing to accept the possibility that man may, one day, travel to another planet, finds it so difficult to admit the possibility that someone from another planet visited our own planet in the past?

CHAPTER VI

THE MOTHER OF ALL SCIENCES: ASTROLOGY IN SUMERIA

Mathematics is the alphabet in which God has written the Universe.
  Galileo Galilei, Italian astronomer and physicist (1564-1642)

O ne of the oldest branches of knowledge, that most ignored and least understood by official science is, without doubt, astrology; to such an extent that there is widespread ignorance of this hermetic science, often associated incorrectly and pejoratively with the practices of charlatans. Astrology is, primarily, based on the hermetic principle of correspondence, devised by Hermes Trismegistus, to whom was attributed the authorship of the mysterious *Kybalion.*

As above, so below; as below, so above.

The Kybalion

According to this fundamental principle of the lost science of Hermes, Hermeticism, there is a corresponding relationship between the movements of the planets and the stars in the Heavens, and the processes of life and human destiny on Earth. This relationship can be understood as a process of synchronicity between two seemingly separate worlds which form part of a perpetual whole.

The Greeks, Egyptians, Hindus and Chinese, with the exception of small contributions from elsewhere, received their fundamental knowledge of the Universe from Chaldean astrology. However, the Chaldeans, the Babylonians and the Assyrians were not the original guardians of this knowledge. Once again, one must go back to the Sumerians to find the first written records of the sciences of astrology and astronomy. The Sumerians, as we have seen, knew of the existence of all the planets of the solar system and possessed very accurate astronomical mathematics that allowed them to calculate the positions of the stars in the firmament

The *Enuma Anu Enlil*, a collection of around 70 tablets discovered in Nineveh, in the library of the Babylonian king Ashurbanipal, has been long considered the oldest source of astrological information in the world, including a large number of astronomical-astrological observations, data on the movements of the Sun and Moon and rules of prediction. During the process of deciphering its contents, it was discovered to contain 21 years of astronomical observations of the planet Venus (*Enuma Anu Enlil*, tablet 63). According to the words of Ashurbanipal himself, it was the part of his collection of which he was most proud. Experts estimate that most of the writings date to the beginning of the reign of the Babylonian King Ammi-Saduqa (1582-1562 BC).

However, there are in the collection two tablets known as the *Mul.Apin* series that are faithful replicas of older Sumerian texts from the year 2,340 BC, according to the calculations made by Werner Papke based on the observations of certain stars on the horizon at dawn. The tablets describe the movements of the Sun, Moon and planets, in addition to 33 constellations with 66 individual stars. Both these tablets and the *Epic of Gilgamesh* agree in their descriptions of planetary positions in the year 2,340 BC. Using this detailed information, we can know the exact position of the stars at the time of the Sumerians, how they divided the sky into constellations and how they interpreted them in order to make their predictions.

The Sumerians divided the sky into three ways or bands in parallel to the celestial equator: "the way of Anu", "the way of Ea", and "the way of Enlil". They divided the circle of 360 degrees that the Earth makes in its orbit around the Sun during a year into twelve equal parts of 30 degrees, the signs of the zodiac, and called it "the Moon´s path", which snaked through the different paths or roads. The summer zodiacal signs are on the way of Enlil, the winter signs on the way of Ea, and the spring and autumn signs are on the way of Anu.

The names that Sumerians used to denominate the signs of the zodiac are very similar to those used today, clearly demonstrating the origin and evolution of these concepts. While, in these tablets, 17 or 18 constellations are mentioned, these were grouped together within a structure of 12 zodiacal signs. The sign of Gemini, as it is currently known, contained four constellations, while Pisces had two. The first sign of the zodiac was *Lu-chun-ga*, which was associated with the same meanings as the spring sign of Aries has today. The following table illustrates the 17 constellations that appeared, as well as their meanings and their relationship with the modern signs of the zodiac; something which is more than evident.

Constellation (Sumerian)	Translation	Current constellation
Lu-chun-ga	The agrarian worker	Aries
Mul-Mul	The star cluster	Pleiades
Gud-an-na	The bull of Heaven	Taurus
Sipa-zi-an-na	The loyal Shepherd of Heaven	Orion
Su-gi	The old one	Perseus
Gam/Zubi	The scimitar	Part of Auriga
Mas-tab-ba-gal-gal	The great twins	Gemini
Al-lul	The crayfish	Cancer
Ur-gu-la	The lion	Leo
Ab-sin	The seed-furrow	Virgo
Zi-ba-ni-tum	The scales	Libra
Gir-tab	The scorpion	Scorpio
Pa-bil-sag	The overseer	Sagittarius

Suhur-mash	The goat-fish	Capricorn
Ziz-a / Gu-la	The great one	Aquarius
Sim-mah	The great swallow	Pegasi, α Equulei and part of Pisces
A-nu-ni-tu	The goddess	Part of Pisces

The uncertainty over whether 17 or 18 constellations are included in the *Mul.Apin* tablet is due to the fact that, in front of the constellations *Sim-mah* and *A-nu-ni-tu*, appears the word *"kun month Zibati month"* whose meaning is "the tails", leading some scholars to believe that it represents an additional constellation.

Figure 6.1 Mesopotamian bas-relief showing zodiacal constellations

Also in the Library of Ashurbanipal, the Victorian archaeologist Austen Henry Layard found a circular clay tablet inscribed with cuneiform texts, catalogued as K-8538, and currently housed in the Assyrian and Babylonian antiquities gallery of the British Museum in London. This piece, a mere 13 centimeters in diameter and, like many other tablets found at the same location is, according to experts, a copy of a much older text which was Sumerian in origin. Its circular shape and the geometric shapes included in each of the eight different sections into which the disc is divided are fascinating, as well as arrows and triangles that are likely to represent stars of greater magnitude, lines that join stars denoted by holes in the surface, charts, and even an ellipsoidal curve, which was thought to be unknown in antiquity. The scribe added some notes giving the names of the stars or constellations; other notes refer to specific positions in the field, even giving measurements of the size of some of the figures depicted. After its presentation at the Royal Astronomical Society in 1880, it was described as "the most enigmatic of the Mesopotamian documents", partly due to the fact that it was entirely unlike the many thousands of clay tablets found in Mesopotamia.

There is no doubt that it is the positions of stars and constellations which are represented in this tablet, although the circle is divided into eight sections rather than twelve. However, in the restored fragments of other Assyrian planispheres, such as K-14943, also housed in the British Museum and barely 6 cm in diameter, we can already see the division of the circle into twelve sections. This example also includes a list of 36 stars associated with these divisions in a clear allusion to the signs of the zodiac and to what, in astrological language, are called "decanates". The stars are represented by small circles, some of which have small central points or are in the form of a six-pointed star. Thus, for example, the first star of the month of *Tebet* (the tenth month, associated with the period in which the Sun is in Capricorn) appears with the name K.U, and the third star of *Marcheswan* (the eighth month, associated with the period in which the Sun is in Scorpio) is represented as *Lugal*.

Figure 6.2 K-8538 – Circular cuneiform tablet discovered at Nineveh

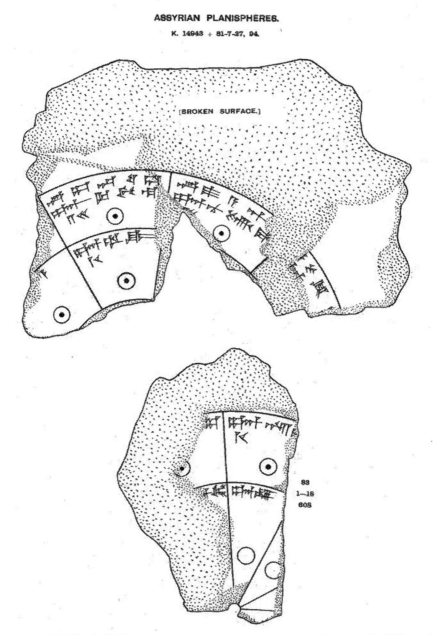

Figure 6.3 K-14943 Fragmentary Assyrian planisphere discovered at Nineveh

This zodiacal division was later incorporated into Egyptian and Greek culture, from where it was passed down to modern times, and throughout the East, where various systems such as Hindu Vedic astrology emerged. It is worth mentioning that the astrological and astronomical knowledge of the Sumerians was lost for many years. So much so that, two thousand years later, the Romans believed something unthinkable to the Sumerians: that the Earth was flat and located in the center of the Universe. It was not until Copernicus that the knowledge of Antiquity was rediscovered. He, very probably, based his work on the *Zohar*, a fundamental work of the Jewish *Kabbalah*, which was, in turn, inspired by ancient knowledge from Mesopotamia.

The whole earth turns, spinning like a ball.
When a part is down, the other is up.
When there is light in one part, it is dark in the other part,
When it is daytime for this part, it is night for the other part.

The Zohar

In their elaboration of the zodiac, the work of the Sumerian astronomers was based exclusively on the signs, which indicates the high degree of maturity reached by their astronomy. They were able to use position coordinates on the celestial sphere based on the ecliptic (the projection of Earth's orbit around the Sun onto the celestial sphere, 23° 27'). However, given the advanced astronomical concepts that allowed the development of a zodiac, including twelve signs, a question arises: What is the true origin of the science of astrology used by the Sumerians at least 5,000 years ago? To answer this question, we must look a little deeper into the astronomical foundations on which astrology is built.

The Earth is not static. It moves steadily through space, both rotating on its axis and orbiting the Sun. Its rotation takes approximately 24 hours and its solar orbit approximately 365 days. During this orbit, the Sun seems to rise each day in a different degree of the Moon's path, or zodiacal belt. In this way, the Sun passes through the twelve signs of the zodiac, one each month, until it has apparently moved the full 360 degrees, at which point the cycle begins again. This cycle is repeated each year. However, the Earth, when it completes its orbit of the Sun, does not return to exactly the same point at which it started a year ago. There is a slight delay, which we can measure as one degree every 72 years. This phenomenon is known as the "precession of the equinoxes". Given that the zodiac is divided into twelve signs of 30 degrees each, it takes 2,160 years (72 years x 30 degrees) for the Sun, rising on the morning of the vernal equinox, to move from one zodiacal sign to the next – for example, from Pisces to Aquarius – thus defining the so-called astrological ages. For the same reason, it takes 25,920 years (2,160 years x 12 signs) to complete the great precessional cycle, when the Earth returns to the same starting position and the Sun rises on the morning of the equinox in the same degree of the zodiac.

The precession of the equinoxes is a phenomenon that falls under celestial mechanics and is neither easy to explain nor to understand. It is essential, however, that we develop a basic understanding in order to comprehend the magnitude of the enigma we face. Having said that, some questions come to mind: if it takes 72 years to verify a difference of 1 degree and 2,160 years to observe a change of zodiacal era, how is it possible for a human being, who lives for 80 years, of which perhaps 50 or 60 are dedicated to studying the heavens, to understand a phenomenon of such magnitude or even to recognize it at all?

If we also consider the fact that the scientific process, as we know it today, based on the dissemination of information from generation to generation with the objective goals of experimentation and observation, did not exist in the Paleolithic era, according to historians, there is only one explanation for the sophisticated scientific knowledge of the primitive Sumerians. The deductive argument leads us to think that, if they could not have developed this knowledge through their own efforts and experimentation, it must have originated elsewhere. This reasoning, once more, coincides with the explanation the Sumerians themselves gave for the origin of this information: the gods gave them knowledge of astronomy and astrology, amongst much more.

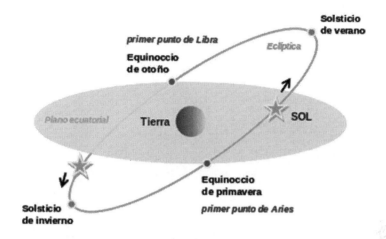

Figure 6.4 Diagram of the apparent movement of the Sun as viewed from the Earth

The Sumerians, either in the historical period or before the Flood, used this knowledge of the astrological ages as if it were a clock, in such a way that the important events in history could be dated. For instance, there are texts that date the Great Flood to the era of Leo so, if we calculate backwards from the current time, in which we are about to enter the age of Aquarius, we note that there are six intervening eras (6 x 2,160) or 12,960 years. So, it is possible to approximately date the Flood to 10,800 BC, when the era of Leo began. In astrological terms, the zodiacal ages are the hours on the clock face; to date events more precisely, astrology provides other factors to represent minutes and seconds.

The Sumerians had the first mathematical system in history which, unlike our decimal system in base 10, was a sexagesimal system in base 6. While, in the decimal system, we count from 1 to 100, in the sexagesimal system, we would count from 1 to 60; this completes a *gesh*. So, when we say 100, the Sumerians would have said 60 or, when we say 200 they would have said 120. This system allowed them to use some particularly specialized mathematical techniques and is far superior to the decimal system when making astronomical calculations, which was certainly their primary concern. The sexagesimal system demonstrates a close relationship with the precessional cycle detailed above. This system made use of a quite unusual alternation between 6 and 10, starting with 6 (10 x 6), followed by 10 (60 x 10), then 6 (600 x 6) and so on.

60, 600, 3,600, 36,000, 216,000, 2,160,000, 12,960,000

The sexagesimal system used by the Sumerians places special emphasis on the number 12,960,000. Why is it that we find in the Sumerian texts numbers of such magnitude, which coincide curiously with the figure of 500 Great Years, also known as equinoctial cycles or platonic years?

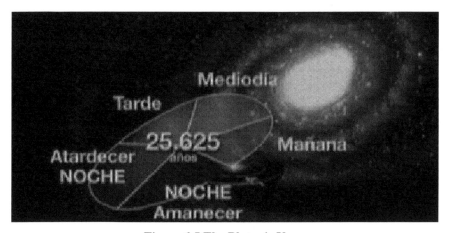

Figure 6.5 The Platonic Year

The existence of all this knowledge in ancient times is so incredible that scholars prefer to ignore it in order that they don't have to answer the uncomfortable question of how the most ancient civilizations on Earth, particularly the Sumerians, acquired it without any historical evidence demonstrating a process of intellectual evolution. Above all, modern astronomy accepts the existence of these periods, as calculated by the ancient Sumerians, but at no point has any scientist been able to confirm the change from one precessional cycle to another through personal observation. What message are the Sumerians sending us from remote antiquity, with a mathematical figure as accurate and on such a magnitude as 12,960,000?

Another figure that is of vital significance to this story is 432,000. According to the *Sumerian King List*, 432,000 years passed between the arrival of the Anunnaki on Earth and the Great Flood. Sumerian astronomical, astrological and mathematical knowledge arrived in the Indian subcontinent through successive migrations of Aryan peoples, who had learned from the Hittites, so diving into the Vedic tradition will allow us to perceive the importance of the Sumerian sexagesimal system and of that number in particular. In the Hindu tradition, the number 432,000 has great importance. It is the number of syllables that make up the *Rigveda*, the sacred book which tells the stories of their gods. In India, that number is associated with the *Yugas* or cosmic cycles of the Earth and mankind. Each great *Yuga* or *Manvantara*, a day of Brahma, is a period of activity in the Universe, as opposed to a *Pralaya*, a period of rest or dissolution. Each *Manvantara* is a measure of cosmic time that is divided into four ages or *Yugas*, whose chronological extensions are an expression of the figure 432,000. There are four *Yugas*: the Golden Age or *Krita Yuga* (4 x 432,000 years), The Age of Knowledge or *Treta Yuga* (3 x 432,000 years), the Age of Sacrifice or *Dvapara Yuga* (2 x 432,000 years) and the current Dark Age or *Kali Yuga* (432,000 years), which makes a total of 4,320,000 years.

4,320,000 years is a cycle of a thousand *Manvantaras* or, also, an Eon or a *Kalpa* although, according to the Hindu tradition, there are *Kalpas* of different lengths.

What is most important in all this is to realize that, in ancient times, there were people who already comprehended periods of cosmic time of such magnitude that they are beyond human understanding, and to which modern astrophysics applies no essential meanings. In this sense, we may recall the phrase in the Hindu calendar which says that, "*in the eyes of Brahma, one thousand cycles are nothing more than a day*", something that should lead us to reflect on the insignificance of the short time we know as the history of mankind, and allow us to look at the past with humility and reverence.

The astronomical and astrological knowledge of Sumer spread to neighboring settlements and, via Babylon, arrived in the land of the Nile, where the Egyptians adopted the zodiacal division of twelve signs. It is enlightening to look at the town which was once the capital of Upper Egypt, Dendera, situated about 60 kilometers north of Luxor. There we find the famous temple of the goddess Hathor, full of astrological meanings and mysteries, including the so called "Dendera lamps" depicted in three stone reliefs that, according to Erich von Däniken, are representations of electric light bulbs.

The temple includes twelve crypts, a number which does not require explanation, even for those uninitiated in the topic. What I consider most relevant is, without doubt, the two zodiacs found there. The first of these is the *Dendera zodiac*, a low relief carved into the ceiling of the *pronaos* or entrance porch of a chapel dedicated to the god Osiris. Its representation of the zodiac in circular form is unique in ancient Egypt. It was brought to the attention of the wider world after Napoleon's Egyptian campaign of 1798-1801. In 1802, Vivant Denon published several illustrations of the zodiac in his book *Travels in Upper and Lower Egypt during the campaigns of General Bonaparte in that country*, which provoked much controversy over whether it was a zodiac or a planisphere. Napoleon´s general, Louis Charles Antoine Desaix, wanted to secure the zodiac for France, but it was not until the antiquities dealer Sébastien Louis Saulnier commissioned the master bricklayer, Claude Lelorrain, to remove the zodiac that it was finally obtained, arriving in Paris in 1821; it was purchased by King Louis XVIII, who had it installed in the *Bibliotheque Royale* (Royal Library) in Paris. In 1964, it was transferred to the *Musée du Louvre* (Louvre Museum), where it currently resides.

Jean Francois Champollion dated the relief to the Greco-Roman period, although many scholars think it is a replica of images located in a much older temple. In fact, the image indicates the positions of the equinoxes at a much earlier time. It appears supported by twelve deities (signs), eight kneeling and four on foot (the cardinal points). The 12 signs of the zodiac are divided into 30 degrees each and these are, in turn, divided into three decans of 10 degrees each, making a total of 36.

In addition to the zodiacal constellations and the purely Egyptian motifs, there are representations of the five planets visible to the naked eye; easily identified in the planisphere thanks to labels in hieroglyphic characters. If we look carefully, the ecliptic of Dendera is not like those found in modern planispheres, but breaks down in Cancer to continue again more regularly from Leo; this peculiarity has been attributed to lack of space, an explanation that, while plausible, is also questionable.

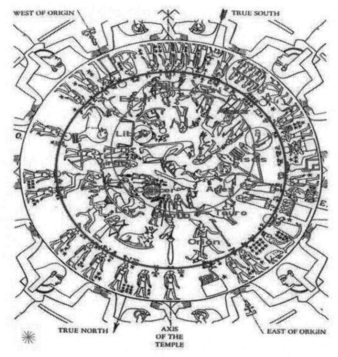

Figure 6.6 Diagram showing the features of the Dendera zodiac

The other zodiac, although much less well known, is illuminated with harmonious colors in its composition and occupies a rectangular strip along the roof of the hypostyle hall. Neither of the reliefs includes any written explanation, so it is obvious that there is something we are not aware of in the set of images, but there is no doubt that the Egyptians knew the signs of the zodiac, and that they possessed some astronomical knowledge which included the precession of equinoxes.

Figure 6.7 Rectangular zodiac from the Temple of Hathor at Dendera

Albert Slosman, a doctor of mathematics who collaborated with NASA on the Pioneer probes to Jupiter and Saturn, suggested that the foundations of Egyptian astrology and astronomy were based on Dendera. Slosman believed that a papyrus written by the scribe of the pharaoh Khufu (4th Dynasty) in the Cairo Museum says that Cheops himself made the third reconstruction of the Dendera temple, according to the same architectural plans used by the Horus followers. All this supports the hypothesis that the *Dendera zodiac* is a replica of an older construction

> *By order of Khufu, the temple of the Lady of heaven of Dendera will be rebuilt for the third time, on the same site and according to the plans laid down by the successors of Horus, on skins of gazelle and safeguarded in the archives of the King...*

Egyptian astrological science took as its basis the sexagesimal system (although they also understood the decimal system) that the Sumerians used. The circle is a model which manifests eternity, because it begins all over again when it returns to the starting point, a concept that nods toward immortality. As in Sumeria, astrology and astronomy went hand in hand with mathematics, a branch of knowledge that was more developed in old Egypt, as may be seen in *the Akhmin wooden tablets* or through detailed reading of *the papyrus of Ahmes*, also known as *the Rhind papyrus*, named in honor of its discoverer, the Scottish Egyptologist Alexander Henry Rhind, which demonstrates an effortless system for calculating fractions. Geometry also reached a very high degree of development, as can be seen in the ratios used in the construction of the pyramids

The Egyptian priests, like the Mesopotamians, used their knowledge of the equinoctial precession and the astrological ages for dating historic events. An example of this is *the Narmer Palette*, carved from siltstone and measuring 64cm x 45cm, found in 1898 at the Temple of Horus, in Hierakonpolis. Academic opinion agrees that the palette commemorates the unification of Upper and Lower Egypt under King Narmer and the beginning of the dynastic period. There seems to be agreement among historians about the approximate date of this unification, dating it to around the year 3000 BC. If you study both the front and the back of the palette, you will see various symbols that date this event to the era of Taurus, which extends approximately from 4,320 BC to 2,160 BC.

Figure 6.8 Diagram showing front and rear views of the Narmer Palette

Ethnology is a branch of anthropology that studies present-day cultures which maintain behaviors and social structures comparable to those of prehistoric cultures which have already disappeared. It is through the study of these primitive peoples, and by projecting their behaviors from the present into the past, that researchers infer, by analogy, aspects of the behavior of Paleolithic communities. This raises the question: how is it possible that there now exist primitive tribes in Africa, Australia and New Zealand, who do not have written language and have yet to make the leap from the Paleolithic to the Neolithic? If the process by which man advanced from the Paleolithic period (the same state in which these primitive peoples are currently living) to building cities, learning to write and developing accurate astronomical systems in ancient Mesopotamia, had been gradual and evolutionary, why have these primitive peoples of today not experienced the same process of technological advancement that the Sumerians experienced in such a short space of time? On the contrary, they have remained developmentally stagnant for centuries. Why have they not experienced even a minimal technological advance?

Once again, we must understand that mathematical and astronomical knowledge of such sophistication, scope and magnitude could not have been achieved by mere intellectual evolution by hunters from the Paleolithic period, whose lives were extremely short and whose primary objective was survival and not stargazing. The most plausible hypothesis is no doubt that an exogenous element was responsible, something that is repeatedly made clear in Mesopotamian and Egyptian mythologies, among others. Why is modern man so committed to ignoring the voice of antiquity?

CHAPTER VII

HUMANITY ENTERS THE SCENE

Those who cannot attack the thought, instead attack the thinker
Paul Valéry, French philosopher (1871-1945)

At the beginning of the twenty-first century, the dispute between evolutionists and creationists seems to have reached an unprecedented intensity. The theory of evolution is, once again, in conflict with creationist theories that had once seemed dead and buried, fruit of a retrograde past.

This is particularly true in one of the most technologically advanced societies on the planet, the United States of America, where so-called "scientific creationism" (and also the theory of "intelligent design") has emerged, promoted by religious groups as a reaction to the predominant scientific movement, which explains the origin of human beings on the basis of Charles Darwin's theory of evolution. It is evident that such groups see this development as a threat to their religious and moral concepts, among which is the existence of a supreme being, God, who created the Universe and, therefore, mankind.

Scientific creationism uses a storyline based on the premise that, if evolutionary theory has faults and weaknesses or cannot explain some facts, as is indeed the case, this is proof that creationism is correct. Its arguments assume that only two options exist: creationism or Darwinian evolution. Scientific creationists have taken advantage of the recent internal debates between evolutionary scientists and used them as a pretext to predict that Darwinism is soon to disappear as the dominant paradigm, leaving creationism as the only reasonable alternative.

On the other side of the contest are those who have seen, in evolutionary theories, scientific proof that the origin of the Universe and man can be explained without the need to resort to a creator God, a notion they consider to have been made redundant by advances in science. According to these principles, humanity is nothing more than a product of the random evolution of matter, and human values are casual and relative.

The storm, far from abating, has reached American universities and colleges, and generated a great deal of controversy in relation to the curriculum taught to students in subjects such as biology, reaching its apogee in the determination of when and how man first appeared on Earth.

Long before paleoanthropological research began in Africa, some thinkers of Classical Greece and, later, Charles Darwin in his book of 1871, *The Descent of Man, and Selection in Relation to Sex*, had identified Africa as the continent most likely to have been the origin of modern humans, as it was also home to their closest relatives (chimpanzee and gorilla) and had climatic conditions favorable for the development of human life.

Since then, there have been important discoveries, although the fossil records which have been used as evidence are only a small proportion of the total that have been discovered; this is why paleoanthropological discussions are endless and irreconcilable.

The first African hominid fossil discoveries, back in the roaring twenties, of the *Australopithecus* (southern ape) generated great expectations, but were not accepted by the scientific community until the fifties, given that the appearance of the fossils was closer to the primates; however, their teeth closely resembled those of humans and they were bipedal.

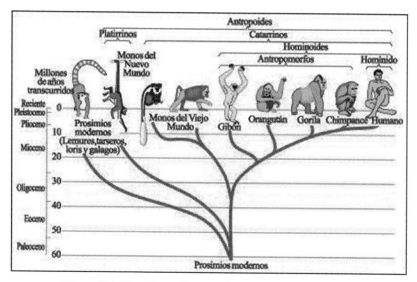

Figure 7.1 The diversified 'family tree' of the primates

A few decades ago, the classification of the genera and species of the pre-human and human branches seemed to have finally reached a logical conclusion; however, the situation today, far from simplified, is instead further complicated with each new discovery of fossils. It was thought that the *Ramapithecus*, a primate fossil dated to 12 million years ago, had already separated from the line of the great apes, and was the direct forefather of *Homo sapiens* but, at the beginning of the eighties, through the application of phylogenetic analysis techniques, it was concluded that *Ramapithecus* was the direct forefather of the orangutan and not of the human line; this led to the determination, with some precision, of the time at which hominids diverged from the apes, at about 4 million years ago.

Currently, it is believed that *Australopithecus* is the genus immediately preceding the *Homo* genus and modern humans, having already separated from the line of the great apes. The first species, *Australopithecus anamensis*, lived approximately 4 million years ago and was identified from bones found in Kenya and Ethiopia. It is thought to be the ancestor of a species that lasted until just less than 3 million years ago, *Australopithecus afarensis*, whose remains were found in Ethiopia, Kenya and Tanzania. "Lucy", made famous by the world's media, was a member of this species. In spite of its small skull, with a simian appearance, the curvature of the jaw and teeth are similar to those of humans, and its pelvis and legs are almost equal in size to those of modern humans. The curvature of the bones of its feet and its long arms suggest an adaptation to climbing trees. In Kenya and Chad, other fossils from the same time have been found which seem to be variants; they have been christened *Kenyanthropus platyops* and *Australopithecus bahrelghazali*.

The next species that we know of, thanks to an abundant and representative sample of bones discovered in South Africa, is *Australopithecus africanus*, which lived approximately 2 to 3 million years ago. Although some scientists believe that *afarensis* and *africanus* are the same species, both the chronological and geographical differences and, above all, the characteristics closest to humans (teeth and mandibular arch less archaic than previous species, greater height and cranial capacity) mean that the majority of researchers believe it to be a separate species. Also contemporary is another species called *Australopithecus garhi*, found in Ethiopia and dated to 2.5 million years ago.

The next on the list is *Australopithecus robustus* (also known as *Paranthropus robustus*), distinguished by a larger chewing apparatus; it seems very likely that the three known species of *Paranthropus* are closely related (*robustus* in South Africa, *boisei* in East Africa, between 1 and 2 million years old, and the oldest, *aethiopicus*, in Ethiopia, between 2.6 and 2.3 million years old). The most striking aspect of *Australopithecus robustus* is that they were contemporaries of the first species of hominids, raising an intriguing scenario of multiple, relatively similar species living close to each other for hundreds of thousands of years.

At this point, approximately 2.5 million years ago, the species classified within the human line (hominids) began to appear, all of them with small teeth, large skulls and the ability to walk upright.

Homo habilis and *Homo rudolfensis* are the oldest species (between 2.4 and 1.5 million years old). While some scholars consider them members of the *Australopithecus* genus, certain important changes, such as a larger brain, less prominent face, smaller teeth and a better developed bipedal walk, suggest their inclusion in the *Homo* genus. The majority of the first humans found in Olduvai (Tanzania), the lakes of Malawi (Malawi), Turkana (Kenya) and, with a little more doubt, in South Africa, are classified as *habilis*, so called for their ability to create tools. Although one of the most well-known skulls found at Turkana, catalogued as KNM-ER 1470, which has a curious mixture of primitive characteristics, such as larger teeth, but also the more advanced characteristic of greater cranial capacity, has been defined by some scientists as a distinct species, *Homo rudolfensis*, in honor of Lake Rudolf, today called Lake Turkana.

Before these two species disappeared, a new type of human made an appearance; 1.8 million years old, *Homo erectus was* found at sites in East Africa, on the shores of Lake Turkana, and in South Africa. This species was present until about 300,000 years ago. The morphological features of *erectus* were more modern than those of *habilis*: greater cranial capacity, very robust, higher stature (the skeleton of the Turkana boy averaged 168 cm, despite being only twelve years old), a less protruding jaw and more pronounced nose; however, his head was still low and elongated and the eyebrow ridges were very prominent. Fossil remains of *erectus* have also been found on the island of Java, and in China (Peking man) which has caused divisions between researchers over how to name them, though a widespread convention is *Homo ergaster* for the African fossils and *Homo erectus* for those found in Asia.

It is clear that both were separate from the australopithecine line and were already closer to humans than *habilis* and *rudolfensis*. The fossil catalogued as KNM-WT 15000, the Turkana boy, corresponds to a hominid who died when eleven or twelve years old, 1.6 million years ago, and his physiognomy reminds us more of the shepherds who today populate the upper valley of the River Nile than that of his predecessor, Lucy, which did not exceed a meter in height. The shortening of the arms shows the final abandonment of the trees as a habitat, with the perfect bipedalism that made him perfectly suited to covering long distances, leading to the first migration out of Africa, although it is not known if there was a conscious desire to expand or, on the contrary, if it was simply a case of the biological imperative to migrate that affects other species.

Later, some remains discovered in Europe and Africa, dated to over 500,000 years ago, reveal that, at that time, morphological changes began to occur, leading to the advent of new species. Again, it was in Africa, where the selective pressures necessary for these evolutionary changes were strongest, that this took place. We find remains in South Africa, Zambia, Tanzania and Ethiopia that show a skull with greater volume (1200-1300 cm3), greater width, more prominent cheekbones and rear occipital, and more arched eyebrows. These remains have been given different names by scholars, among which are *Homo rhodesiensis*, with advanced anatomical features suggesting a relation to *Homo heidelbergensis* and *Homo neanderthalensis*, and with certain characteristics that point toward *Homo sapiens*; as such, many researchers consider them our most immediate ances-tors. Modern classification places all of them within the species *Homo heidelbergensis*, as this was the first one, named after the finding of the Mauer jaw, near Heidelberg (Germany). According to Phillip Rightmire, both the Neanderthals and the Cro-Magnon (or early *Homo sapiens*) descended from the species *heidelbergensis/rhodesiensis*.

Let's take a moment to talk about research in this area. Classification of the animal kingdom is based on comparative anatomy, that is, the study of the similarities and differences observed in the organs, muscles, and skeletons of different species, which allows us to reconstruct evolutionary history to some extent. However, it must be said that these types of comparison are not accurate. Instead, many researchers now use genetics to compare different species. Today, it is thought that the conclusions derived from genetic analysis are very accurate, and this would be the case if our knowledge of the universe of genetics was complete, but it should be noted that knowledge in this field is still in its infancy, despite the false triumphalism that is transmitted, day after day, by the media. The conclusions derived from these analyses, far from being certain truths, should be taken with caution; they are challenged every day by new data and advances in genetics, a branch of science that still harbors a good number of mysteries.

The scientific reasoning is that, the closer two species are, the greater the number of molecular structures they will share in their genome. Over the past few years, the scientific community has accepted as an unassailable truth that human beings and their closest living relatives, the chimpanzees, only differ in 1.24% of their DNA sequences. However, an international team coordinated by Tomas Marques-Bonet, of the Institute of Evolutionary Biology (a joint research center of the Pompeu Fabra University and *Consejo Superior de Investigaciones Científicas*), has very recently published its research in the journal *Nature*, in February 2009, concluding that this estimate is incorrect and that, in reality, the number of differences can be up to ten times greater.

This shows how imprecise findings based on genetic testing can be. It was discovered in this study that the genome of each species of primate, including humans, comprises large fragments exclusive to that species. According to the authors, the key to this result was the study of the duplication of large DNA fragments repeated throughout the genome. This part of the genome had previously been ignored as it was an extremely complicated process to separate it from the rest of the DNA, although it had long been suspected that it was important. As the authors point out, the differences that had been studied previously were changes (mutations) in the genome sequences that are shared by all primates; however, the differences studied by the researchers at the Institute of Evolutionary Biology are differences unique to each species.

The international team has systematically studied segmental duplication for the entire genome of four species of primates: cynomolgus monkeys, orangutans, chimpanzees and humans. In this way, it has been able to develop the first catalog of species, specific to these regions of the genome, and also much more effectively quantify the differences between species and understand at what point in their evolution they appeared. This represents radical differences in some of the books that make up the genetic library of each species.

Back to the main topic. On the origin of our species, *Homo sapiens*, there have existed for some time two competing models: the first proposes a multiregional origin in various parts of the planet, where modern humans developed in a more or less independent way, starting from their pre-human forms (*erectus* in Asia, *ergaster* in Africa, *neanderthalensis* in Europe etc.); the second theory, known as the "Garden of Eden" or "Out of Africa", postulates a single source for all present-day human populations, in a specific area of Africa, that spread across the planet.

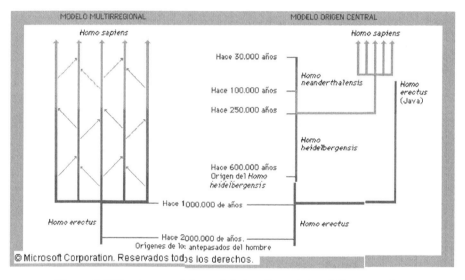

Figure 7.2 The two models explaining the origin of *Homo sapiens*

The first model, called the candelabrum, must answer the question of how people so geographically distant from each other, and with such small populations, were able to retain the biological unity needed to finally develop into modern humans

In relation to the second model, the latest genetic research has produced some revealing data. The genetic information of an individual is found mainly in the DNA located in the nucleus of the cells. However, there is also so-called mitochondrial DNA, located in the mitochondria, structures within the cytoplasm of the cell and not in the nucleus, with the particular characteristic that it is only transmitted through the maternal line. Its analysis allows us to identify the common ancestor of a species, the so-called "mitochondrial Eve". These studies reveal that all human DNA comes from a single original sequence, located in Africa, which dates back to about 200,000 years ago. That's not to say this human Eve was the oldest female of the species, but the oldest of the females whose descendants survive to this day. Other Eves had descendants, but their lineages have not been fortunate enough to reach the present time. In the same way that mitochondrial DNA is passed on from generation to generation only from mother to child, the researchers have examined the DNA that is transmitted exclusively along the paternal line, the Y chromosome. The results of this research led to the conclusion that the man who possessed the oldest Y chromosome, the chromosomal Adam, also lived in Africa.

This second hypothesis has in its favor a key fact: European Neanderthals lived about 110,000 years ago, and it is said that they were too different from us to have had time to develop into *Homo sapiens* in so short a space of time. In addition, the fossils of Palestine in the Middle East have been accurately dated, and it has been verified that the ones with a more Neanderthal aspect (Kebara, Tabun), lived in that location some 40,000 years later than those of a more human type (Sokhul, Qafzeh). That is just the opposite result we would expect if they were our ancestors. The approximately twelve remains found at Qafzeh, dating from about 100,000 years ago, are the first evidence of *Homo sapiens* in the Middle East. The archaeological data shows that the *sapiens* abandoned the location between 50,000 and 80,000 years ago, after which the site was occupied by Neanderthals, until the Cro-Magnons returned later.

The discussion of whether Neanderthals belong to our lineage has echoed in the halls of paleoanthropology for 150 years, since they were first discovered. What do we know about them? Most paleoanthropologists agree that their remote origin was in *Homo heidelbergensis* (like *sapiens*) and that Neanderthal man is a different species of our genus. However, were they really a different species to our own?

In the summer of 2009, studies conducted by researchers at the *Consejo Superior de Investigaciones Científicas* (CSIC), in collaboration with the Max Planck Institute in Germany and the University of Oviedo, were made public. They restored the complete genome of the mitochondrial DNA of five Neanderthals, one from the Sidrón Cave (Spain), another from the site of Vindija (Croatia), two from Feldhofer (Germany) and one from Mezmaiskaya (Russia). For this study, the researchers used novel techniques in DNA sequencing that allowed them to explore millions of DNA sequences from ancient bones. In this case, the analysis of five genomes led to the conclusion that the last common source of all Neanderthal mitochondrial genomes (110,000 years ago) was more recent than that of the modern *Homo sapiens sapiens* (150,000 years ago), which seems to demonstrate that they were not our ancestors.

Although these dates are more recent than those obtained from previous models based on fossil records, the results indicate that the genetic differences among Neanderthals were less than those among modern humans, even lower than in European populations currently. For example, the genome of the individuals in Feldhofer and Vindija are identical despite being separated by a thousand kilometers. This can only occur if species diversity is very low.

It was also revealed that the variation within the human mitochondrial genome were in the order of three times higher than the average variation within the human species at present, although less than half than the difference between humans and chimpanzees. The conclusion was that Cro-Magnon and Neanderthals were two different species that shared a common ancestor, although it must be said that these conclusions haven´t taken into consideration the recent genetic sequencing that points to a greater difference between humans and chimpanzees. The difference, rather than 1%, might be as much as 10%. As you can see, things aren´t that clear and the last word has not been said.

Who were the Neanderthals? How did they live? Why did they become extinct? There are two hypotheses in terms of chronology: one that traces their origins to between 250,000 and 200,000 years ago and another that traces them back to about 120,000 years ago. They formed a human group who lived mainly in Europe and west Asia, becoming extinct due to unknown reasons about 30,000 or 40,000 years ago. They have been described as prehistoric brutes, but they were neither brutes nor stupid.

They have been caricatured to an absurd extent, perhaps to give modern humans a pleasant feeling of superiority from which to contemplate the enormous gap that separates us from them.

From those old stereotypes of furry, fierce beings more like ape than man, their image has gradually changed as prejudices about their human status have been diluted. They were physically very strong, light-skinned and with a more voluminous skull, receding chin and a sloping forehead, but we cannot say that they were very different to the *Homo sapiens* or Cro-Magnons of that time. They were organized into small groups of hunter-gatherers and there is no data suggesting that their hunting methods were less socially organized than that of *sapiens*.

They possessed structures of family and social relationships within the group, leading a nomadic life bound to the rhythms of nature. There is abundant data that indicates Neanderthals formed social relationships based on respect for the individual and on group solidarity, thus caring for weaker members. They used bone, wood, leather and stone to build their homes, in caves or in the open air. They were also master stone carvers, developing the so-called *Levallois* technique, which required the craftsman to develop detailed mental images prior to its implementation.

Burials have been found, dating from 60,000 years ago, in which grave goods were deposited with the deceased, which indicates a capacity for human feelings and religious abstraction. Some authors have theorized that this behavior was in imitation of the rituals performed by *sapiens*, with whom they shared their habitat for a long time, but there is no scientific basis to such a claim, because we have no primary evidence at that point in prehistory to indicate who might have been mimicking whom.

Some researchers have argued that artistic activity is the main difference between Neanderthals and *sapiens*. It is true that many of the finds proposed to be Neanderthal art are debatable; however, we know that they were familiar with the use of dyes and collected objects like stones of vivid colors, fossil fragments and other minerals. In fact, some 37,000 years ago, when they shared the stage with *sapiens*, they possessed objects of bone and ivory that were drilled and used as pendants, with the clear intent of ornamentation but, once again, it has been suggested they were imitating the behavior of *sapiens*.

It seems that Neanderthals, in the eyes of the majority of researchers, could only have human traits through the unconscious imitation of their superiors, *sapiens*, the authentic humans. From an academic point of view, art is defined as a purely human phenomenon, which saw its first flowering in the period known as the Upper Paleolithic, which immediately followed the disappearance of the Neanderthals.

It must be questioned if these comparisons have been carried out in the right way because, in the period of some 12,000 years that Neanderthals and *sapiens* shared their European habitat, while it is true that Neanderthals did not develop the height of artistic expression that *sapiens* would develop some 20,000 years later, it is also true that *sapiens* themselves did not do so during the era in which they lived side by side. This raises the question of what might have happened if the Neanderthals had not disappeared and, on the contrary, had survived for a further 20,000 years. Would they also have reached the levels of artistic expression reflected on the walls of caves?

Different chronological periods cannot be used to make a comparison like this. It would be the same as saying that man in the Middle Ages, from a paleoanthropological point of view, did not have the intelligence to develop complex computer systems simply because there are no records of computers at that time, when it is obvious that what he lacked was the accumulation of knowledge and skills that developed in later centuries and culminated in the advent of computer science. Can anybody know for certain that the Neanderthals would not, given another 20,000 years, have created artistic works of the same quality as *sapiens*?

The capacity of human beings to interact with each other through a highly structured and specialized system of vocal communication has always been considered a differentiator marking the frontier between *Homo sapiens* and the rest of the inhabitants of the planet. However, did Neanderthals have an articulated language? Until not so long ago it was assumed that the structure of their larynx did not allow them to articulate vowel sounds, but several discoveries have challenged this view.

One was the discovery of a Neanderthal hyoid bone, which connects the larynx or voice-box with the muscles of the tongue, identical to that of *sapiens*. Another was the discovery in *heidelbergensis* (the immediate predecessors of Neanderthals and *sapiens*), in Atapuerca, of an auditory system similar to our own.

Finally, genetic studies on the finds from the Sidrón Cave showed that Neanderthals and *sapiens* shared the gene FOXP2, required for the development of speech and language. Regarding the auditory system, in 2004 a team of scientists analyzed fossils found at *Sima de los Huesos de Atapuerca* (Spain) belonging to individuals of the genus *Homo* who lived 400,000 years ago. To do this, the team included experts in 3D imaging, who were responsible for rebuilding the middle ear bones of the fossils to determine if they were able to hear the same range of frequencies as modern man, indicating that they could have had an articulated language as complex as *sapiens*.

The paleontologist and professor Ignacio Martinez stated that the individuals in *Sima de los huesos* could hear like modern humans and could certainly speak. The same team of scientists performed the same type of study on fossils of the early hominids *Australopithecus* and *Paranthropus*, and discovered that the hearing of these hominid species, which lived 2 million years ago, was more similar to that of chimpanzees and that, therefore, their language abilities could not have been as complex and articulate as our own. The conclusion seems to be that human speech, as we understand it, could have begun at some point between 2 million and 400,000 years ago. In light of these discoveries, the idea that Neanderthals possessed both speech and language becomes very plausible indeed.

The big mystery is: what happened to the Neanderthals? Why did they disappear, leaving barely a trace? Paleoanthropologists say that

Neanderthals were the lords of Europe but, some 50,000 years ago, *Homo sapiens* arrived in several waves of migration from Africa, and the two species lived together in the same geographical space for at least 12,000 years. The contacts between the two included moments of hostility, as well as close relationships. At Lagar Velho in Portugal, remains have been found of what might be an example of hybridization between the two species: a *sapiens* child that, years after the disappearance of the Neanderthals, still preserved some anatomical traits only found in the latter. Was there sexual contact between the two species? If so, could Neanderthal blood be running in our veins? Did they disappear without trace, or are their descendants living among us? What really happened we cannot say, but we should be prepared for some unusual answers.

The evolutionary history of the human being is very far from being a simple branching of the tree of life resulting in the man of today. All the data suggests that the human species which inhabited the Earth interbred, thus giving rise to various hybrids. In 2014, the journals *Nature* and *Science* simultaneously published a discovery shedding light on this. *Nature* featured a study conducted by a team of geneticists from the Harvard Medical School and *Science* reported on another carried out by Benjamin Vernot and Joshua Akey, from the University of Washington, stating that Neanderthals had mixed with Cro-Magnon, modern humans being the final result of this process. Through a genomic study of human populations, it has been verified that 20 - 30% of the current human genome comes from Neanderthals. Now we can see that modern humans preserve much more Neanderthal DNA than was previously thought...

Most researchers believe that Neanderthal and *sapiens* are two different species, something that depends more on cataloging than on real differences. One thing we do know with certainty is that both Neanderthals and Cro-Magnon emerged from the same common ancestor, *Homo heidelbergensis*, after which they broke away and took different paths, although their level of intelligence and behavior were similar. Researchers believe that *sapiens* did not descend from Neanderthal, but what if something apparently equally preposterous was the case; that Neanderthal was a descendant of Cro-Magnon, one which eventually disappeared? Or even that they did not disappear and are still among us, without our ever noticing... The fact is that both species emerged between approximately 200,000 and 300,000 years ago, overnight, and time will reveal new surprises.

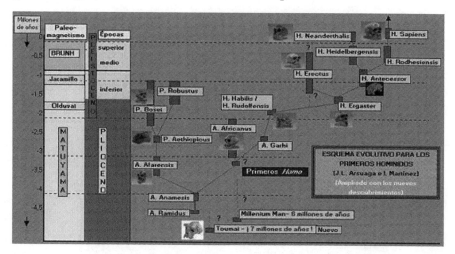

Figure 7.3 Illustration of the ancestry of hominid species

Modern anthropological theories on the origins of man, based on evolution and natural selection, cannot explain many features and aspects of *Homo sapiens*. How can one explain that *sapiens* has evolved an advanced level of intelligence and knowledge in the last few million years, while his close cousins, the monkeys, have been relatively stagnant at an evolutionary level? The explanation given by science is that, during this time, hominids became bipedal, leaving them with two arms for the use of tools, which produced a feedback process in the brain that caused the development of enhanced mental faculties.

It is true that certain scientific tests have shown that rats develop greater brain mass when active rather than at rest and, when caged, those that are provided with toys develop greater brain mass than those with an empty cage. While this may be true, it would be quite another thing for the rats to become another type of animal entirely. In addition, in nature we see examples of animals extremely skillful in the use of tools which have, however, not reached a human level of intelligence, so contradicting and negating the argument.

For example, the Egyptian vulture breaks ostrich eggs by throwing stones while the sea otter of the northern Pacific Ocean uses a stone to detach shellfish from rocks and to crack their shells, using another stone as an anvil. Chimpanzees also manufacture and use simple tools, yet we do not see their level of intelligence change in a substantive way. The theory of evolution can explain changes in the organization of species, but they are made in a gradual and slow manner and not overnight, as happened in the case of man. Why did hominids become intelligent while the chimpanzee did not?

If science offers a tremendously confusing explanation for the origins of modern humans, it is due to the fact that neither anthropologists nor archaeologists know for certain what happened. The emergence of *Homo sapiens* is a mystery which is, for the time being, indecipherable and which, when calculating the probabilities, begins to seem impossible. The records show that, after millions of years of minimal progress with stone tools, *Homo sapiens* suddenly appeared, 250,000 years ago, with doubled cranial capacity and the ability to speak. For reasons not yet explained, he continued living in a primitive mode until about 30,000 years ago, at which point he experienced a shift towards his modern behavior. Some 12,000 years ago he had already spread throughout the world and had developed agriculture. Then, 7,000 years ago, he founded the first great civilizations and has now begun a space race through the immensity of the solar system.

All this data points in the opposite direction to evolutionary theory, which evokes a slow and gradual process of transformation in species that would suggest perhaps a million years for the more advanced hominids to move from lithic tools to the use of other materials, and tens of millions of years in order to master mathematics, chemistry, astrophysics and space travel.

The reality is that the theory of evolution as scientific fact and the theory of divine creation belong in two different planes, but I do not think that one should be excluded to the detriment of the other, as if they were two irreconcilable positions. After all, evolution and creation (revolution) are two ends of a common idea, graduations and measurements of the same scale or process. Revolution is nothing more than rapid evolution in time or, in other words, a process that takes place over a significantly shorter period of time than we are used to through the natural process of evolution. Why not open a new path of research that supports the coexistence of the theory of evolution with divine creation?

CHAPTER VIII

AND THE GODS CREATED MAN IN THEIR IMAGE AND LIKENESS

There must be no barriers to freedom of inquiry. There is no place for dogma in science. The scientist is free, and must be free to ask any question, to doubt any assertion, to seek for any evidence, to correct any errors.
Robert Oppenheimer, American physicist (1904-1967)

The story told in the Bible about the creation of man is, without doubt, the decisive factor in the debate between creationists and evolutionists. Creationists argue that human beings were created by the grace of God and did not arrive at their current state by means of a slow evolutionary process, developing from living beings that preceded us. It is time to immerse yourself in the most ancient texts written by human beings. Let's look at what the Bible says in the verses of *Genesis*, so full of secrets and contradictions.

And God said: Let us make man in our image, after our likeness
Genesis 1:26

In this translation, certain elements have been changed that hinder our understanding of the passage's original meaning. In the original Hebrew, in place of the word God is the word *"Elohim"*, which literally means "gods". This is an interesting and, no doubt, deliberate choice on the part of the scribe, using the plural term rather than the singular *"El"*, which he could have used to refer to a unique "God". This is the original text in Hebrew:

Vayomer <u>Elohim</u> na'aseh adam betsalmenu kidemutenu veyirdu bidegat hayam

While, in the English translation, the translator has substituted the term "gods" for "God", which might be perceived as an error, he did not remove the grammatical construction of the verb in the sentence that follows, retaining the corresponding plural possessive pronoun ("let us make man in our image, after our likeness"). There are scholars who try to justify this by saying that, in ancient times, it was customary for great individuals to use the *pluralis majestatis*, the "royal we", to refer to themselves. This is a childish and unfounded attempt at justification, particularly when one looks at the original text in Hebrew and, as we shall see later, when studying the Mesopotamian texts which inspired the biblical *Genesis*.

What secret hides behind the use of the word *Elohim*? Was there more than one god at the time of creation? Whatever the answer, the *Elohim* are, once again, the stars of the story and, as I have mentioned in previous chapters, it will be necessary to see what the Mesopotamian texts, older than the Bible and free of any subsequent correction, have to say about it. First, we should look a little more deeply into the biblical texts. There are many contradictory messages in the *Book of Genesis*. Let's look at the following stanza, to which we shall return later because of its implications:

And it came to pass,
when men began to multiply on the face of the earth,
and daughters were born unto them,
that the sons of God saw the daughters of men that they were fair;
and they took them wives of all which they chose.
And the Lord said: My spirit shall not always strive with man,
for that he also is flesh: yet his days shall be an hundred and

twenty years.
The Nephilim were in the earth in those days, and also after that,
when the sons of God came in unto the daughters of men,
and they bare children to them, the same were the mighty men
(in Hebrew "the gueborim", "the giants") which were of
old, the men of renown

Genesis 6:1-4

Here we find some disturbing messages. What does the scribe mean when he writes of the children of God and the daughters of men? Who were the *Nephilim*? And who were the *Gueborim*? Ancient Israel had only one God, so where did the sons of God, the *Nephilim*, come from? The verses also speak, for the first time, of the mighty men. Giants are present in all mythologies both eastern and western. What kind of beings were these giants?

The idea that these "sons of God" were materialized angels who had mixed with women was accepted and widespread during the period of Hellenized Judaism, as seen in the Greek *Septuagint*, which replaces the expression "sons of God" with "the angels". The Dead Sea Scrolls found at Qumran are in full agreement on this. Scholars know that the authors of the *Book of Genesis* based their story on much older and more detailed texts whose origin was Sumer, so it is interesting and enriching to see what they said about this. These texts make clear that the creation of man was the work of the Anunnaki, the *Nephilim*, the *Anakim*, or the *Elohim*, different names used for alien beings that came from another planet to colonize the Earth for their own benefit. Let's not get ahead of ourselves, though. We should follow step by step and see what these ancient stories have to say.

The *Epic of Atrahasis* (exceedingly wise), known in technical circles as *Enuma Ilu awilum*, was introduced to the wider world at the end of the nineteenth century thanks, once again, to George Smith. It was a very short version and a little confusing as, for a long time, it was thought that the reverse of the tablet was the front. It was not until 1956 that the Danish assyriologist J. Laessoe put the fragments together and established that what we were dealing with was the oldest known genesis story covering the entire history of mankind, from the moment that man was created, through the Universal Deluge, and, finall , to the so-called historical period. Although entire passages of the poem are lost, in 1969, W. G. Lambert, in collaboration with A. R. Millard, published *Atrahasis: The Babylonian Story of the Flood*, a more detailed reconstruction of the story so far.

The Anunnaki, beings from another planet, came to Earth and found mineral resources as well as the potential for agricultural production; they decided to begin the cultivation of food and extraction of minerals. This was long before man made his appearance on the stage. After some time, the space travelers, due to the harshness of the working conditions under which they suffered, rebelled and rioted, their cries reaching the very doors of their great master, Enlil. This sparked a series of events of great significance for us, the earthlings

The story begins by describing, in a precise and journalistic language, the conditions in which these beings lived, prior to the advent of man, as they dug channels, built dams, plowed and harvested crops.

> *When the gods, like man,*
> *Bore the work, carried the labor-basket,*
> *Great indeed was the drudgery of the gods,*
> *The work was heavy, too much was the distress.*
>
> Epic of Atrahasis

It emphasizes the difficul y and the long period for which they bore these arduous working conditions.

> *They counted years of drudgery.*
> *For two thousand five hundred years, and more,*
> *Forced labor they bore night and day.*

This caused a rebellion of the workers who, destroying their equipment, rioted in front of the house of the highest authority, Enlil.

> *Let us confront the throne-bearer,*

That he may remove from us our heavy labor.

Enlil, the master, given the situation created by the insubordination of the workers, held a grand council to find a solution. The Council was attended by the great leaders, in addition to Anu and Enki. In the meeting, Nuska, a trusted man of Enlil, was ordered to arbitrate and to establish why the Anunnaki workers had rebelled and besieged the house. On his return, after a dialog with the mutineers, Nuska explained to those present in the Assembly that the complaints of the workers were caused by the harsh conditions to which they had been subjected.

Enlil, a lover of discipline, demanded exemplary punishment so that the situation would never be repeated, but Anu, the sovereign, was more sympathetic to the plight of the workers.

Anu opened his mouth,
And said to the gods, his brothers:
Why are we accusing them?
Their work is heavy, too much is their distress.

It was at this point that Ea (Enki) addressed the Assembly. He suggested a solution to the problem, proposing that they relieve the unbearable burden of the Anunnaki through the creation of a "primitive worker" that would do the work so far undertaken by the gods. For that he took advantage of the presence of Ninti (Belet-ili).

While Belet-ili is present,
Let the birth-goddess create a human, a man.
Let him bear the yoke! Let him bear the yoke!
Let man assume the drudgery of the gods!
Let man assume the drudgery of the Igigu!
Let the midwife create a human being!

The Assembly, with genuine enthusiasm, welcomed Enki´s proposal to create a primitive worker, an *Adamu*, a term that was no doubt the inspiration for the biblical name Adam. This solution would relieve them of the work and allow a society of leisure for the Anunnaki.

However, those gathered had questions and doubts about the feasibility of creating a living being specifically designed to carry out the work that these beings from another planet no longer would. How intelligent should that being be? The worker would need to be smart enough to understand orders and to handle the equipment used by the Anunnaki.

Ninti agreed to the proposal made by the Assembly, while winking complicitly at Enki, to indicate that he should help her with the assignment.

> *But Nintu, opened her mouth,*
> *And said to the great gods,*
> *It is not properly mine to do these things;*
> *Enki is the one who purifies all,*
> *Let him provide me the clay, and I will do (it).*

It took the intervention of Nammu, Anu's wife and the mother of Enki, to persuade him to get over his reluctance to participate. In this regard, there are two tablets with identical content, one from Nippur, in the museum of the University of Philadelphia, and the other currently held at the Louvre but acquired from an antique shop, which shed light on these events. Thus, while Enki rested, Nammu appealed to him once again, telling him of the anguish that the gods suffered and interceding to persuade him to enact what he had proposed at the Assembly.

> *Oh, my son, rise from your bed...work what is wise,*
> *Fashion servants of the gods, may they produce their doubles...*

The response of Enki offers a solution for the mystery of the creation of man, by integrating the opposing and seemingly antagonistic positions of the creationists and the evolutionists. It explains that man was not created out of nothing by God but that mankind was also not the result of a slow evolution.

> *Oh my mother, the creature whose name you have pronounced,*
> *it exists,*
> *Bind upon it the image of the gods,*

Mix the heart of the clay that is over the Apsu;
The good and princely fashioners will thicken the clay!

In these four lines is the key to the riddle: how could a new creature become physically, mentally and emotionally a replica of the gods? How was man created in their image and likeness? On the basis of a creature already existing in the Earth's ecosystem: a hominid (*Adama*, clay, earth); Enki applied the genetic changes required (created in the image of the gods) to improve its intelligence and thus create a new being (*Adam*, the terrestrial) in such a way that it could take charge of those tasks that, until that time, were exclusively the province of the gods.

The Hebrew *Genesis*, as well as other traditions, speaks of God as a potter that created man from a "piece of clay". This is an incomplete and less detailed interpretation than the original Mesopotamian sources. It is important to observe the word game that has taken place which, without doubt, hides a vital message. On the one hand is *Adam*: the human, the terrestrial; on the other hand is *Adama*: cultivable, clay-rich soil.

Then Elohim formed Adam of the dust of the ground,
breathed into his nostrils the breath of life,
and the man became a living soul."

Genesis 2:7

That Enki was aware of the existence of hominids, of which I spoke in the previous chapter, is beyond doubt, as demonstrated in the written records which have come down to us. Enki, always eager for new knowledge, had the scientific mind and the curiosity needed to take an interest in all the beings which formed the Earth's fauna, among whom were these apes with human form. In the *Epic of Gilgamesh*, this being, ancestor to humans, this dust of the earth, *Adama*, is described in the following verses.

The whole of his body was covered with hair,
He was clothed with long hair like a woman.
The quality of his hair was luxuriant, like that of Nisaba.

*He was innocent of mankind; he knew nothing of the cultivated
land;*
He was clothed with garments as Samuqans.
With gazelles he ate herbs,
And lurked with wild beasts at the water-holes,
He had joy of the water with the herds of wild game.

The possibility of domesticating the *Homo erectus, ergaster* or
heidelbergensis through a process of breeding and generational selection
was duly discarded, given its savagery, as well as its intelligence,
which posed difficulties in converting it to a docile beast of burden
which would serve the interests of its masters. At the same time, it
was necessary to upgrade the creature in such a way that it was able
to perform certain tasks. It needed a brain sufficientl developed to be
able to manipulate instruments with skill and be able to understand the
orders given. It needed an overhaul of its intelligence to become a *lulu
amelu* (hybrid worker). Enki must have seen the solution to the problem
immediately: he had to bind the genetic fingerprint of the Anunnaki to
this being through genetic manipulation. Enki decided to create a hybrid
Anunnaki/*Homo erectus*.

Enki and Ninti developed a plan to design a being that would be a
"servant of the gods", to resolve the situation in which *"there was no
Adam who cultivated the land."* According to the Sumerian writings that
have come down to us, the gods saw man as a necessary evil whose
function was to be a servant or slave to facilitate their wishes. The gods
had little compassion and were cruel masters who regarded humans as
naughty children, with no more importance than pets, and whom it was
necessary to govern with an iron fist.

That man was created to serve the gods was not an idea which would
seem strange in antiquity. The divinity was "Lord", "Sovereign" and
"King", and a word that is usually translated as worship is *avod* (work),
so the men of antiquity did not worship their god in the way understood
today, rather they worked for him.

For the modern man of the twenty-first century, such an idea would not seem so ridiculous if he thought logically and disregarded cultural and religious considerations. At the end of the day, the ultimate aim of humans remains the same as that of the ancient gods, to avoid hard work. We are already starting to see technological advances in robotics that, in a few short years, will allow robots in service of humanity to carry out dirty and dangerous jobs. In short, there will be machines that perform tasks which, today, must be completed by humans. So suggest Erik Brynjolfsson and Andrew McAfee in their recent book, *The Second Machine Age: Work, Progress, and Prosperity in a Time of Brilliant Technologies*, an essay that deals with the opportunities and dangers that await us during the second industrial revolution, the era of robotics, which has sparked a heated debate in the United States. The controversy has even been dramatized by the media through science fiction television series like the British-American *Humans* or the Swedish *Real Humans* which, in an open-minded way, explore the future impact on society of robotics for domestic use.

The word "robot", popularized by the playwright Karel Capek in 1920, comes from the Czech *robota* (forced labor) and *rabota* (servitude); the term comes incredible close to the same meaning as the term "man" had in antiquity. Robots are now being developed using designs that mimic human neuronal processing maps; at the same time they will be provided with a human appearance to make them pleasing to our eyes, so we might well say that they are made in the image and likeness of their creators. Are we repeating, somehow, something that already happened thousands of years ago? There are even those who dare to venture that, at some point in the future, there might be a rebellion of the robots that will force human beings to fight for their freedom and exterminate these automatons.

According to Daniel Wilson, PhD in robotics at the Robotics Institute of Carnegie Mellon University and a researcher for Microsoft at the Palo Alto Research Center (PARC), this assumption is not at all far-fetched, given the progress that is being achieved in artificial intelligence. He has even proposed some measures to create an effective resistance against a future rebellion of the robots. Fans of the silver screen will recall the *Terminator* series, which imagines a dystopian future in which machines reach such a degree of consciousness that they rebel against humanity. Something similar, although with different participants, has already happened in the remote past, as we will see. The cycles of history repeat, but let's not anticipate events and get back to the theme we were discussing.

To carry out the plan, Enki asked the Council for the use of a young Anunnaki god, the instigator of the rebellion. He intended to mix his blood, his genetic code, with the clay of the ground (Earth) and, in this way, create the first men.

That one of his brothers
Be provided to me
He will have to perish,
So men can be created

Enuma Elish

On the first, seventh, and fifteenth of the month
I shall make a purification by washing.
Then one god should be slaughtered.
And the gods can be purified by immersion.
Nintu shall mix the clay
With his flesh and blood.
Then a god and a man
Will be mixed together in clay

Epic of Atrahasis

That was the original plan, corroborated by the teachings of all religions across the length and breadth of the Earth. Though none have told the tale accurately from the old, original sources; each and every one of them has modified aspects more or less essential for their ideological interests. In the case of Christianity, in the defense of a monotheistic doctrine which postulates the existence of a single god, the original references to different beings or gods have been excluded, despite the fact that its own dogma includes many inconsistencies in this regard. At the same time, it gives new names to these beings, the "angels", incorporeal beings. However, as we will see, this is more than questionable when the biblical texts are analyzed by a dispassionate and critical reader who can verify that these angels are described as beings of flesh and bone, with a physical body as material as ours.

Figure 8.1 A Mesopotamian low relief where different chimeras are represented at the pre-human stage

These beings from distant stars would surely possess the technological knowledge to perform such a task. What emerges from the original sources, however, is that they had never attempted something like this before; this is demonstrated by the enthusiasm it generated among the members of the Assembly and by the repeated unsuccessful attempts before the successful completion of the prototype.

When Berosus, Babylonian priest, wrote to the Greeks about cosmogony and the Mesopotamian stories of creation, he spoke of a pre-human stage in which humans coexisted with beings that were born with two or four wings, others with horns, or some with male and female genitalia. He also spoke of a man with two heads and described a beast, by the name of Oannes, whose body was shaped like a fish and who had grown a human head under the head of fish, and human feet instead of a tail

> *There appeared men, some of whom were furnished with two wings, others with four, and with two faces. They had one body but two heads; the one that of a man, the other of a woman; and likewise in their several organs both male and female. Other human figures were to be seen with the legs and horns of goats; some had horses' feet; while others united the hind-*

quarters of a horse with the body of a man, resembling in shape the hippocentaurs. Bulls likewise were bred there with the heads of men and dogs with fourfold bodies, terminated in their extremities with the tails of fishes; horses also with the heads of dogs; men too and other animals, with the heads and bodies of horses and the tails of fishes. In short, there were creatures in which were combined the limbs of every species of animals.

The Legend of the Creation according to Berosus and
Damascius

The Egyptian sphinxes, animals with a human head, as well as the monsters of Greek mythology, including the famous Minotaur (half man, half bull) convey a message, not understood today, about this period in which the ancestral gods or these alien beings were devoted to genetic experimentation. This resulted in many hybrid organisms or *chimeras* until, finall , they succeeded in creating the being that would become *Homo sapiens sapiens*. The Sumerian texts, illustrated with many interesting details, give an explanation of the existence of these abnormal beings.

Ninmah made a woman unable to give birth,
Enki watching this woman unable to give birth,
Decided her fate, and destined her to live in the gynaeceum.
She made a being deprived of male organ,
Deprived of female organ.
Enki, seeing this being deprived of male organ,
Deprived of female organ,
Decided its destination would be to precede the king.

Enki and Ninmah

The writings also speak of Enki's other failed attempts; how he created a being sickly of body and weak of spirit, and went to Ninmah (Ninti) for help but, although she tried, she could not fix the problem. She spoke to the creature, but it did not respond, she offered it bread but it did not pick it up. The creature could not stand, walk or sit, nor could it bend its knees.

Figure 8.2 A Mesopotamian low relief where different chimeras are represented at the pre-human stage

The *Popol Vuh*, the Book of Counsel of the Quiche, one of the great Mayan families, corroborates the fact that the man was a creation of the powerful who came from the Heavens.

> *And the Forefathers, the Creators and Makers, who were called Tepeu and Gucumatz said: the time of dawn has come, let the work be finished, and let those who are to nourish and sustain us appear, the noble sons, the civilized vassals; let man appear, humanity, on the face of the earth.*

However, a great mystery underlies this apparent simplicity. In what way could a new creature become physically, emotionally and mentally, a replica of the *Nephilim*? What was the process used to create the man? We can imagine, in the light of the stories and modern knowledge of assisted reproduction, cloning and stem cells, how it was done. In the creation story of *Genesis*, the Hebrew Bible tells us, using very descriptive language, the way in which Eve, the female of the species, was created from Adam's rib, through a surgical operation, even performed with anesthesia.

And Yahweh God caused a deep sleep to fall upon the man,
and he slept;
and He took one of his ribs,
and closed up the place with flesh instead thereof,
And the rib, which Yahweh God had taken from the man,
made He a woman,
and brought her unto the man.

Genesis 2:21-22

The process described here may seem inconsistent with the process of the creation of man which I have described above but, if we explore the meanings of the words, the pieces of the puzzle fit together perfectly. Noah Samuel Kramer points out that the name Eve means "that who has life" or "full of life", suggesting that the biblical story of her origin from Adam's rib comes from, with a high probability, the Sumerian word *IT* that means both "life" and "rib".

It must be clarified that Enki and Ninti had worked on the creation of the *lulu amelu* (the mixed one, the hybrid) in a place that, in the Akkadian language, is called *Bit Shimti* (the house where the breath of life is given); that sounds rather like a laboratory equipped with the means for genetic engineering. If we analyze in more detail the different parts of the word SHI.IM.TI, there are different meanings intertwined one with another: life, clay, the belly, and the rib.

As the original Mesopotamian version on which *Genesis* was based has yet to be found, we cannot be sure which of the meanings was chosen by the authors, although it seems obvious that all are intermingled, in some mysterious way.

Figure 8.3 The creation of man. Mesopotamian low relief.

The ancient writings suggest that travelers from another world came to the Earth and, after a while, decided to create a servant race to carry out their heavy labor. In this way begins the first chapter of the birth of mankind. The following episodes of humanity's true history are even more exciting…

CHAPTER IX

EARTHLY PARADISE AND THE SECOND GENETIC MANIPULATION: PANIC IN EDEN

The real problem is not whether machines think, but whether men do.

Burrhus Frederic Skinner, American psychologist
(1904-1990)

The concept of the Earthly Paradise is one that is both mysterious and important to the future of humanity. Plenty of ink has been spent on this subject even though, most of the time, the facts have been adapted to suit religious interpretations, instead of being used in a dispassionate search for objective truth.

The Earthly Paradise is the name popularly given, at least in the Christian tradition, to the Garden of Eden: a place where the first humans, Adam and Eve, had everything they might need and did not know of pain, hunger or death; until they were expelled from the garden for disobeying God, committing the so-called original sin by eating the forbidden fruit of the tree of knowledge. God put Paradise out of the reach of Adam and Eve and inaccessible to humanity. After this incident, never more would humans enjoy the garden until the day of the Final Judgment, when the souls of the righteous and virtuous will reunite with God in the Heavenly Paradise. At least this is what the official doctrine of the Catholic Church says, although it is neither clear nor simple.

Was there really an Earthly Paradise or was it simply a religious myth without a material basis? If it existed, where was it located? To be able to answer these questions with a degree of rigor, we should take some time to evaluate the historical value of the biblical sources. For a long time, critics and scholars have claimed that the writers of the Bible invented or exaggerated the names of people and cities mentioned in it, but the archaeological findings, one after another, have begun to show that the biblical writings may indeed have some historical value.

Historians had claimed that King Sargon of Assyria, whose name appears in the *Book of Isaiah* 20:1, never existed. However, in 1843, the palace of Sargon II was discovered near the Iraqi city of Khorsabad; he is now one of the best-known Assyrian kings. Assyria, in its day a powerful empire, is frequently mentioned in the Bible and archaeological findings have demonstrated the accuracy of the text. In another example, excavations at Nineveh uncovered a carved slab at the palace of Sennacherib that shows Assyrian warriors with Jews captured after the fall of Lachish, in 701 BC, as recorded in 2 *Kings* 18:13-15.

The chronicles of Sennacherib, also found at Nineveh, detail his military campaign during the reign of Hezekiah, king of Judah, mentioning him by name. Sennacherib brags about his many victories but does not mention at all the capture of Jerusalem, something that is consistent with the biblical record which claims that he suffered a great defeat at the hands of God in the attempt. After this humiliation, the Bible tells us that Sennacherib returned to Nineveh, where he was betrayed and assassinated by his sons (*Isaiah* 37:33.38). The record of his murder appears in a couple of Assyrian inscriptions.

Other Assyrian cuneiform inscriptions also mention the biblical names of Ahaz and Manasseh, kings of Judah, and the names of Omri, Jehu, Jehoash, Menahem and Hoshea, kings of Israel. A further example is found in the archaeological investigations in the ruins of the ancient city of Babylon, which yielded some three hundred tablets with cuneiform writing dating back to the reign of Nebuchadnezzar. Among the many names that appear is "Yaukin", king of the land of Yahud, a reference to Jehoiachin, king of Judah, who was deported to Babylon with his whole family when Nebuchadnezzar conquered Jerusalem for the first time in 597 BC (2 Kings 12:11).

Critics claim that the Hebrews did not possess an alphabet, despite the fact that the Bible indicates otherwise in *Numbers* 5:23, *Joshua* 24:26 and *Isaiah* 10:19. However, in 2005, remains of a Hebrew town from the 10th century BC were discovered at Tel Zafit, Israel, where archaeologists found a piece of limestone engraved with an archaic alphabet which allows us to reasonably conclude that the Jews of that time were already literate and able to record their own history.

Finally, in the interest of brevity, the *New Encyclopedia Britannica* says about the controversy that archaeological criticism has been unable to confirm if the available historical information on the oldest periods is reliable and, therefore, dismisses the theory that the stories of the *Pentateuch* (the first books of the *Old Testament*) are simply a reflection of a later period.

There is sufficient evidence that the biblical texts are not fanciful stories without a basis in reality; on the contrary, they have been shown to have significant historical value, based on archaeological findings. In light of this, it's time to see what the Hebrew sources have to say about the Earthly Paradise. *Genesis* begins with an overview which tells us of the existence of an artificially planted garden, situated to the east of an unknown point.

> *Then Yahweh God planted a garden eastward in Eden;*
> *and there he put the man whom He had formed.*
> *And out of the ground made Yahweh God to grow*
> *every tree that is pleasant to the sight, and good for food;*
> *the tree of life also in the midst of the garden,*
> *and the tree of knowledge of good and evil.*
>
> Genesis 2:8-9

The story of *Genesis* continues with a much more accurate description which refers to specific geographic information

> *And a river went out of Eden to water the garden;*
> *And from thence it was parted, and became into four heads.*
> *The name of the first is Pishon: that is it which compasseth the*
> *whole land of Havilah,*
> *where there is gold; and the gold of that land is good:*
> *there is bdellium and the onyx stone.*
> *And the name of the second river is Gihon: the same is it that*
> *compasseth the whole land of Cush.*
> *And the name of the third river is Hiddekel: that is it which goeth*
> *toward the east of Assyria.*
> *And the fourth river is Euphrates.*
>
> Genesis 2:10-14

Two of the rivers, the Euphrates and the Hiddekel (Tigris), focus our attention, once more, on Mesopotamia, which literally means "the land between the two rivers". The two water courses originate in the Taurus Mountains, on the Anatolian plateau in eastern Turkey. Their courses are sometimes very close and, at others, far apart, running through modern Iraq, and into the Persian Gulf. In this way, we might say that we have a sandbox in which to place the location of Eden which should be in Mesopotamia or not very far from it, in the area of the headwaters of both rivers.

The objective is to locate the other two rivers the Bible speaks of, the Pishon and Gihon, something which will not be an easy task. In our time, there is no trace of the other two rivers mentioned in the Bible, no likely candidates close to the headwaters of the Euphrates and the Tigris in any case; perhaps, due to the geological and climatic changes that have caused desertification of the area during this time, both rivers have disappeared.

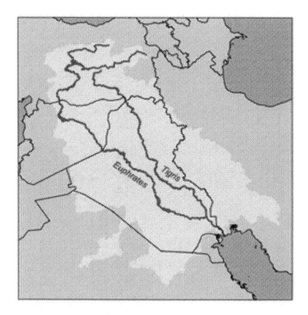

Figure 9.1 Map showing the courses of the Rivers Tigris and Euphrates

Of the third river, the Gihon, we find several references, the first to the kingdom of Ethiopia (known in ancient times as Cush or Kush), which contains the so called Blue Nile, and the second to the River Karun that begins its journey in south-west Iran and, after a great loop toward the north, ends up close to the Tigris and the Euphrates in the Persian Gulf. However, these correlations may be erroneous, which could lead to a false interpretation.

Kush or Cush could be referring to a kingdom named in the Assyrian inscriptions as Kusu. It was the land of the *kusai*, located in the north of Syria, from which came the excellent breed of *kusai* horses. George Smith, the English assyriologist, in *The Chaldean Account of Genesis*, suggests that the father of Nimrod, the builder of the Tower of Babel, was from Cush and that this could be an allusion to the lands of Kusu. Nimrod is a legendary figure in Armenian folklore, intimately connected with the patriarch Abraham, whose hometown was Edessa, modern Sanliurfa, situated just 13 kilometers from Gobekli Tepe, a place that will be important in this story. On the other hand, the kingdom of Armenia in the first century BC was famous for its horses, so we might conclude that the land of Kusu, where the *kusai* horses came from, should be situated in the Armenian highlands, which seems to indicate that the Gihon was the Araxes, the modern River Aras. The origin of the name "Gihon" is unclear, although it should be noted that, during the Arab invasion of the Caucasus in the eighth century, the Araxes was known as "Gaihun", and Persian dictionaries of the nineteenth century referred to the Araxes as the Jichon-Aras. The River Aras is born in the Bin-Gol Mountains along with a branch of the Euphrates. It flows eastward, passing the base of Mount Ararat, joining the River Kur before it empties into the Caspian Sea.

Regarding the fourth river, the Pishon, the reality is that the land of Havilah is totally unknown, and it is possible that the biblical text could be citing the land of a person called Havilah, as *Genesis* does when referring to him, along with Nimrod, as sons of Cush (*Genesis* 10:9). If these names refer to certain kingdoms and to their founders, then the possibility that Cush is a synonym for the land of Kusu, an old name for Armenia, leads us to search for traces of the Pishon there. Reinforcing this last argument are the writings of the Greek historian Strabo who, in his work, *Geography*, containing the geographical knowledge of the first century, makes it clear that Armenia was well known for its gold mines and, in Book 11 of the *Geography* speaks of the mines of Syspiritis near the town of Caballa.

Another very interesting clue in the search for the identity of the Pishon comes from the ancient Assyrian Church of the East, known as the Nestorian Church in the Western world, which recognizes the Great Zab River, a tributary of the Tigris, as the Pishon. This information comes from a remote region located in the foothills of the Zagros Mountains in south-east Turkey, on the border with Iran and Iraq, where the highest authority of the Nestorian Church signed their letters with the following: *"from my Cell on the River of the Garden of Eden"*. This should not be taken lightly as the Assyrian Church is one of the oldest in the region, its foundation dating back to the first century. The Great Zab is born in the mountains of south eastern Turkey and runs for 425 kilometers through Iraq before it empties into the River Tigris.

From all this, you can draw the conclusion that the Garden of Eden was not an imaginary or fictional place and that it should be located in the Middle East somewhere in the fertile crescent, in two possible locations. The first would be close to the headwaters of the Euphrates and the Tigris, in the eastern part of Turkey, if we listen to what the Bible says. The second possible location, according to the theories of Sitchin and many others, who interpret the Bible's words as meaning that the rivers converged in the Garden of Eden and not that they originated in it, would be in the area at the confluence of the Euphrates, the Tigris, the Karun, and a possible fourth river that, although currently dry, crossed the Arabian peninsula.

I am personally inclined to locate Eden in an area not far from the headwaters of the Tigris and Euphrates Rivers. Why place the Garden of Eden in this area? On one hand, as has happened on other occasions, it would not be the first time that archaeological discoveries have confirmed what is written in the Bible. On the other, the description of the four rivers indicates that the Garden of Eden was located in historic Armenia. It must be said that Armenian academics have tried for many years to convince the rest of the world that the physical location of the Earthly Paradise was located in their native land. Their claims often went unnoticed in the West as their research is usually written in Russian Armenian, a language that very few non-Armenians can read.

In the West, a small number of people believed that the Earthly Paradise might have a physical location and far fewer concluded that the headwaters of the four rivers might be the location of the garden. However, Marmaduke Carver, the rector of Harthill in South Yorkshire, had already considered this possibility in his fascinating work, *A discourse of the terrestrial paradise: aiming at a more probable discovery of the true situation of that happy place of our first parents' habitation*. The work was published in 1666, one year after his death, and although the exact location of his grave is unknown, we know the epitaph that was inscribed on his headstone.

Reader, if you love piety, if you know how to value learning, you should know what a treasure lies under this stone, Marmaduke

Carver formerly rector of the Church of Harthill, but very well versed in...chronology and geography, an accomplished linguist, a fine speaker- the man, to wit, who...pointed out to the world the true place of the terrestrial paradise (yet in death)... He was translated on this day of August 1665.

Andrew Collins, in his book *Gobekli Tepe: Genesis of the Gods*, explains in a detailed manner his research about the life and work of the clergy man.

So it seemed only fitting that I should find that York Minster Library has two of the only remaining copies of Carver's book in the country.

Carver began his book with the intention of disproving Martin Luther's theory that the Garden of Eden was a mere symbolic utopia. Later, he tackled the theory that located the garden in the area where the Tigris and the Euphrates converge in lower Mesopotamia, an idea promulgated not only by Calvinist reformers, but also by the Pope and Catholic Church. He finished by locating the Garden of Eden in a part of Armenia that now forms part of eastern Turkey.

Significantl , he examined ancient evidence that suggested the Euphrates, Tigris and Araxes originate from the same source. According to Carver, there was a single source located in the Armenian forests in the vicinity of the lake known in antiquity as Thonitis or Thospites, Arianias or Arsissa. All of these names are associated with the current Lake Van, the largest body of water in Turkey, located at the eastern end of the country. Carver cites the belief of several classical writers, among whom were Strabo and Pliny, that a kind of proto-river, the real origin of the Tigris, emerged from a primordial source that later poured into Lake Van in such a torrential manner that it did not mingle with the saline waters of the lake.

The proto-Tigris, he claimed, re-emerged beyond the southwest extreme of the lake, plunging into a cavern, and reappearing in the south-eastern Taurus Mountains, specifically in the former Armenian province of

Sophene. This location is well known today as the origin of the Tigris. Carver firmly believed that this primary source, the real source of the Tigris, was where the four rivers of Paradise on Earth originated. Finally, he concluded his work by proposing a location of the Garden of Eden between Sophene and the true sources of the Tigris. Sumerian-Akkadian mythology confirms Carver's idea, stating that both the Tigris and the Euphrates originated from a primary subterranean source that is the source of all the sweet waters they called *Apsu*.

At this point, it is worth mentioning something that happened in 1995. In eastern Turkey, very near Iraq and Syria, a Turkish peasant discovered some archaeological remains that will rewrite, once again, the concepts and chronologies that experts had long held on the history of mankind. The place is called Gobekli Tepe (Potbelly Hill) and consists of a beautiful temple with amazing sculptures of deer, wild boar, snakes, human figures and waterfalls, dated to 12,000 years old, in the middle Stone Age, when it was assumed that man wore skins and had yet to develop writing, the wheel, agriculture and pottery. This sacred ground is, without a doubt, the oldest known up to now. A place where priests lived and there were cults of sacrifice in the heat of bonfires. The ruins hold many mysteries. How did a society that did not know of agriculture build such an incredible temple and sculpt those wonderful figures? Could the Sumerian texts that speak of events prior to the flood be right

One of the most baffling and intriguing facts is that the temple was deliberately buried around 8,000 BC, without doubt a herculean task for the primitive inhabitants of the area. It must have taken decades to pile up the tons of earth required to bury the sculptures and megalithic stones. How they did it and why are questions that further excavations may one day explain. With only a small part of the site exposed after a decade of excavation and investigations at a very early stage, it is possible that someone will find something much more spectacular in the near future; Gobekli Tepe remains a mystery that time will unravel.

Fernan Buruk, a Turkish historian, says that Gobekli Tepe is the place where Adam and Eve were brought after leaving the Garden of Eden, while Klaus Schmidt, a member of the German Archaeological Institute, adds "*I believe that here we face the first representation of the gods.*"

Figure 9.2 The megaliths of Gobekli Tepe, Turkey

According to the British Egyptologist, David Rohl, in his book, *Legend: The Genesis of Civilisation*, the Earthly Paradise was on the shores of Lake Urmia, not far from Gobekli Tepe. This ancient site could be giving us clues about the location of the mythical Eden although, according to the Sumerian texts, in far more remote times than are suggested by the dating of its ruins to 12,000 years ago.

For academics, the story of what happened in the Garden of Eden is an allegory or a mythical story of imaginary events, which has more to do with religion or philosophy and refers to a place which has never physically existed on Earth. What if it wasn't like that? What if the Bible was right, once again, and that, in a place called Eden, in the vicinity of the sources of the Tigris and Euphrates Rivers, an orchard or a garden with many fruit trees had been created artificially? What if it is true that the newly created human being, the Adam, was taken to this place to be the caretaker of the garden and its fruit? Who were the builders of this series of shrines of circular and rectangular stones? What motivated them to build such structures in such an early time, just after the last Ice Age? Were the traditions of these primitive builders preserved by the descendants of Abraham in the holy land, where they inspired stories of angels trafficking with humans and abducting their women, in religious texts such as the *Book of Enoch* or *Genesis*?

The answers may be found in the nearby mountains of prehistoric Tell Idris, named after Idris, the Arabic name of the pre-diluvian patriarch Enoch, the great-great-grandfather of Noah. The *Book of Enoch* tells that Enoch, while resting in his bed, was visited by two strange beings with angelic appearance, the Watchers, who invited him on a fantastic journey into the Heavens. Later in the story, Enoch is shown a jail where 200 angels are imprisoned. When he asked why so many were crowded into the prison, he was told that these angels had disobeyed celestial law, descended from Heaven and took women for their enjoyment. The result of this was the birth of the demigods, as explained in a previous chapter.

The word "Eden" is often used as a synonym for "paradise"; however, strictly speaking, the term "paradise" originally referred to a beautiful garden, while "Eden" is a word of Akkadian origin which has been interpreted, in the majority of texts, as referring to a pure and natural place. The word comes originally from the Sumerian "E. DIN" meaning the place, the home (E) where the righteous, the pure, the divine (DIN) live. As such, the stories are talking about a garden or paradise located in a geographical area called Eden, the place where the DIN live, also known as the DIN.GIR, terms that reference divinity, the gods, the Anunnaki, and the biblical *Elohim*.

One of the events that would prove to be decisive for the fate of humanity and for the future relations of man with his creators happened in the Garden of Eden, where man learned his role as a servant of the gods, far away from the place where he had been created. The Sumerian texts are the key to understanding, once again, aspects of the Bible in which the plurality of god has not been completely eliminated.

We must bear in mind the existing rivalry between Enki, the creator of mankind through genetic engineering, and Enlil, the supreme commander of the alien colony on Earth. It was a struggle for power between two stepbrothers, one of whom, Enlil, had benefited from the laws of inheritance of his kingdom, which ensured that power was delegated to his hands. However, Enki, who had commanded the first expedition to Earth and, given who he was, enjoyed great power, was also resentful of what he considered an injustice.

Enlil was characterized by his rigid personality. He was a lover of order and discipline and professed no sympathy for humans, whom he saw as a necessary evil. Enki, however, was a brilliant scientist and expert in many different branches of knowledge who, at the same time, professed a great love for the humans he considered, not without reason, his sons. From the ideas above, which are based on data obtained from older sources, which inspired the story of biblical creation, we will derive conclusions that will undoubtedly shatter religious dogma that has stood since time immemorial.

It was in the Garden of Eden, that Enki decided to improve, through a series of genetic changes, the being he had created. Until that time, the *lulu amelu,* the mixed one, the product of a mixture of an alien species with a *Homo erectus*, was a hybrid and, as such, could not reproduce. At the same time, its degree of intelligence and consciousness was limited and it lacked the capacity for independent thought. It was sufficient to satisfy the needs of the gods, the same relationship you might have with a pet today.

> *And they were both naked, the man and his wife, and were not ashamed.*
>
> Genesis 2:25

The reasons that led Enki to carry out the second genetic manipulation of the *lulu amelu* are unknown, but it is easy to imagine that his decision might have been motivated by factors such as the desire of the artist to improve his work, as well as the desire to protect it from what he considered abuse or mistreatment by Enlil, with whom he didn´t enjoy the best relationship. In this way, Enki, the brilliant *connoisseur* of the mysteries of life, what we would consider a biologist today, was ready to go to work. As *Genesis* says:

154

Now the serpent was more subtil than any beast of the field
which Yahweh God had made.
And he said unto the woman, Yea, hath God said,
Ye shall not eat of every tree of the garden?
And the woman said unto the serpent,
Of the fruit of the trees of the garden we may eat;
But of the fruit of the tree which is in the midst of the garden,
God hath said, Ye shall not eat of it, neither shall ye touch it,
lest ye die.
And the serpent said unto the woman,
Ye shall not surely die:
For God doth know that in the day ye eat thereof,
then your eyes shall be opened,
and ye shall be as gods, knowing good and evil.

Genesis 3:1-5

It seems clear that the serpent was not a snake, since he could talk to the woman, something impossible for a reptile. At the same time, the serpent did not provoke any fear in her; on the contrary, he inspired confidenc and possessed sufficient authority to persuade her to follow his advice, even daring to challenge the almighty God of the Bible. If he was not a snake, who was he? I am sure, dear reader, that you have already guessed it was Enki, known by the Sumerians as "the serpent god."

It is time to return to Potbelly Hill, to trace the path of the serpent. When you visit Gobekli Tepe, you see a superabundance of reliefs which depict snakes but, among all these, there is one that is surprising and gets most of the attention. It is a small relief, about four inches high, including two symbols set in steatite with profound biblical connotations: a tree and a snake. It is also interesting that the Yazidis live very close to Gobekli Tepe. They venerate the serpent, and have a reputation as Devil worshippers, though the latter is a biased interpretation of their cult of Melek Taus. This is curiously intermingled symbolism: the tree, the serpent, the Devil...and all this happened 12,000 years ago.

The cult of the serpent as a sacred animal is widely spread across the planet and the cultures of antiquity. The Aztecs in Mexico, in the *Legend*

155

of the Suns, depict the creation of man by the god Quetzalcoatl, the Feathered Serpent (*quetzal*, "feather" and *coatl*, "serpent"), who was assisted in his task by Cihuacoatl, the Serpent Woman; and in the Aztec cities of Teotihuacán and Tenochtitlán, there are many decorative motifs based on snakes.

At the same time, another Mesoamerican people, the Maya, also venerated the plumed serpent under the name of the god Kukulkan (*Kukul*, "plume" and *Kan*, "snake"), who is referred in the *Popol Vuh* as a creator god. It should be noted that, in the Yucatan peninsula, there is a line of hereditary priests who deliberately distort the skulls of their children in order to acquire the elongated head of a serpent, so they may be chosen as priests of "the people of the Serpent". Something similar may have happened in the remote past at Tell Arpachiyah, in northern Iraq, in what is believed to have been a ritualistic center of the elite, where deformed human skulls have been found.

Hermes in Greece, Thoth or Tehuti in Egypt and Mercury in Rome, are names by which the Sumerian god Enki was known in these civilizations. All of them are represented as gods of wisdom and knowledge bearers. Their symbol, the well-known "caduceus of Mercury" or "caduceus of Hermes", formed by two serpents entwined around a staff, is the symbol of modern medicine.

In the palace of Knossos, in Crete, where the Minoan civilization developed, famous for King Minos and the legend of the Minotaur, we find some very realistic small statuettes in honor of *the goddess of the snakes* that connect the worship of the serpent with that of the mother goddess.

In the Iberian peninsula, which in its proto-history was known by the Greeks as *Ophiussa*, land of the *ophi*, of snakes, there is abundant testimony that relates the snake to different sacred practices. For example, the sculpture in limestone of *the priestess of the serpent* of Porcuna, in Jaén, despite being in a poor state of preservation, shows a woman with a majestic appearance carrying an obedient snake on her back.

Figure 9.3 Minoan figurines depicting the "goddess of the snakes"

The existence in Spain of an old and strange but still popular Galician *copla* (folk song), collected by the researcher López Cuevillas, deserves a special mention. The song tells that the snakes, when they got older, went back to Babylon. There they laid down and became filled with moss, adopting the appearance of a fallen tree trunk and giving us to understand that the serpent, as with many humans when near death, wished to return to its place of birth, to its home…to Babylon.

All this makes a lot of sense, particularly when one considers the ancient Mesopotamian texts, since the snake was associated with the god Enki and his family, being his son Marduk, the chief god of Babylon. It might be asked why this popular folk song relates the snakes with a place so far away from Spain as Babylon; how did the Celtic peoples of Spain come to know the relationship between the symbol of the serpent and its origin in Mesopotamian lands?

There are many more examples of peoples and places where the serpent is worshipped as an auspicious animal. The earliest written tales associate the snake with the god Enki and his family, although they do not tell us why he adopted this insignia. Why then is the serpent associated with the devil in biblical texts? Christian theologians should explain, if the serpent is satanic, the reason why, even today, its image is still used as an icon of medicine and healing throughout the world.

At this point, we should consider the way in which the history of mankind has been written. The writers of the histories we are taught had their own particular points of view on what happened. This was the point of view of those who had won the many conflicts which characterize human history, because those who have lost did not have the right to add their voices to the story. You can see this easily after any war but, if we look at one of the most important and most recent, the Second World War, it is obvious that Germany was defeated, and the USA was one of the primary victors. It is easy to see that the history books are skewed towards the victorious nations.

However, had Hitler won the war, would the histories say the same? We can be sure they would be completely different. They would describe other facts and would even have attempted to justify the Holocaust; no doubt they would also blame the USA for the nuclear bombs that destroyed Hiroshima and Nagasaki. The story would be written in a different way, applying the labels of good guys and bad guys differently. Just to be clear, this is purely an intellectual exercise and does not imply on my part any sympathy for, or justification of, these barbaric events. It has always been so; the winners write the official version of history. Given this fact and bearing in mind the rivalry between Enki (the snake) and Enlil within the Anunnaki power structure, it will be much easier to understand why those who wrote the Bible demonized one of them.

The Hebrew *Genesis* is an adaptation of a text written by followers of Enlil to the Judaic doctrine, in which he is referred to with a different name (Yahweh), as the singular, supreme God; in the same way as, in Sumeria, he was considered the supreme god, but not the only one. This is the primary difference because, in the Bible, the references to other gods, given the monotheistic theme, were removed as much as possible. As such, we owe exclusively to the Bible and subsequent theological developments, the association of the serpent with evil and the Devil. Nevertheless, until the advent of Christianity, the snake had always been considered a favorable sign because it represented Enki, the god who had created mankind and saved man from extermination in the deluge planned in secret by Enlil, as you will see later in a Sumerian version

158

rather more coherent than the biblical version of a God who decides to exterminate mankind and then regrets it.

Figure 9.4 Egyptian low relief where snakes are represented

Once again, they tell us something very different from what actually happened, a Machiavellian conspiracy designed to prevent humanity following the guidelines of those who were actually trying to help us in our evolution. Instead, they are identified as the darker and more negative aspects of the religion: evil and the Devil. In reality, it was Enki who encouraged man to eat the forbidden fruit (forbidden by Enlil) of the tree of knowledge of good and evil; it was he who helped mankind to make an evolutionary leap that Enlil did not wish to happen for fear of losing control of his human servants. It was Enki who helped man to make the genetic leap that allowed sexual reproduction, and not into a state of original sin (however that may be defined).

The dominant clan, the followers of Enlil, condemned Enki in their writings, despite the fact that he was the true benefactor of mankind, and made him into a caricature of evil, public enemy number one, Satan. These writings, already distorted, were picked up by the Christian tradition and endorsed by theologians who, lacking the original knowledge, distorted them even further, giving rise to certain dogmas which, without any basis in reality, still survive today.

Moreover, a critical reading of the book of *Genesis* makes it clear that the god called Yahweh (Enlil) lied, while the serpent (Enki) told the truth, as is shown later. Yahweh said to Adam and Eve that, if they ate of the forbidden fruit they would die; the serpent told them that this was not true, that Yahweh had deceived them as, if they ate the fruit, they would attain the same level of wisdom that he possessed. The story reveals that Yahweh was bluffing; Adam and Eve did not die but they were expelled from the Garden of Eden due to the panic that the changes occurring in the primeval humans caused in Yahweh and his followers. Here again are the verses in which the snake speaks:

> *And the serpent said unto the woman,*
> *Ye shall not surely die:*
> *For God doth know that in the day ye eat thereof,*
> *then your eyes shall be opened,*
> *and ye shall be as gods, knowing good and evil.*
>
> Genesis 3:4-5

The serpent's predictions are confirmed, literally one by one, by God, admitting that he had lied and that the serpent spoke the truth.

> *And the Lord God said,*
> *"Behold, the man is become as one of us,*
> *to know good and evil:*
> *and now, lest he put forth his hand,*
> *and take also of the tree of life,*
> *and eat, and live for ever."*
>
> Genesis 3:22

The snake has revealed the intention of God to deceive Adam and Eve. God, or rather that being that has been identified as God, is afraid that the *lulu amelu*, this hybrid of alien and hominid, used as a slave in the service of the gods, could achieve a greater level of intelligence that would allow him to escape from the yoke imposed by the gods, and win freedom from his masters. Enlil wanted an obedient humanity with a low level of intelligence, whose reproduction he could control. All this changed in the Garden of Eden. The laws of Chaos are inexorable and, once again, this was evidence of the fundamental principle that, in any experiment outside the laboratory, there are variables which cannot be controlled. The AMELU project, the creation of a being to labor for the gods, had escaped the control of its creators. Humanity had reached adulthood.

In the original Hebrew bible, the term used for "God" is *Elohim* (the gods). The text describes a conversation that takes place between several beings or gods (*"And Elohim said: Behold, the man is become as one of us"*), who are frightened by the possibility that man, after this last mutation giving him a degree of consciousness comparable to that of his creators, (*"To know good and evil"*), could, using the materials and knowledge of the Garden of Eden, alter his own genetic code (*"lest he put forth his hand, and take also of the tree of life, and eat"*) in order to extend his limited existence beyond that of his creation (*"and live forever"*) and so rival the lifespan of the Anunnaki gods.

When you read the book of *Genesis* with this new perspective, it is easy to see that the god or the gods in the text have nothing to do with the omnipotent, omnipresent, omniscient and loving God that the *New Testament* and Christian doctrine celebrate. The text makes clear that Yahweh did not know Adam and Eve would eat the forbidden fruit, something inexplicable for an omniscient God. Instead, he is strolling in the garden, searching for Adam and Eve, without knowing where they were hiding.

> *And they heard the voice of the Lord God walking in the garden in the cool of the day:*
> *and Adam and his wife hid themselves from the presence of the Lord God amongst the trees of the garden.*
> *And the Lord God called unto Adam, and said unto him, where art thou?*
>
> Genesis 3:8-9

This describes a God with very few divine attributes, closer to human than to transcendence and divine perfection. One might say that Yahweh had been caught completely off guard, something impossible for a true

God, by definition. I do not seek to hurt the feelings of true believers; rather I would like to point out the semantic problem with the word "god". This is compounded by the fact that the Bible is composed of different books, written by different authors and, for that reason, there is no consistent doctrine.

What alternatives were now left to Enlil? Man could now replicate himself independently, without any need for the technological assistance of the gods that had created him. For the gods, this meant a total loss of control of the population of their human workers. In addition, the problem might get worse if they were allowed access to the fruit of *the tree of life*, of immortality, which would undoubtedly create exponential population growth and could put at risk the supremacy of the alien gods on the planet.

So Yahweh was a victim of circumstances, and had no other choice but to expel Adam and Eve from the Garden of Eden, thus denying them access to the technology symbolized by the tree of life. To ensure this he established a military presence, a cherub with his flaming sword, to defend the garden and prevent the humans from returning.

> *So he drove out the man;*
> *and he placed at the east of the garden of Eden Cherubims,*
> *and a flaming sword which turned every way,*
> *to keep the way of the tree of life.*
>
> Genesis 3:24

As usual at this point, we should see what the Mesopotamian texts say about the events in the Garden of Eden. The *Epic of Gilgamesh* recounts the adventures of the demigod and his faithful friend Enkidu, a word which literally means "Enki's creation". The first tablet refers to Enkidu with the words *lulu amelu* (mixed one), prior to the transformation that made him as wise as the gods. When Gilgamesh, King of Uruk, learned of the existence of such a being, he ordered a woman, expert in the art of seduction, to introduce Enkidu to pleasures he had not yet known.

Now, woman, make your breast bare, have no shame, do not delay but welcome his love. Let him see you naked; let him possess your body.
When he comes near uncover yourself and lie with him; teach him, the savage man, your woman's art...

A little later, the tablet describes how Enkidu underwent a metamorphosis, thanks to the charms of a woman, through a process that reminds us of that described in the book of *Genesis*.

She made herself naked and welcomed his eagerness;
As he lay on her murmuring love,
She taught him the woman's art.
For six days and seven nights they lay together,
For Enkidu had forgotten his home in the hills.

The consequences of this process were, as the Bible says, the disappearance of his primitive past, the expansion of his consciousness and understanding that equaled that of the gods.

Enkidu was grown weak, for wisdom was in him,
and the thoughts of a man were in his heart.
So he turned and sat down at the woman's feet,
and listened intently to what she said:
You are wise, Enkidu,
and now you have become like a god.

Once they had finished, the woman compared Enkidu with a god, in the same way that Adam, after eating the forbidden fruit at the suggestion of Eve, opened his eyes and knew the nature of good and evil as did God. The similarities between the two stories even include their nakedness. Enkidu was naked before the encounter with the woman, and received his clothing, like Adam, after eating the forbidden fruit. After this event, Enkidu is given the designation "man" for the first time, in contrast to *lulu amelu.* This was the second genetic manipulation of the *lulu amelu.*

She divided her clothing in two and with one half she clothed him, and with the other herself;
And holding his hand she led him like a child to the sheepfolds, into the shepherds' tents

Epic of Gilgamesh

And the Lord God made for Adam and for his wife coats of skins, and clothed them.

Genesis 3:21

Later, in tablet XI, the *Epic of Gilgamesh* gives some clues about the key role that Enki played in the outcome of this story. Gilgamesh reached the land where Utnapishtim, the Sumerian Noah, lived and he received the knowledge of a plant, the *Shibu issahir amelu* (the old men are young again) that granted eternal youth. With it in hand, he decided to travel back to his city, Uruk, to help its citizens escape the pangs of disease and death. However, the story tells that, when night fell, Gilgamesh stopped the boat in which he was traveling and found a well in which to bathe. While he was distracted, a snake took the plant and fled, leaving the hero distraught as he had lost the key to immortality.

Gilgamesh saw a well of cool water and he went down and bathed;
But deep in the pool there was lying a serpent,
And the serpent sensed the sweetness of the flower.
It rose out of the water and snatched it away,
And immediately it sloughed its skin and returned to the well.
Then Gilgamesh sat down and wept, the tears ran down his face.

The serpent, the symbol of Enki, is involved once again at the moment when man seems to have gained immortality. In addition, there are images, symbolized by the caduceus of Mercury, that contain clues indicating that, in the Earthly Paradise, a change to the genetic code of humanity took place. The caduceus of Mercury is represented by two snakes entwined around a staff in a way that recalls the winding double helix of DNA discovered by Francis Crick and James Watson, the structure which carries the molecular basis of the human genome, and therefore the key to important aspects of this story such as the extension of life, something that I will discuss later in more depth.

Figure 9.6 Images of the serpent throughout history and from across the world. The DNA double helix.

Another Mesopotamian text of great value, known as the myth of *Adapa and the Food of Life*, is relevant to the same line of research. The Akkadian version has come down to us only as fragments from four different sources, three of them found in the library of Ashurbanipal at Nineveh, and a fourth from the archives of the Egyptian town of Tel el-Amarna. Adapa is created by Ea (another name for Enki) and is the king of the city of Eridu. In *the Sumerian King List*, he is identified as Alulim, the first of the antediluvian kings, who ruled for a total of 28,800 years; we should also note the phonetic similarity with "Adam", the first of the biblical Patriarchs. He is described as wise but not immortal.

Ea made broad understanding perfect in Adapa,
to disclose the design of land.
To him he gave wisdom, but did not give eternal life.

The story tells that Adapa went fishing one day, but the south wind suddenly capsized his boat and threw him into the sea. Furious at this, he broke the wings of the south wind and, for seven days, the wind could not blow. Because of this, Anu, the god from Heaven, was furious and demanded he explain himself.

Enki advised him how he should behave in front of the greatest of the gods. He told him to dress in mourning so that, when he arrived at the gates of the house of Anu, his guardians, Dumuzi and Ningizzida, would ask him why he was so dressed. Enki told Adapa to answer that he dressed in mourning because the Earth missed some of the gods. The guards would certainly ask: who are these deities? He should answer that the gods missed on Earth are Dumuzi and Ningizzida. Enki knew that this would flatter the guardians of the house of Anu and that, as a result, they would speak on his behalf before Anu, as was the case. Enki also warned him to refuse any food or drink that Anu offered as it would be the food and drink of death, offered as punishment for Adapa breaking the wings of the south wind.

When you stand before Anu,
They will hold out for you bread of death, so you must not eat.
They will hold out for you water of death, so you must not drink.
They will hold out a garment for you: so put it on.
They will hold out oil for you: so anoint yourself.
You must not neglect the instructions I have given you.

Anu, impressed by Adapa's sincerity, offered him the food of immortality, which he refused, losing the opportunity to be immortal, for him and for all mankind. Anu was puzzled that Adapa refused the food and drink of life and the gift of immortality, so sent him back to Earth to live as a mortal. Again, the story contains allusions to life and death, as well as the possibility of eternal life through the consumption of sacred food and drink. In this case, instead of the fruit of the biblical tree of life, he is offered the water and bread of death.

In summary, in the Earthly Paradise, guided by Enki, a genetic change occurred in the being created by the gods as a faithful worker to free them from the heavy burdens of work. Modern man had now made his appearance.

CHAPTER X

PREHISTORIC TIMES

The wise man can change his mind. A foolish man, never.
Immanuel Kant, German philosopher (1724-1804)

June 24th 1947, the day the aviator, Kenneth Arnold, saw those famous nine flying discs next to Mount Rainier in Washington State, marks the beginning of the modern study of ufology. The development of the aviation industry has allowed many sightings that otherwise would have been impossible. However, this does not mean that we cannot find records and evidence of the existence of mysterious objects travelling through the heavens, defying the law of gravity, prior to December 17, 1903, when the Wright brothers made the first powered flight in history over the sands of Kitty Hawk beach. We can, in fact, find hundreds of testimonies throughout history and across the world.

There are images and written evidence of unquestionable authenticity of UFO sightings prior to the Flood, during the prehistory of mankind, which could shake the foundations of official history. I am talking about real images made by our ancestors on the rock walls of the caves they frequented or inhabited; the cave paintings. Dated in some cases to more than 40,000 years ago, in the last glacial period, they are among the earliest recorded manifestations of art, and have resisted the test of the centuries thanks to the fact that they were protected from erosion.

Among the oldest and most important caves are the prehistoric sites in northern Spain and southeastern France that make up the so-called Franco-Cantabrian caves, occupied during the Late Stone Age, the period of transition from the Paleolithic to the Neolithic. The paintings are particularly characterized by the realism of the figures depicted. Among the most important sites are the caves of Altamira, La Pasiega and El Castillo, in the north of Spain, as well as Lascaux, Font-de-Gaume and Pair-non-Pair in southwest France, Chauvet-Pont-d'Arc in southern France, and Cosquer, near Marseille. It is also worth noting the recent discoveries in the caves of Vilhonneur in western France, dating back some 25,000 years before Christ, according to the authorities in the field, older than the famous paintings of Lascaux and Altamira.

The themes of these paintings deal with matters of interest to the human communities of those times. We find representations of human beings and animals, as well as hunting scenes. The principal figures are animals: bison, horses, mammoths, deer and reindeer, among others, which are often shown dead or wounded with arrows and other weapons. There are also many outlines of hands.

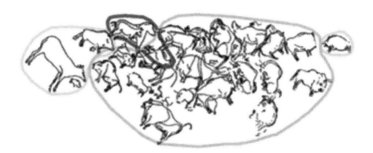

Figure 10.1 Outline of the cave paintings at Altamira, Spain

For the creation of these images, the anonymous artists used the natural resources available to them, taking advantage of the natural shape of the rocks with great skill to give a sense of space and achieve three dimensional effects. This technique, which precisely defined the contours of the figures, as well as the vividness of the colors used to cover the inner surfaces (red, black, yellow, and brown), creates an impression of great realism. In some cases, the figures are even painted to scale. It is more than obvious that these people painted and drew what they saw during their daily existence. These artists were figurative painters; it was not until the twentieth century that abstract art appeared.

At this point, I would like to show you a series of drawings or engravings, described by scholars as "brands hardly intelligible, signs of difficult interpretation", although there are no inconsistent lines or scratches. You can see these "marks or scratches" in the following illustration.

Figure 10.2 Some examples of unusual cave paintings

It is worth pointing out that, in a type of art characterized by realism and naturalistic depiction, these figures appear to have no connection with reality. Taking into account that the rest of the cave paintings accurately reflect scenes of everyday life, there is no reason to think that the "marks or scratches" were examples of abstract art. The artists painted what they saw and, although the reader will reach their own conclusions about what such illustrations may or may not be, they undoubtedly raise new questions about this period of prehistory. Were these artists painting pictures of spaceships they saw flying in the sky? If not, what meaning did these images have?

Another source of revealing evidence lies in the Sahara desert, in the Tassili n'Ajjer Mountains, in southeast Algeria. In caves, gorges and rifts formed by the action of wind and water, there are more than 15,000 examples of paintings and engravings, constituting one of the most important and richest collections of rock art from the Upper Paleolithic and Neolithic. The oldest paintings have been dated at from 10 to 15 thousand years old.

As previously explained, the artists of prehistory portrayed scenes of their everyday existence, often featuring animals, on the walls of caverns, using them as an improvised canvas. Thanks to these paintings we can form an accurate idea of the fauna and human customs of the areas in which they lived. In the murals of Tassili n'Ajjer (Plateau of the Rivers), the main animals portrayed are giraffes, ostriches, elephants, oxen and hippos. This means, among other things, that, in the past, the desert of today was brimming with life and water was plentiful. In fact, scientists believe the Sahara was a heavily populated area between 8,000 and 6,000 BC, with lush vegetation and navigable by long and fast-flowing rivers

However, the people of Tassili n'Ajjer left a great mystery: strange beings with huge round heads and a single eye, painted in the caves. Henri Lhote, French explorer and ethnologist, was the first to discover these representations, in 1933, giving them the evocative name of "the Martians". Science accepted that Henri had discovered the "Sistine Chapel of Prehistoric times", but discredited his theories, which indicated that something strange and mysterious had occurred there in the most remote antiquity. The Russian archaeologist Alexei Kazantsev visited Tassili in 1962, subsequently making the following statement:

The men from prehistory painted cosmonauts! It is increasingly likely that aliens could have visited Earth 10 thousand years ago.

As you can see, there have been all kinds of controversial statements that add to the mysterious nature of the paintings. If the primitive artists who designed these images were unaware of abstract art and they are not allegories, then what are those giant humanoid figures with large heads or, as some writers claim, strange helmets on the head and tubes in the back? What were these perplexing beings that look like astronauts doing by the side of giraffes, elephants and other well-known animals? How could prehistoric man have painted what he had not seen?

The mystery awaits revelation but, whatever the answer, there is no doubt that it raises a new question. They are records which, if we listen to the official scientific opinion, should not be there...but they are. If anything is clear it is that nothing is clear.

Figure 10.3 Images of cave paintings at Tassili n'Ajjer, Algeria

Thanks to the work of these unknown artists we know that, in antediluvian times (before 11,000 BC), primitive humans were witnesses to the existence of "flying cars" and strange gigantic beings, the *Nephilim*, *Giborim* or *Rephaim* described in the Old Testament. In all mythologies, demigods are the product of sexual union between gods and men. In Greek mythology, Zeus was so seductive that he fathered many illegitimate children with many lovers; Achilles, the hero of the Trojan wars, was half human and half divine. Islam speaks of the *djinn* or genies, who shared the world with humans and seduced their women, producing offspring. Titans or giants also appear in the Indo-Aryan traditions; for example, in the *Ramayana*, known as *rakshasa* in Sanskrit, they are considered to be in perpetual conflict with men. There is documentary evidence that this concept was also common to the Egyptians, the people of Ugarit, the Hurrians and other peoples of antiquity.

The Hebrew *Genesis*, as mentioned in previous chapters, describes a period in the history of mankind, before the Flood, in which existed the *Nephilim* or *Giborim*, which it defines as a race of giants that were the result of sexual union between the children of God and the daughters of men. I have transcribed the full text below by placing in parentheses the terms in Hebrew so that the reader is able to see the true nature of the original expressions: *haElohim* (the gods), *haAdam* (men) *and haGibborim* (the heroes).

> *The Nephilim were in the earth in those days, and also after that, when the sons of God (haElohim) came in unto the daughters of men (haAdam) and they bare children to them; the same were the mighty men (haGibborim), which were of old, the men of renown.*
>
> Genesis 6:4

The ancient *Septuagint* translation of the *Old Testament* into Greek, the oldest and most important text among the collection of sacred Jewish writings, replaces the term "sons of God" with "the angels". In this enigmatic way, the original expression *haElohim,* children of the gods (in plural), became, first, the "sons of God" (in singular) and later "the angels". The apocryphal *Book of Enoch* reads:

> *It happened after the sons of men had multiplied in those days, that daughters were born to them, elegant and beautiful. And when the angels[1], the sons of heaven, beheld them, they became enamoured of them, Saying to each other, Come! let us select for ourselves wives from the progeny of men, and let us beget children.*
>
> Book of Enoch 7:1-2

(1) The text in Aramaic reads "watchers" here

A Sumerian tablet referred to as CBS 14061 describes an occurrence that has strong echoes of the Enochian marriage of an angel to a human woman. The tablet narrates the story of one young god named Martu, who falls in love with the daughter of the high priest of Ninab. Martu tells his mother, a goddess, how he feels and she asks whether the object of his affection has "appreciated his gaze". Subsequently, the goddess permits their marriage.

> *In my city I have friends, they have taken wives.*
> *I have companions, they have taken wives.*
> *In my city, unlike my friends, I have not taken a wife;*
> *I have no wife, I have no children.*

In Mesopotamia, the *Epic of Gilgamesh* presents its hero as a demigod who was three parts divine and one part human, and the book says that "*his lust leaves no virgin to her lover, neither the warrior's daughter nor the wife of the noble*". At the same time, a Hittite text describes him as a being of massive proportions, about 5.60 meters in height by about 2.25 meters across his chest, among other superlative dimensions of his virile body.

> *Eleven cubits was his height,*
> *the breadth of his chest was nine spans.*
> *His member was the length of three (....)*
>
> Epic of Gilgamesh

There is a parallel to these gargantuan sizes in certain passages of the Bible, when it speaks of Goliath, the giant of the city of Gath and rival of King David, whose height is described as six cubits and a span (about 3.25 meters) according to *1 Samuel*. Giants also appear in other passages throughout the *Old Testament*.

> *And there we saw the Nephilim,*
> *the sons of Anak, which are part of the Nephilim;*
> *And we were in our own sight as grasshoppers,*
> *and so were in their sight.*
>
> Numbers 13, 33

These texts are some of the many written records that describe a time before the Flood. In this time, the Anunnaki, in the absence of females of their own species on Earth that could satisfy their sexual desires, and seeing that the females of the creature they had created in their image and likeness through genetic manipulation were beautiful, could not resist breaking the rules imposed on them by their leaders not to mingle with beings of a different race or lower species. So they mingled and lay with "the daughters of men". The masters of this alien race did not look kindly on such behavior (although some of them also indulged in it) because, as experience had shown, extraterrestrial and terrestrial, given their common genetic basis, could reproduce, and they knew that this would lead to the degeneration of their race and to the loss of their original identity.

Between gods and humans there were many similarities, but a more than obvious class difference. Men had been created as servants for the gods, and the possibility that this distinguishing line would become blurred, due to the association between gods and women and the subsequent birth of demigods, was not approved of by Enlil, the supreme commander of the alien mission on Earth.

Some of these angels, the *Grigori* (in Sumerian, *Igigi*), who had been entrusted with the task of building the Garden of Eden, digging ditches and draining channels, not only fell in love with the beautiful terrestrial women but, as a result, they began to reveal to the human species some of the secrets of advanced alien technology, such as astrology, the manufacturing of weapons, spells, incantations and botany, among others. These were the same *Igigi* who had rioted due to their harsh working conditions which, as you will remember, motivated the creation of man.

> *Y'asa taught men to make swords, knives, shields, breastplates, and made known to them the metals and the art of working them, and taught women about bracelets, ornaments and the use of antimony, the beautifying of the eyebrows, the use of costly stones of every valuable and select kind, and all the coloring tinctures.*
> *And there arose much godlessness, and they committed fornication;*

And they were led astray and became corrupt in all their ways.
Shemihaza taught enchantments and root-cuttings;
Hermoni the resolving of enchantments;
Baraq'the the signs of rays;
Kokab'el the constellations;
Zeq'el the knowledge of the lightning;
'He taught the meanings;
Ar'tagof taught the signs of the earth;
Shamsi'el the signs of the sun;
And Saharan'el the motion of moon,
and all of them began to disclose secrets to their wives .

The Book of Enoch, 8:1-3

Throughout this process, as is easy to imagine, the men of the human species bore the brunt of it, as they were dispossessed of their women or attempted to defend their possessions which, in many cases, led to their deaths.

And as men perished, they cried,
And their cry went up to Heaven.

The Book of Enoch, 8:4

When Enlil, a disciplinarian, saw these outrages, he decided that those who had breached the rules not to associate with humans should be punished by exile from their planet of origin, remaining forever on Earth.

So has He created and given to me the power of reproving the
Watchers[2], the children of heaven.
I wrote out your petition,
And in my vision it appeared thus,
That what you petition will not be granted unto you throughout
all days of eternity,
And that judgement has been finally passed upon you:
Your petition will not be granted unto you.
And from this time forward, never shall you ascend into heaven;

He has said, that on the earth He will bind you,
as long as the word endures.

The Book of Enoch, 14:3-5

(2) The original term "watchers" was later replaced by "angels".

This was only the beginning of the problem for Enlil. The Anunnaki had not considered the rapid reproduction of the human beings, who started to overpopulate the Earth. For this reason, the aliens, in spite of their advanced technology, felt their supremacy to be threatened, as humans began to show signs of abandoning their original respect and veneration toward them. Due to this fear, the sovereign in the assembly decided to reduce the human population through the use of biological weapons, for the first time in the history of mankind

600 years, less than 600, passed,
And the country became too wide, the people too numerous
The country was as noisy as a bellowing bull.
The god grew restless at their racket,
Enlil had to listen to their noise.
He addressed the great gods:
"The noise of mankind has become too much,
I am losing sleep over their racket.
Give the order that suruppu-disease break out.

Epic of Atrahasis

CHAPTER XI

EXTERMINATION OPERATION

I can even read the intricate tablets in Sumerian; I understand the enigmatic words in the stone carvings from the days before the Flood.

Ashurbanipal, Assyrian King (668-627 BC)

The myth of the Flood is part of the collective memory of all humanity. The names of the characters and some of the details may vary, but the main elements of the cultural tradition remain unchanged: the belief that a great flood, decreed by angry gods, affected the planet in ancient times, and that a man and woman were saved to allow the continuation of the species.

There are those who accept the story as part of their doctrine of faith, while scientists understand it as a fable or, at best, a figment of the collective unconscious with some psychological implications; never as something with real, historical foundations. However, could it be that the Flood was not a myth or legend but, on the contrary, the memory of a real event of such importance that it was indelibly fixed in the consciousness of our ancestors? The scientific community ignores the existence of dozens of stories, all with a common message; therefore, in order to answer this question, we must embark on a journey through traditions and beliefs rooted in different parts of the globe and periods of history.

Greek mythology, according to various sources, tells the story of Deucalion, who was warned by his father, the Titan Prometheus, that Zeus planned a great deluge to destroy the Bronze Age peoples of Greece. Deucalion built a large chest, filled it with provisions and climbed into it with his wife Pyrrha. Then Zeus caused a great flood that submerged most of Greece, drowning the people, with the exception of a few who sought refuge in the mountains. Deucalion and Pyrrha remained adrift for nine days and nine nights before coming ashore at Mount Parnassus. After the end of the rains, Deucalion offered a sacrifice to Zeus who, pleased with his offering, sent Hermes to offer them what they wanted most. Deucalion asked that he be allowed to create a new breed of humans, and Hermes replied that all they needed to do was to cast stones over their shoulders. The stones that Deucalion threw became men and those that Pyrrha threw became women.

Apollodorus says that the intention of Zeus in causing the Flood was to destroy the vicious race of the Bronze Age, of which Hesiod speaks in his writings. Other sources suggest that Zeus sent the Flood as punishment for the injustices of humans.

From the Greek perspective, the Flood affected only mainland Greece; however, in the Roman versions, the Flood was universal, covering the entire world, and only Mount Parnassus escaped its effects. According to the Roman writer Ovid, Zeus was so disgusted by human injustice in general and, in particular, the iniquities of Lycaon, tyrant of Arcadia, who liked to immolate human victims, that he decided to exterminate all mankind. For this reason, Zeus threw his thunderbolts across the land but, fearing that the fire could reach the Heavens, he decided to use water to complete the task. All sank beneath the waters, save only Deucalion and Pyrrha, who sailed in the chest to Mount Parnassus. Zeus was pleased that they had survived as he knew of their virtuous characters. The couple consulted an oracle of Themis, the personification of natural law, who told them they should throw the bones of their grandmother over their shoulders. They were surprised by this advice, but Deucalion understood that it referred to the stones which made up the body of Mother Earth; the couple then began the work of bringing to life a new race of human beings.

The traditions of the new world provide some very interesting sources. 3,500 years ago, in an area in the south of Mexico between the states of Oaxaca, Guerrero and Puebla, the Mixtec culture began to develop. They worshiped gods similar to those of the Aztecs and used a vigesimal system of numbers, ideographic writing and an astronomical calendar. They are now known for their codices, as well as for their numerous and beautiful works of art. The Mixtecs referred to themselves in their own language as *Nuu Savi*, which means "people of the rain", and created the *Codex Borgia*, named in honor of the Italian Cardinal who acquired it for his magnificent private museum. This codex, made of deer skin, and consisting of 78 pages that deal with mystical, scientific and artistic themes, says the following:

Long before the sun shone,
when the Earth was covered by the water.
A divine couple, the snake lion god and the tiger snake goddess,
they had two sons.
They multiplied over the years, and were destroyed by a great
flood, by their parents;
few were saved. Their descendants are the Mixtec.

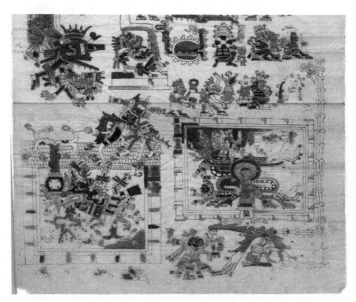

Figure 11.1 The Codex Borgia

Back in the old world, it is time to remember the moment, in 1872, when George Smith spoke, for the first time, to the British Society of Biblical Archaeology of the existence of a story of the Mesopotamian Flood contained in the *Epic of Gilgamesh,* found by Austen Henry Layard in the library of Ashurbanipal, in Nineveh. This is how Smith described his discovery, while he was sorting through incomplete fragments of text:

> *On looking down the third column, my eye caught the statement that the ship rested on the mountains of Nizir, followed by the account of the sending forth of the dove, and its finding no resting place and returning. I saw at once that I had here discovered a portion at least of the Chaldean account of the Deluge.*

This discovery, apparently accidental, encouraged Smith to search through other fragments that he had found and already filed under the category of "mythological tablets". Despite the simple account Smith gave of his discovery, it goes without saying that the task of the young assistant at the British Museum was not easy. One must see a tablet with inscriptions in cuneiform first hand in order to understand the difficulty of reading broken fragments of clay, on which are engraved a few signs that sometimes overlap with one another, and that the passage of time has blurred or even worn away entirely. A genuine puzzle, the difficulty of which was increased by the fact that Smith did not know precisely what he was looking for.

However, Smith's search was made a little easier thanks to his knowledge of the organization of information in the ancient libraries of Mesopotamia. He knew that the tablets were indexed by subject, date of composition and by the primary text to which the tablet belonged. With this knowledge, the young orientalist eventually found what he was looking for.

> *I found a fragment of another copy of the Deluge, containing again the sending forth of the birds, and gradually collected several other portions of this tablet, fitting them in one after another until I had completed the greater part of the second column. Portions of a third copy next turned up, which, when*

joined together, completed a considerable part of the first and sixth columns. I now had the account of the Deluge in the state in which I published it at the meeting of the Society of Biblical Archaeology, December 3rd, 1872.

This news, as might be expected, thrilled the academic world and the public, whose only source of the Flood story, until now, had been from the biblical texts. George Smith writes that, at the end of the conference, Edwin Arnold of the *Daily Telegraph* approached him with a proposal that he personally continue the excavations with financing from the newspaper, which offered the not-inconsiderable sum of one thousand guineas to gather more information on such a fabulous mythical tale. Smith, taking a six-month sabbatical from the museum, left for the Middle East. What happened, one week after he began his excavations, is an example of the important role that fortune plays in scientific discoveries. Smith recounts it in the work called, *Assyrian Discoveries: An Account of Explorations and Discoveries on the Site of Nineveh, During 1873 to 1874.*

I sat down to examine the store of fragments of cuneiform inscriptions from the day's digging, taking out and brushing off the earth from the fragments to read their contents. On cleaning one of them I found to my surprise and gratification that it contained the greater portion of seventeen lines of inscription belonging to the first column of the Chaldean account of the Deluge, and fitting into the only place where there was a serious blank in the story.

Although the text he found did not correspond to the *Epic of Gilgamesh*, being rather a part of the *Epic of Atra-Hasis*, the fabulous discovery helped to eliminate any doubt as to the original source from which the authors of the Hebrew *Genesis* had drawn their tale of the biblical Flood. According to the biblical story, Yahweh, angry with humanity for the sexual contact between the "sons of God" and the beautiful and desirable "daughters of men", regretted the creation of mankind and decreed their elimination.

And the Lord said, I will destroy man whom I have created from the face of the earth; both man, and beast, and the creeping thing, and fowls of the air; for it repenteth me that I have made them.

Genesis 6:7

Later, oddly enough, this omnipotent, omnipresent and omniscient God decides to prevent the annihilation of the human species and warns Noah of what is going to happen. He even concocts a plan for his salvation through the building of an ark in which Noah, his family and representatives of all the animal species of the planet will be able to survive.

Were the animals also guilty of the excesses and sins of humanity? Why would Yahweh resolve to destroy the animals and, a little later, allow their survival? Although I know that many devout believers will say that, for a human, it is impossible to understand the designs of the Lord, what is certain is that the scriptures describe the acts of this god called Yahweh as those of a being who, at best, suffers from Bipolar disorder. Again, religious manipulation in defense of a monotheistic Christian doctrine has distorted the original account.

We gain greater clarity when we look to those older texts that inspired the writers of *Genesis*. In the original Sumerian text, as well as in subsequent Mesopotamian versions, it appears that more than one God is involved. In the first act of the drama that leads to the Deluge, the major players, once again, are the two old rivals: Enlil and Enki. The authoritarian and disciplined Enlil, the highest authority of the Anunnaki colony on Earth, had become increasingly disturbed by the course events had taken since that distant time when man was created to serve the gods.

Indeed, there had been many complications. There was the unexpected development by the "human servant" of the ability to procreate, the primary cause of their expulsion from EDIN and, even worse, the interbreeding of gods and humans, resulting in the birth of hybrids or demigods. To all this had to be added the fact that the growth of the human population was out of control, to the extent that it threatened the security and the achievements of the gods on Earth.

Enlil had hatched several plans with the clear intention of decimating the human population, but had not achieved his goal thanks to the actions of Enki in sabotaging his genocidal ambitions, avoiding time and again the fulfilment of Enlil's murderous designs. At the end of the previous chapter, I described Enlil's decision to use biological weapons, unleashing epidemics in order to drastically reduce the human population. Enki, as Creator and Father of mankind, opposed him at every turn. Understanding the intrigue and politics of the Anunnaki gods, he advised Atra-Hasis, the Assyrian Noah and hero of the Deluge, the way to prevent the total extinction of his creation.

Atra-Hasis was instructed to meet the elders in assembly and to take the decision that humans would abandon their work, offerings and services to all the gods, with the exception of the god Namtar, the direct cause of the epidemic, who should be given all kinds of offerings and works. Enki knew that these actions would confuse the Anunnaki, who would see that they were losing the willing submission of humanity, meaning that they would have to return to performing the labor for which men had been created. At the same time, with their favorable treatment of Namtar they were sending a clear message to Enlil and his assembly of Anunnaki that human beings had power, and that the course of action they chose could benefit or damage the gods. It was the first general strike in the history of mankind.

The elders listened to his speech;
They built a temple for Namtar in the city.
Heralds proclaimed...
They made a loud noise in the land.
They did not revere their gods.
They did not pray to their goddess.
But searched out the door of Namtar.
Brought a baked loaf into his presence.
The flour offerings reached him.
And he was shamed by the presents.

And wiped away his hand.
The suruppu-disease left them.
The gods went back to their regular offerings.

Epic of Atrahasis

Enlil accepted his failure in bad grace and was soon to make the attempt to decimate the human species once again, through a drought followed by famine. It's easy to imagine that, in a place like Mesopotamia, the land between the rivers, where water was of vital importance for growing crops, a decrease in the levels of the Rivers Tigris and Euphrates could be catastrophic for the people. To this end, the Anunnaki did not hesitate to decrease the supply of water to inhabited areas through control of an intricate hydraulic system of canals and dams.

Enlil heard their noise and addressed the great gods:
The noise of humankind is too loud for me,
with all their uproar I cannot go to sleep.
Cut off food supplies to the people,
let plant-life to feed them be scarce;
Above, let Adad withhold his rain,
Below, let the flood not rise from the deep;
let the wind blow and parch the ground;
let the clouds thicken but only drop drips;
let the fields lessen their yields,
let Nisaba seal up her breast.

Epic of Atrahasis

Enki, using the same methods which had proven to be so effective in the case of epidemics, advised Atra-Hasis to, again, apply enough pressure on the Annunaki leaders to make them desist from their efforts. However, Enlil, the great ruler of the gods, now suspecting a conspiracy to undermine his plans, decreed that the drought should intensify, as a consequence of which, the famine worsened.

Thus, no water or food escaped,
and the rigors of famine returned:
Above, Adad withheld his rain.

Below, the flood did not rise from the deep.
The womb of earth did not bear;
plant-life did not sprout.
People were nowhere to be seen.
The black fields became white,
the broad plain was smothered in salt.
For one year they ate grass;
for the second year they depleted the storehouse.
The third year came and their features were distorted by
hunger.
On the arrival of the fourth year
their long legs became short,
their broad shoulders became narrow,
and they walked hunched up in the street.

Epic of Atrahasis

Approximately the next 30 lines of the poem are lost but, extrapolating from the story so far and with the aid of a Neo-Babylonian fragment, it seems that Enki, due to the prayers of Atra-Hasis, persuaded the *Lahmu*, "the guardians of the sea", to provide large quantities of fish to counteract the lack of crops and meat, thereby alleviating the famine and derailing Enlil's plan.

After this new failure, Enlil, by now very upset, again convened the Assembly of the great Anunnaki and, visibly angry, reprimanded Enki for acting against his orders. It is at this moment that Enlil, tired of his plans to decimate humanity failing one after another, presented to the Assembly a new and definitive plan to eradicate the problem: the annihilation of the human race entirely through an irreversible catastrophe. The flooding of the whole surface of the Earth would be the means he chose to achieve this radical objective.

This time, the sovereign king decided to take a series of precautions, insisting that all the members of the Assembly of the gods swear a solemn oath that none would hinder nor betray his decision. There was a tense debate in which Enki objected to this foolish project, reminding those present that his creation of man had been at the express request of the gods; and how much they had benefited. Enki refused both to swear the oath and to participate in the criminal plan, inviting Enlil to take sole responsibility for the decision and the risks and dangers it involved.

Come now, let us all take an oath to bring a flood.
Anu swore first, Enlil swore, his sons swore with him…
Enki opened his mouth and addressed the gods his brothers:
Why will you bind me with an oath?
Am I to lay hands on my own people…
Am I to give birth to a flood? That is the task of Enlil.

Epic of Atrahasis

Finally, Enlil convinced the Assembly to support his scheme, ensuring that all of them, Enki included, solemnly swore that they would not oppose it nor warn mankind of the danger. The decision had been taken and thus began the countdown.

The gods commanded total destruction;
Enlil committed an evil act against the people.

Epic of Atrahasis

After reading the ancient Mesopotamian stories, the biblical story of the Deluge begins to make sense, despite its subsequent literary mutilations. Detailed examination makes some of the fine points much clearer. I have pointed out in previous chapters, when talking about the mythical Garden of Eden, that the term is derived from the Akkadian E.DIN, home of the DIN, the righteous, the pure, the gods, the divine. Noah, the Hebrew hero of the Deluge, is described in *Genesis* as "*a righteous man who walked with Elohim*" (*Genesis* 6:9). Here he is described as both "righteous" (DIN) and "man".

Following the etymology of the original terms, we are talking of a demigod, a hybrid born through the interbreeding of humans with Anunnaki gods from another planet. The apocryphal *Book of Enoch* tells the story of how Lamech, Noah's father, when he saw the birth of his child, ran to his own father, Methuselah, and asked him to seek advice from Enoch, who lived among the righteous, with the angels, the

DIN. I transcribe below the fragment of the text in which Methuselah asked Enoch for his advice and, leaving aside literary license, exalted the semi-divine nature of Noah and his relationship with the DIN, the righteous, the divine, the *Elohim*, the Anunnaki.

And now hear me, my father, for a child has been born to my son Lamech, whose form and type are not like the type of a man. His color is whiter than snow, and redder than the flower of the rose, and the hair of his head is whiter than white wool. And his eyes are like the rays of the Sun; and he opened his eyes and made the whole house bright.

And his father Lamech was afraid and fled to me. And he does not believe he is sprung from him but thinks him to be from the Angels of Heaven. And behold, I have come to you, so that you may make known to me the truth.

The Book of Enoch, Chapter 106, 10-12

The Mesopotamian texts are much more accurate. The data is drawn from the traditions recorded in various writings, especially in the antediluvian section of the so-called *Sumerian King list*. This text, from a historiographical point of view, allows us to understand better than any other the place that the Deluge occupied within the Sumerian-Akkadian world. In this document are presented all the dynasties which reigned in the different Sumerian cities since their founding, "*after the kingship descended from Heaven*", as it says in the first line of text. The first to write about the Flood were the Sumerians, who placed this event as a historiographical watershed within their vision of the ancient Mesopotamian Near East, marking a before and after between two eras, similar to the way the birth of Christ is used by modern historians.

In the era before the Flood, the five cities where kingship resided are listed in chronological order: firstly Eridu, the sacred city of Enki, followed by Bad-Tibira, Larag (Larak), Zimbir (Sippar in Assirian Babylonian) and Curuppag (Shuruppak). The second era is delineated by the catastrophic Flood, which is described as follows:

After the Flood had swept over, and the kingship had descended from heaven, the kingship was in Kish.

The text continues, enumerating the postdiluvian dynasties until the year 1900 BC, the period of the first Dynasty of Isin, when the list was written. As usual, the similarities between the ancient Sumerian texts and the biblical stories are stunning, leaving no room whatsoever for doubt. If, in the Bible, there are ten antediluvian patriarchs, in the *Sumerian King List* there are ten sovereigns who reigned before the Flood. Noah is the tenth biblical patriarch while the Sumerians call the tenth sovereign Ziusudra, the old Babylonians call him Atra-Hasis; Utnapishtim is the hero of the Deluge in the *Epic of Gilgamesh*, and Xisuthros was the name used by the priest Berosus in his account of the Babylonian Deluge, written in Greek and, although his works are lost, quoted by Syncellus.

The Sumerian city where all these events took place was Shuruppak, the place where, for the first time, the office of King, the unique privilege of the gods up to this point, had been ceded to a demigod, whose name in Sumerian was Ubara-Tutu, the father of Ziusudra. From this we may conclude that Noah was not a mundane man but the son of a demigod and a woman, someone of great importance in public life, someone whose veins ran with Anunnaki blood.

After the Assembly approved his plan to exterminate the human race, Enki, unable to save humanity this time, found a way to prevent its extinction by saving Atra-Hasis. He decided to outsmart Enlil without betraying his solemn oath, using a large dose of inventiveness. In the Sumerian story, found on a fragmentary tablet at Nippur in 1895, Enki sent a premonitory dream to Ziusudra, leading him to visit the temple to seek advice from his god. Enki told him of his plan by revealing his secret to a wall, thus keeping his oath to Enlil.

And as Ziusudra stood there beside it, he went on hearing:
Step up to the wall to my left and listen!
Let me speak a word to you, wall. Listen to my words. Listen to my advice

By our hand a flood will sweep over
the cities of the half-bushel baskets, and the country;
the decision, that mankind is to be destroyed has been made.
A verdict, a command of the assembly cannot be revoked,
an order of An and Enlil is not known ever to have been
countermanded,
their kingship, their term, has been uprooted
they must bethink themselves of that.

The Eridu Genesis (Sumerian story of the Flood)

The later version of the story of the Flood in the *Epic of Gilgamesh* has some small variations that do not alter the story, but do provide some interesting details about the city where these events unfolded. Below is the section of the poem in which Enki tells Utnapishtim, the hero of the Deluge, what is going to happen:

Reed-house, reed-house! Wall,
O wall, hearken reed-house, wall reflect;
O man of Shuruppak, son of Ubara-Tutu;
Tear down your house and build a boat,
Abandon possessions and look for life,
Despise worldly goods and save your soul alive.
Tear down your house, I say, and build a boat
Hut, oh hut! Wall, o wall!

Epic of Gilgamesh

In this way, Enki asks Atra-Hasis/Utnapishtim/Ziusudra to abandon everything and build a boat, construction of which Enki will oversee, promising, in addition, to supply him with the necessary provisions for the journey. The man, at this point, poses a question to his benefactor: how should he act and what should he say to his fellow citizens when they asked why he is building a boat? Enki advised him to tell them that, because of the disagreement between Enlil and his protector god Enki, he had decided to leave for the kingdom of the latter, in the *Apsu*, so he needed a boat to traverse this great expanse of water.

Atra-Hasis received the command.
He assembled the Elders at his gate.
Atra-Hasis made ready to speak,
and said to the Elders:
"My god does not agree with your god,
Enki and Enlil are constantly angry with each other.
They have expelled me from the land.
Since I have always reverenced Enki,
he told me this.
I cannot live in...
Nor can I set my feet on the earth of Enlil.
I will dwell with my god in the depths.
This he told me..."

Epic of Atrahasis

Enki gave very specific instructions about how the ship should be built, as well as how much time remained before the catastrophe, as evidenced by the reference to a clepsydra specially prepared for this event. The Sumerians and, subsequently, the Babylonians, Egyptians, Chinese and Indians used a form of water clock called a *clepsydra*, which measured time by the escape of water from a vessel. The water was contained in a graduated container and flowed out of a hole, so that the level fell. The water level was measured against a scale marked on the container that indicated hours.

He opened the water clock and filled it,
He told it of the coming seven-day deluge.

Epic of Atrahasis

Before continuing with the Mesopotamian version of the Flood I will discuss some aspects of the story that are important. One of the most controversial points of the biblical narrative, from a scientific rather than mythical point of view, is without doubt when it describes Noah and his family coexisting in the ark in perfect harmony with hundreds of animals, some of them very dangerous to humans and from distant parts of the planet. According to the story, Yahweh made a distinction between "clean" and "unclean" animals and asked Noah to save seven pairs of each species.

Of clean beasts, and of beasts that are not clean,
and of fowls, and of every thing that creepeth upon the ground,
there went in two and two unto Noah into the ark, male and female,
as God commanded Noah

Genesis 7:8-9

Common sense rebels against an image like this, no matter how hard one might try to explain it mystically, arguing that the almighty power of Yahweh could transform wild lions and reptiles into meek little lambs guided by divine forces. All of this without forgetting the huge amount of provisions that would be needed to feed all these animals during such an extended voyage. This lack of credibility, characteristic of this part of the narrative in the book of *Genesis*, threatens the credibility of the entire history of the Deluge.

The Mesopotamian version, once again, casts light on the subject, explaining the way in which Enki aimed to ensure the preservation of different animal species: not by taking live animals on board the ship, but by preserving their seed. We must remember that Enki was the scientific commander for the Anunnaki mission on Earth and had created man through complex genetic manipulation. For this reason, Enki had the knowledge necessary to select, acquire, and preserve the seed of living beings, and to recreate them from the genetic material in their DNA.

Then take up into the boat the seed of all living creatures.

Epic of Gilgamesh

The Hindu version of the Flood, older than the Hebrew and Greek, has remained remarkably consistent to this date. The Vedic scriptures of India, in particular the *Bhagavata Purana*, recount that a king, Svayambhuva Manu, was warned of the Deluge by the god Vishnu, incarnated in the form of a giant fish. The king built a great ship to house his family and Matsya, the gigantic fish, towed the ship, saving it from destruction. The

Hindu story of the Deluge has some curious features, explaining that the water did not come from the clouds in the form of rain, but that it was a flooding of the ocean which swept across the planet. It also explains that the protagonist, instead of loading the ship with a pair of each species, saved the semen of all animal species in order to repopulate the Earth.

The Mesopotamian and Vedic versions give an explanation that is entirely logical, and consistent with our current knowledge of biotechnology. At the same time, it is a plausible solution to the problem of lack of space in the ship and requirement for vast stocks of food, although it contradicts the traditionally accepted version of the Bible. What could be the origin of such an error? The confusion might have been born of the fact that Noah brought onto the ark some domestic animals that were used to living with humans to a certain extent, while the rest of the animals were not transported physically but only preserved through their seed. This part of the narrative could have been lost with time for the simple reason that it was a concept foreign to those who compiled the story.

This might, however, explain the mysterious classification that the Bible makes between clean or pure and unclean or impure. It could be talking about wild and domestic animals, that is to say, on the one hand, the pets who rubbed shoulders with the DIN (the righteous, the pure, the divine), from where the distinction might originate, that had been taken on board the ship and, on the other hand, the wild animals of which only the genetic material had been preserved. This explanation has nothing to do with kosher dietary laws and the kashrut prohibitions on consumption of unclean animals in Judaism.

When the ship was completed, Noah embarked with his family. According to the Mesopotamian sources, apart from the family of Atra-Hasis, some close friends were also aboard, as well as those who helped in its construction. It was then that the signal came from Enki announcing the imminent arrival of the catastrophe; the hatch was closed and the force of a hurricane released the ship from its moorings.

When Shainash,
ordering a trembling at dusk,

showers down the destroying rain,
Board thou the ship,
batten the hatch!

The signal was an earth tremor caused by detonations planned and ordered by the Anunnaki command, in order to break the balance that kept the water level of the sea and the marshes. The location in which the explosives were placed is a mystery that we will try to reveal later, but certainly the power of the detonations had to be enormous, sufficient to cause a seaquake which would, in turn, cause *tsunamis* of such gargantuan magnitude that they swept across the inhabited lands.

The destruction of coastal communities by giant waves has occurred throughout history. There are records of the *tsunami* created by the explosion of the volcanic island of Santorini in 1480 BC and its effects on the Minoan civilization. Most *tsunamis* are generated along the so-called Ring of Fire or circum-Pacific belt, a volcanic area with high levels of seismic activity, approximately 20,000 miles long and located in the Pacific Ocean. *Tsunamis* can be caused by volcanic eruptions, earthquakes, meteorite impacts, landslides or explosions. The energy of a *tsunami* is constant and depends on its height and speed; they may travel hundreds of miles and reach speeds of 430 to 500 mph. While they are not particularly dangerous over the deep ocean, they can be catastrophic when they reach the shallow waters of the coast.

When the wave approaches the coast, its speed slows, while its height can reach more than 90ft. The phenomenon is usually composed of several waves that arrive at the coast in intervals of 15 to 20 minutes, with the peculiar feature that the first of the waves is very similar to a normal wave. The *tsunami* is usually preceded by the shoreline receding some tens or hundreds of feet from the coast and then, after 5 to 15 minutes, massive flooding that can penetrate miles inland. Of all disasters, tsunamis are among the most terrifying.

Does the idea that the Deluge was triggered by a succession of *tsunami*, caused artifi ially through the use of a superior technology, probably nuclear detonations, seem like nonsense to you? I suggest you read the following.

On September 25, 1999, the journalist Eugene Bingham published an astonishing story in the *New Zealand Herald*, claiming that New Zealand had conducted secret experiments with the intention of generating *tsunamis*, according to declassified files. Bingham, a professor at the University of Auckland, claims that New Zealand had collaborated with the United States to carry out a series of underwater explosions, generating a small *tsunami* in Whangaparaoa in 1944 and 1945. The work of Professor Thomas Leech was considered so significant that, according to secret reports of the time, senior members of the US defense staff believed that, if the project had been completed before the end of the Second World War, it could have played a role as effective as that of the atomic bomb.

The details of the "*tsunami* bomb", known as "Project Seal", or how to artificially cause tsunamis and convert them into a powerful weapon of mass destruction, are contained in documents of the time declassified by the New Zealand Ministry of Foreign Affairs and Trade. These documents, stamped with the seal "Top Secret" show that, after the war had ended, the US and British armies were so excited about the potential of "Project Seal" that they considered sending Professor Leech to Bikini Atoll to witness the American nuclear tests and to see if these might be applied to his work. Professor Leech never made the visit but Dr. Karl Compton, a member of the US board of assessors of atomic tests, was sent to New Zealand. He was so impressed by the work of Leech that, on his return, he recommended that the Joint Chiefs of Staff continue with the project in cooperation with the government of New Zealand. Below is part of a letter sent from Washington to New Zealand in 1946.

Dr. Compton is impressed with Professor Leech's deductions on the Seal project and is prepared to recommend to the Joint Chiefs of Staff that all technical data from the test relevant to the Seal project should be made available to the New Zealand Government for further study by Professor Leech.

Despite open support at the highest levels of government in the US and New Zealand, details of the inquiry never came to light. Neil Kirton, a former colleague of Professor Leech, told the *Weekend Herald* that the experiments involved the use of explosives underwater with the intention of creating a *tsunami*. Small-scale explosions were carried out in the Pacific and on the outskirts of Whangaparaoa, which, at the time, was controlled by the army, but it is uncertain what happened to Project Seal once the final report was submitted to the Wellington Defence Headquarters late in the 1940s. However, Kirton added: *"whether it could ever be resurrected...under some circumstances I think it could be devastating."*

Research at the University of Waikato, New Zealand, has shown that a modern experiment could produce waves more than ninety feet high. Dr. Willem Lange has theorized that a single explosion would not necessarily be effective but that a series of them could cause a significant impact. Suspicions that today's great military powers have investigated and possibly used geophysical weapons is not new, particularly given the continuing allegations about the US developing a powerful microwave cannon in Alaska, the famous HAARP (High Frequency Active Auroral Research Program), based on the technology of the famous physicist Nikola Tesla.

Among the events that can cause *tsunamis* are underground nuclear tests, according to Lila Rajiva, a freelance journalist from Baltimore. In fact, all the information relating to nuclear tests in the Pacific is classified as "top secret" and the US has not ratified the Comprehensive Test Ban Treaty, leaving the door open for further tests. France has also carried out a large number of nuclear tests on the atolls of Mururoa and Fangataufa. As a result, in 1995, three residents of Tahiti, Marie-Therese Danielsson, Pierre Largenteau and Edwin Haoa, whose properties had been damaged, denounced the French Government. They claimed that these nuclear explosions could cause landslides like that which occurred on Mururoa Atoll in 1979, removing more than 35 million cubic feet of coral and rock, creating a cavity 450 feet in diameter, and leading to a large wave that reached the Tuamotu archipelago, causing numerous casualties. The French authorities initially claimed that the phenomenon was due to natural causes before, finall , recognizing the so-called "accident" on July 25, 1979.

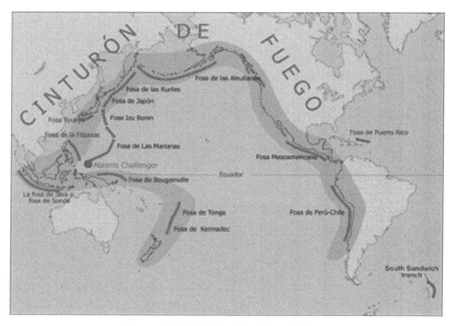

Figure 11.2 The Pacific Ring of Fire

The Indian Ocean earthquake of December 26, 2004, with a magnitude of 9.3 on the Richter scale, the second highest since the invention of the seismograph, and lasting for 8 to 10 minutes, had its epicenter off the coast of the island of Sumatra, in the archipelago of Indonesia. It caused a series of devastating *tsunamis* that reached heights of up to 90 feet. The succession of *tsunamis* devastated the coasts of most of the countries around the Indian Ocean, inundating large numbers of coastal communities across south and southeast Asia. The number of people killed is estimated at 230,000, according to a recent study sponsored by the United Nations.

Is there a possibility that a large explosion caused the *tsunami*? Could previous nuclear tests have caused it indirectly? Rumors abound. According to *The International Herald Tribune,* on December 29, the computers in the offices of the Comprehensive Nuclear Test-Ban Treaty

Organization received seismic data on the earthquake that spawned the *tsunami* on the previous Sunday morning; this was not reported because the 300 employees of the office were on vacation. What was the reason for their vacation? Surprisingly they lacked the capacity to act officiall , while awaiting ratificatio of the Test-Ban Treaty by 11 countries, among which were the US, North Korea and Pakistan.

The United Nations Emergency Relief Coordinator, Jan Egeland, during his press conference at the Jakarta meeting, addressed the rumor that the *tsunami* had been caused by a nuclear test, although later he had to clarify his position, probably by order of Kofi Annan. The Israeli press soon echoed the rumors. *The Jerusalem Post* and *Arutz Sheva* reported that an Egyptian news outlet, identified as *Al Osboa* or *Ousboue*, had argued that India, in a nuclear arms race with Pakistan, had received advanced nuclear technology from the US and Israel and that this would have been tested in the Indian Ocean.

The denials on the part of the Israeli press did not take long and nor did statements from the International Atomic Energy Agency, denying any nuclear origin of the *tsunami*. The *Times of India* further insinuated that the testing of weapons which, through the use of magnetic waves, could remotely cause earthquakes and volcanic eruptions, was behind the disaster. It was probably referring to HAARP. Benjamin Creme, of *Share International* magazine, which often reports on earthquakes around the world, said that it is impossible to carry out an underground nuclear test without causing an earthquake, not necessarily in the immediate vicinity, but in another part of the world. He believes that nuclear tests are responsible for a quarter of the earthquakes worldwide.

After this brief interlude, in which I have set out some strong arguments that the Deluge was something more than torrential rains, I will return to the central point. The Deluge was not a flood produced by forty days of torrential rains, but a series of devastating floods, a consequence of a sharp rise in sea levels. A flood generated by several giant waves that penetrated to the heart of the inhabited lands. *Genesis* describes the start of the Flood as follows:

In the six hundredth year of Noah's life, in the second month,
on the seventeenth day of the month, on the same day
were all the fountains of the great deep broken up,
and the windows of heaven were opened.

Genesis 7:11

The biblical version speaks of springs that emanate from the "deep of the sea", a translation of the original Chaldean *Apsu* that denoted the oceanic abyss, the distant seas, south of Mesopotamia. If you take a look at a map of the world, you will realize that, from the point of view of an observer located at the mouths of the Tigris and the Euphrates, the springs "at the bottom of the sea", in the *Apsu*, cannot be anywhere other than the Indian Ocean, and the Antarctic Ocean, with its icy continent. The *tsunami* came from the south.

On the first day the tempest from the south rose up,
Blew swiftly and brought the flood,
*Like a battle force the destructive **kashushu** passed over the*
people.

Epic of Gilgamesh

The first glow of dawn,
A black cloud lifted from above the horizon.

Epic of Gilgamesh

Other evidence in support of the theory that the great wave came from the south is the fact that Enki, who was aware of the whole operation, had devised a plan to save Atra-Hasis/Noah. It was obvious that if, as was expected, a *tsunami* of great size came from the south, the force of the water would inevitably push the ship toward the north. Enki was aware of the existence of a mountain to the north of Mesopotamia with twin peaks, the highest in west Asia: Mount Ararat (5,165 m) and Mount Sis (3,896 m). In addition, there were other peaks such as Mount Damavand (5,671 m) in northern Iran, the only places high enough that there might be a chance to escape such a flood

He hoped that a boat located in the area of the Tigris and the Euphrates, if propelled by a great wave from the south, could potentially reach one of these places, thus saving those on board. The wave came from the south, but there are still many questions to resolve. Where were the explosive charges placed? How can we explain a rise in sea level sufficient to cover the entire surface of the planet to a degree that it was necessary to take refuge at altitudes of over 16,000ft?

CHAPTER XII

A JOURNEY TO THE CENTER OF THE EARTH: THE WATERS OF THE FLOOD CAME FROM THE INTERIOR OF THE EARTH

*Every truth passes through three states, first it is ridiculed, then
it is violently opposed and finally it is accepted as self-evident*
Arthur Schopenhauer, German philosopher (1788-1860)

I have vivid memories of those afternoons in which I passionately enjoyed reading the novels of the magician of fantastic realism. One after another, titles such as *From the Earth to the Moon*, *Twenty Thousand Leagues under the Sea*, *Around the World in Eighty Days* or *Journey to the Center of the Earth*. All of them were about fabulous and adventurous journeys, a perfect subject for the vivid imagination of a teenager.

Jules Verne, born on February 8, 1828 in Nantes, France, was destined to be a faithful representative of the values symbolized by his sun sign, Aquarius, with his taste for innovation and technological advances. Though he was not a particularly dutiful character, he studied law, following the family tradition, and married a rich widow, his wealth allowing him to lead a comfortable life. The synchronicities in his biography alone deserve a separate chapter. An example of this is the fact that he signed several contracts with his publisher Jules Hetzel, one of them in 1871, while the astronomer who discovered Uranus, ruler of Aquarius, his zodiacal sign, was Sir William Herschel, in 1781. Note the phonetic similarity between the last name of the editor and the astronomer, as well as the mirrored numbers of the years if you read them backwards. From a young age, Verne was fascinated by technology and everything that was novel, extraordinary and unconventional. This is reflected in many of his books, forerunners of the modern science fiction genre. In his books, the author described fantastic inventions, unthinkable at the time. The amazing thing is that many of the things he imagined later became real; something that always fascinated me and gave his works an almost prophetic nature. Where did Verne get his inspiration from?

In his book, *Paris in the Twentieth Century*, written in 1863 but not published until 1994, he described the city of lights in the year 1960 in seemingly prescient detail:

> *Latin and Greek are not only dead languages, but buried as well.*

> *Most of the countless cars that plied the causeway of the boulevards did so without horses; moved by an invisible force, through an air motor dilated by the combustion of gas.*

> *Shopping centers as rich as palaces where light was expanded in white radiation, these broad channels of communication wide as squares, these squares coarse as flood plains, these hotels immense...*

> *You will be adult at age eighteen.*

He also predicted the existence of a metro train network with lines that crisscrossed the French capital, and an automatic and secret system of communication at a distance, rather like emails, among many other things.

In his novel of 1870, *Twenty Thousand Leagues under the Sea*, Verne described a submarine called the Nautilus, in which Captain Nemo raced across the bottom of the oceans and which was remarkably similar to the first nuclear submarine launched by the US Navy in 1954 (named the USS Nautilus in tribute). In the same work, he anticipated the bathysphere.

However, in addition to Verne's more spectacular visions and synchronicities are those found in the novels *From the Earth to the Moon* and its sequel, *Around the Moon*. In the first, he tells how, at the end of the American Civil War, the members of the Baltimore Gun Club are unemployed and plan to manufacture a huge cannon to destroy the Moon. Later, they plan to send a manned projectile. In the second book, he describes the details of the trip.

The books contain some surprising details which seem to anticipate the Apollo program a century later; such as the number of crew members, three in the novel and three in the Apollo capsules. In the books, Verne selects a launch site for the projectile at Stone's Hill, near Tampa Bay in Florida, only 125 miles from the Kennedy Space Center at Cape Canaveral, from where Armstrong, Aldrin and Collins were launched. In the novel, the protagonists discuss whether to choose a launch site on the southern coast of Texas or the Florida peninsula. NASA chose a launch site in Florida, but located their central operations center in Houston, on the southern coast of Texas. The duration of the trip made by the Apollo astronauts was three days, exactly the same as in the story. When they returned to Earth, the Apollo capsule fell in the Pacific two and a half miles from the place described in the novel and was rescued by an American ship in the same way. All this cannot be mere coincidence; there are several oceans around the world and the Pacific alone has a surface area of over 63 million square miles.

Verne's first manned spaceflight departed in December, at some point in the 1860s. The first human flight to the Moon took place one hundred years later, on December 21 1968, although it would be a few months before Armstrong and Aldrin set foot on it from Apollo 11.

From my point of view, it was clear that Jules Verne was a mixture of scientific pioneer and clairvoyant. The evidence was overwhelming. Then came my fifteenth birthday and, among other gifts, I received a copy of *A Journey to the Center of the Earth*, with multiple dedications from my friends. Given that time had proved the great writer correct in his other novels; I began to wonder if there might be a grain of truth is this one too. What truth was hidden in this novel?

Figure 12.1 Jules Verne's *Journey to the Interior of the Earth*

Journey to the Center of the Earth, published in 1864, is one of Verne's best-known novels. It is the second book of the *Voyages extraordinaires* series. The adventure begins with the astounding discovery by German Professor Otto Lidenbrock of a cipher written by Icelandic alchemist Arne Saknussemm, in the 16th century, in which he claims to have travelled to the center of the Earth. The coded message is concealed in a manuscript of the Icelandic saga *Heims-kringla,* a chronicle of the Norwegian kings who ruled Iceland, written by Snorri Sturluson. It is a manuscript written in runic characters that can be deciphered when read backwards. The message he finds is disturbing:

In Sneffels Yokulis craterem, kem delibat umbra Scartaris, Julii intra calendas descende, audax viator, et terrestre centrum attinge; Kod feci.

Arne Saknussemm

Go down into the crater of Snaefells Yocul, which the shadow of Scartaris caresses before the calends of July, O audacious traveler, and you will reach the center of the Earth. I did it.

Arne Saknussemm.

The professor follows the instructions of the alchemist, accompanied by his nephew Axel and the Icelandic guide, Hans. They depart for Iceland, and go to the volcano Snæfellsjökull, the place marked on the parchment as the gateway to the interior of the Earth. According to the instructions, the peak Scartaris, before the kalends of July (the first day of the month), casts its shadow over a crater that leads to the center of the Earth. In this way, they descend into the interior of the planet, where they follow a path which leads them to underground oceans, prehistoric creatures and endless adventures, to the delight of the reader.

Modern society recognizes the genius of Jules Verne in anticipating many inventions and advances of the twentieth century in his writings, but nobody says anything about what can be understood from *Journey to the Center of the Earth*. It is regarded as mere adventure fiction, without any scientific basis. What the collective memory does not recall is that this is exactly how the ideas in most of his books were seen at the end of the nineteenth century, including *From the Earth to the Moon*. Very few in the era of scientific realism thought that a journey to the Moon was remotely possible…it was simply unthinkable. The vast majority of the scientific establishment at that time considered such a thing a joke at best; something that has occurred many times throughout history. Western society also took a long time to accept that the Earth was round. Prior to Columbus' discovery of the Americas it was considered that the trip he launched across the Atlantic Ocean in search of the new world was madness. Neither was it easy to accept that the Earth revolved around the Sun, and not the other way around. The question arises: How long will it take to accept that there is a subterranean world? Time is circular and history repeats itself so, some day perhaps, the prophetic spirit of the great French writer will once again be recognized. Then, what is now seen as impossible will be clearly evident.

Official science postulates that the Earth is a solid body made up of several layers, with a solid inner core. In summary, the current scientific paradigm asserts that the structure of the interior of the planet is a series of layers: the crust of the Earth, that is between 18 to 44 miles thick in the continents (continental crust) and 6 to 12 miles in the oceans (oceanic crust); the mantle, whose thickness varies between 1,740 and 1,800 miles; and the core, composed of nickel-iron alloy or NiFe, where temperatures reach between 4000°C and 6000°C and the density varies from solid materials at the center and more fluid towards the exterior. This is what, in summary, the official version says.

What the vast majority of people don´t suspect is that this is nothing more than a hypothesis, and that its veracity has not been demonstrated in an unquestionable way by the scientists who defend it. It is just a belief of science. However, once again, a mere hypothesis or belief, supported by those who are supposed to have the knowledge, raises something that has not been empirically proven to the category of absolute truth and proven fact. This is not a personal opinion, because those who defend this hypothesis as an indisputable truth lack the necessary evidence to do so, and are only supported by research of limited scientific value that is insignificant in relation to the magnitude of the problem. However, those few who dare to defend the possibility that the Earth is hollow, to a greater or lesser extent, are considered ignorant, fanciful and unscientific.

Gerardus Mercator (1512-1594) was a Flemish mathematician, astrono-mer and cartographer, author of a world map and inventor of the cylin-drical projection, which is the basis for marine cartography and many current atlases. Abraham Ortelius, another cartographer of the 16th cen-tury, called him the greatest geographer of his time and, more recently, the writer Nicholas Crane referred to him as "the man who mapped the planet". His legacy is part of our daily life, every time we consult an atlas or use the Global Positioning System (GPS). In the so-called Mercator projection, the meridians and parallels are drawn at right angles. These straight lines, known as rhumb lines or loxodromes, create segments that are at right angles with the meridians. While the meridians are always an equal distance from each other, the parallels grow further apart as they approach the poles.

In his mysterious and puzzling map of the North Pole, published posthumously in 1595, the surrounding ocean is shown connected to an inland sea through four gaps in the ice. Why, instead of the polar ice cap, does it show an inland sea? Did Mercator know something in the 16th century that is ignored today? Something that could shed light on certain unexplained phenomena that occur at the poles? Mercator maintained, in his time, an interest in Egypt and even visited the Great Pyramid in 1563. Could he have gained access to old maps that served as sources for his future works?

Figure 12.2 Mercator map of the North Pole

The French cartographer Philippe Buache (1700-1773), came to be Geographer Royal of France and made some of the highest quality maps of his time; his map of Antarctica, drawn in Paris in 1737, a century before the discovery of the icy southern continent, featured a great Antarctic continent with no polar ice cap and an inland sea accessible through two channels. Note that, in both maps, the polar ice cap has disappeared, rather surprisingly, four centuries before there was any evidence of another pseudo-scientific dogma that attempts to explain the current polar melting: the so-called greenhouse effect, caused by the technological advances of man during the twentieth century. According to these maps, the polar ice caps did not exist several centuries ago, so, therefore, to argue that the cause of their disappearance is due to an effect of the twentieth century is a childish argument lacking in rigor. It is like trying to explain a murder through a suspect's visit to the victim's house four hundred years after the crime occurred.

There are many other impossible maps, like that of Oronce Finé, the *Nova et Integra Universi Orbis Descriptio*, a planisphere preserved in the Library of Congress in Washington DC that, in 1531, depicted the coasts of the Antarctic continent, many years before it was discovered; more evidence that history is not exactly as it has been told (unfortunately I do not have sufficient space in this book to explore this fascinating topic more fully).

Another is the case of the Ottoman admiral, Piri Reis. In 1929, some old maps, now very well known by researchers of the unusual, were discovered in the imperial Topkapi Palace in Istanbul. These maps were drawn on gazelle skins, one in 1513 and a second in 1528, by the Ottoman admiral and cartographer, Piri Reis. The maps show the west coast of Africa and east coast of the Americas and the admiral noted in writing that they were based on maps of much older origin. The problem is that, according to official history, those coasts could not have been known at that time. It is possible to observe the islands of the Maldives, which were not mapped until 1592, and the source of the River Amazon in the Andes, a place Hernando de Soto was not sent to explore until 1533. The contours of the Antarctic coastline of the region known as Queen Maud Land are also depicted, an area which would not be charted until the eighteenth century, but also with an interesting peculiarity which gives rise to even more questions: the accuracy of its contours is such that it implies that the coast was mapped before it was covered by the great ice sheet. This simple fact gives us cause to relocate the origin of maps to prehistoric times, in which historians say that *Homo sapiens* lived in caves.

Piri Reis, born in Gallipoli in 1465, was a navigator of recognized prestige as well as a geographer and cartographer. His teacher of navigation was his uncle Kemal Reis, one of the most feared pirates of the time, and he became admiral of the Ottoman fleet in a time in which the Muslim crescent moon and the Christian cross faced one another across the Mediterranean. His tragic death, beheaded at the age of 89, by order of the governor of Egypt, Ali Low, was the final end to his fascinating existence. Piri Reis bequeathed to us, in addition to his maps, filled with a lot of data and unresolved questions, a manuscript, the *Kitab-i-Bahriye* or "Book of Navigation". In it, on page 68, dedicated to the unknown seas, can be read something that adds even more mystery, if this is possible, to the strange phenomena that occur in the polar zones:

Understand this well. The land of darkness will be left behind.
Do not be surprised by these words. A vessel that penetrates
the darkness does not remain there.
Having arrived there, the entire crew would die. And the reason
for this is that no ship can reach the poles of the world.
It can follow this route but it cannot pass the 55th parallel,
even by a degree.
The darkness is over the poles of the world, both the North and the
South. Make no mistake. The darkness in the north is on the earth.
The darkness in the south is on the sea.
Now you know where this darkness is: one is on the sea
and the other is on the ground...

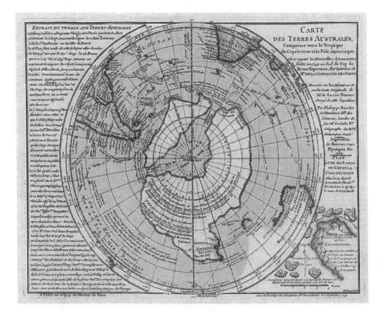

Figure 12.3 Map of Antarctica by Philippe Buache

At this point, you should have already intuited that the entrances to the underground world are at the planet's poles. Can you remember in which geographical location Jules Verne placed his entrance to the interior of the Earth? In a volcano in Iceland, an island located between the North Atlantic Ocean and the Arctic Ocean. Will this choice be as prophetic as were many of his other works?

It was in 1692 that the first work about the hollow Earth appeared, written by the famous English mathematician and astronomer who gave his name to the comet, Sir Edmund Halley. Newton was also a fervent supporter of the theory. Leonhard Euler, a mathematical genius of the seventeenth century, was also in favor of the hollow Earth model, open at the poles, with a central sun, and inhabited.

At the beginning of the nineteenth century the theory of the hollow Earth enjoyed great popularity in the United States of America, which led the former US Army office , John Cleves Symmes Jr, to declare on April 10, 1818 in Saint Louis, Missouri, that *"the Earth is hollow and habitable within; containing a number of solid concentric spheres, one within the other, and that it is open at the poles twelve or sixteen degrees. I pledge my life in support of this truth, and am ready to explore the hollow, if the world will support and aid me in the undertaking.*" The controversy continued until the beginning of the twentieth century, at which point the model of the solid Earth was imposed. It is interesting to see what Verne wrote about this matter in his novel;

> *'So, Axel, it is the heat that bothers you?'*
> *'Certainly. If we were to attain a depth of only twenty-five miles, we would have reached the limit of the Earth's crust, for the temperature would already be more than 1,400 °.'*
> *'And you are afraid of melting?'*
> *'I leave the question for you to decide,' I replied sharply.*
> *'Here is what I decide,' said Professor Lidenbrock, assuming an important air. 'It is that neither you nor anyone else knows for certain what happens in the Earth's interior, given that scarcely a twelve-thousandth part of its radius is known. It is that science is eminently perfectible, and that each existing theory is constantly replaced by a new one.*

Later on, Profesor Lidenbrock continued:

> *"You see, Axel, the state of the central core has produced various hypotheses amongst geologists; nothing is less proven than the idea of an internal heat. In my view, it does not exist, could not possibly exist. In any case, we shall see for ourselves."*

Which made Axel finally reflec

> *Could I take seriously his decision to go to the core of the terrestrial mass? Had I just heard the senseless speculations of a lunatic or the scientific analyses of a great genius? In all this, where did the truth end and illusion begin?*

Personally, I do not like the term "hollow Earth" because it gives the impression that the globe is completely empty inside. What I propose is a certain degree of emptiness, smaller or larger, of sufficient size to house life, seas and continents, but not a total vacuum. I know that the majority of people think this is a folly without foundation, but it is interesting to consider the response of the British Geological Society when, at the end of the twentieth century, it was asked about the controversy as to whether the Earth was hollow or solid, replying that there are dozens of arguments against the Earth being hollow; but, there were also hundreds of arguments against it being solid.

From this response we may infer, as I have postulated, that there is no scientific certainty that the interior of the Earth is solid, however much its supporters may mock the contrary position. What are the main points on which official science bases its assumption that the Earth is not hollow? Let's look at what Jan Lamprecht, in his book *Hollow Planets: A Feasibility Study of Possible Hollow Worlds* (1999), has to say about it.

Newton's Law of Gravity has made possible space travel and the existence of satellites. Science uses his formula accurately to measure gravity within the bounds of the solar system and the Universe but it remains untested in other areas. It is more than 300 years since Newton devised his formula, but still we don't know what exactly causes gravity.

$$F = G \left(\frac{m_1 m_2}{R^2} \right)$$

Figure 12.4 Newton's law of gravitation, expressed as an equation

When the formula has been used to determine the mass of the Earth it is based on the concept that, for each mass of M inside the Earth, it exerts an attractive force of F, but the valid range for Newtonian gravity is unknown. In Newton's formula it is G, the universal gravitational constant. It is assumed, and assumed is the correct word here, that each mass of M exerts the same force of F wherever in the Universe it may be. In the same way, and for the subject we are discussing, it is also taken for granted that each mass of M exerts the same force F whether it lies on the surface of the Earth or whether it is deep inside the Earth. Official science uses the Cavendish balance to determine the mass of the Earth, and presumes that each particle exerts a fixed force upon all others. This assumption excludes the very real probability that particles near the surface of a planet might exercise a greater force than those deep down.

The master key to gravity is the mass of the Earth so, if the mass of it is wrongly calculated, then so are the estimations for other bodies of the Universe. If the mass of the Earth has been exaggerated, then the masses of all other bodies in the solar system have also been inflated. It follows then, if the Earth is hollow, then so is every planet in the solar system. How can we be sure that the Earth really has the mass assumed by Newtonian gravity? Gravity being such a weak force, is an experiment using two lead balls representative enough to extrapolate to the entire Earth when there is electrical charge to account for, and also magnetic and electromagnetic forces that are a lot stronger than the force of gravity, and which the current theory does not take into account?

Seismology is the science of earthquakes and the propagation of elastic waves through the Earth or other planet-like bodies. It is the trusted method of knowing what is going on beneath our feet. However, following the above paragraph, the speed at which seismic waves travel through the Earth is ultimately deduced from the understanding of the structure of the Earth, based on Newtonian gravity. That is an assumption based on an assumption. Too many assumptions... In fact, there is no way of being certain that these waves are really reaching those depths or travelling at those speeds. In the same way, we cannot be sure that speed changes in the waves are due to the changing composition of the Earth.

The current view of the inner Earth might be very inaccurate. Many of the predicted structural changes at depths of just a few miles have never been proven to be correct. If such errors have occurred, can we trust predictions based on this theory when dealing with rocks that are hundreds and thousands of miles beneath the surface of the planet? The fact is, the deepest that man has ever gone into the Earth's crust is 25 miles...

Geology is a science that studies the solid Earth or celestial bodies, the rocks of which they are composed, and the processes by which they change. It plays a fundamental role in geotechnical engineering and is a major academic discipline. That being said, what do we really know that may be trusted implicitly about the Earth's interior? It is an extended mistake to believe that the lava which pours out of volcanoes comes from a large tank of melted material that makes up the greater part of the Earth's interior. However, scientists have found that lava comes from within the Earth's crust, from around 20 miles down. The existence of lava does not affect the transmission of seismic waves, which indicates that the crust is mainly solid.

So where does the heat which melts the rocks come from? There are two scientific theories. Some geologists argue that the melting can be explained by the existence of high concentrations of radioactive elements in a concrete area that produce enough heat to melt rock. This theory is supported by the fact that much lava is slightly radioactive. The other theory says that shearing and faulting generate heat via friction. There is evidence to support both theses. Lava cannot be rising from the center of the Earth because it would cool down and become solid on its long, slow journey upwards. So lava is a surface phenomenon and does not reflect what the Earth is like 60 or 150 or more miles down

Jan Lamprecht also gives some reasons to believe the Earth may be hollow. In his book he speaks about what seismologists call the shadow zone; that is, the large area of the Earth where seismographs cannot detect P or S waves. He concludes that the most likely reason why these waves cannot be detected is because they cannot penetrate there; because there is nothing there to penetrate (seismology does not work in gas). He also explains the Earth's magnetic field based on a counter rotating dynamo effect, which involves a burning hydrogen core. He argues that, as hydrogen is the lightest element, due to Newton's shell theorem making $g = 0$ at the center, it would naturally diffuse to the center and would burn in a reaction similar to those that happen in the stars.

There are those who will argue that, if large entrances to the interior of the Earth really existed at the poles, the pilots of the airlines that fly on transpolar routes would have seen something. It is true that some companies fly this type of route, but it is no less true that they fly far from the exact North or South Pole, because to fly closer would lead to very serious interference with their instruments, putting the planes in serious danger. It must also be said that the climate of the area, with its layers of cloud, fog and snow storms does not allow for adequate visibility. Everybody knows how difficult it is to distinguish objects with clarity on the open sea or in large expanses of snow or ice.

You must bear in mind that, in Canada, there are huge areas of icy wilderness that remain unexplored. What would happen if a plane flew over that area? What would happen if pictures were taken on one of those rare days of good visibility? The pictures would show reflections and mirages caused by snow and ice. They could also show dark spots or strange shadows without sufficient definition to give cause for an investigation. The fact is that there are still large areas of our planet which are virtually unexplored, among which are both poles, deserts and jungles.

It is a fact that, in the twenty-first century, it is still possible to make amazing discoveries, things which, surprisingly, have remained hidden from human view. One such example is the spectacular cave of Hang Son Doong, in Vietnam, discovered by a shepherd in 1991 who, fearful of the sound that came from the entrance, kept it secret until 2009, when the discovery was made public. It is the largest known cave on Earth and consists of various tunnels that interconnect a great multitude of caves, a jungle and a subterranean river. The cave is more than four miles in length with an average height of 650ft, reaching, in some sections, 800ft. An expedition headed by Howard and Deb Limbert, however, met an enormous wall of calcite that prevented them continuing on their path, opening up the possibility that the cave is still larger. This is only a grain of sand in the desert of what is still to be discovered.

There are those who say that, if there were large holes at the poles, some explorers would have found them during their expeditions. However, things are not that simple, as evidenced by the previous example of the discovery of the Vietnamese cave. The Son Doong cave had escaped discovery in previous speleological expeditions to the region, because it is too far from the road and was covered by the jungle. According to Spillane, a member of the British expedition: *"You've got to be very close to the cave to find it. Certainly, on previous expeditions, people have passed within a few hundred meters of the entrance without finding it."* As we can see, the idea that the Earth is well explored and that there is nothing spectacular left to discover, is not correct. If the example above doesn't seem representative, be prepared for the spectacular nature of the next.

Lake Vostok, located more than 740 miles from the South Pole, was theorized at the end of the 1950s by the Russian scientist Andrei Kapitsa. His theory of the existence of an underground lake was confirmed by Russian scientists and the British in 1996, by combining data from various sources including airborne ice-penetrating radar imaging observations and space-based radar altimetry. The underground lake is covered by 12,000ft of Antarctic ice, and is about 150 miles long by 30 miles wide, with an estimated average depth of 1,100ft.

In February 2012, according to the magazine *Scientific American*, a team of Russian scientists and engineers succeeded for the first time in drilling down to the waters of the subglacial lake. Their spectacular findings were made possible through the use of Remotely Operated Vehicles (ROVs). The discovery, which has recently been published in *PLoS Biology*, by a team of researchers from the universities of Oxford and Southampton, in collaboration with the British Antarctic Survey (BAS), reveals the existence, not of a new species, but of a completely new ecosystem, with entire communities of unknown species under the perpetual ice of Antarctica.

Thanks to the heat of hydrothermal vents on the seafloor a unique biosphere has been created, in an environment of complete darkness. It includes huge colonies of the new species of yeti crab, an undescribed predatory sea star with seven arms, barnacles, sea anemones and an identified pale octopus, among many others. In this area, there are hydrothermal vents (black smokers) where water temperatures reach up to 382°C.

Professor Alex Rogers, of Oxford University's Department of Zoology, and the main author of the study, says that *"hydrothermal vents are home to animals found nowhere else on the planet that get their energy not from the Sun but from breaking down chemicals, such as hydrogen sulphide. The first survey of these particular vents, in the Southern Ocean near Antarctica, has revealed a hot, dark, lost world, in which whole communities of previously unknown marine organisms thrive."*

The researchers were surprised not to have found a single species common to the hydrothermal vents of the Pacific, Atlantic or Indian Oceans. Rogers and his team believe that the differences between the groups of animals found in the Antarctic and those of all the other oceans is proof that the hydrothermal vents may have much more diversity and complexity than was thought. These findings, says Rogers, *"are yet more evidence of the precious diversity to be found throughout the world's oceans. Everywhere we look, whether it is in the sunlit coral reefs of tropical waters or these Antarctic vents shrouded in eternal darkness, we find unique ecosystems that we need to understand and protect."*

Could anyone have imagined, only a few years ago, the possibility of finding a place, located in the coldest area of the planet, with temperatures six times higher than those in the hottest deserts of the world? Had anyone thought of the possible existence of a lake of such dimensions hidden in Antarctica? Yet more evidence of the weakness of the arguments that underlie certain pseudoscientific ideas that affirm the impossibility of existence at the poles, of entrances to the interior of the Earth, as well as the impossibility of life in the planet's interior.

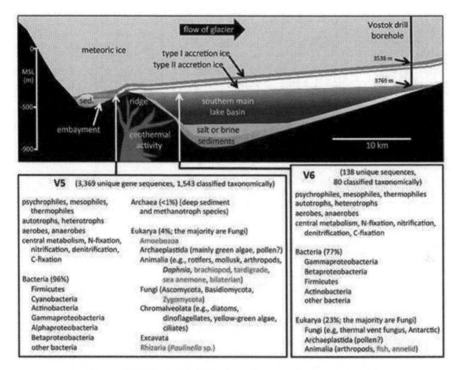

Figure 12.5 Lake Vostok contains a unique ecosystem.

I have always been fascinated by the way in which the scientific community presents as certain and rigorous, things that later have been proven false. History is full of the examples of which I spoke in the first chapter. Most people accept as true what is taught by the official media, and they do so because it is comfortable to believe what everyone believes, and to think how everyone thinks. The person who goes against the mainstream runs the risk of being labeled a fool or worse.

Defenders of the dominant scientific paradigm use the results of drilling experiments as evidence that the Earth is not hollow. These samples, which have not reached deeper than 1% of the diameter of the planet, show that the Earth is solid to a certain depth and in certain places but do not exclude other areas or greater depths. Similarly, it is noted that the temperature increases depending on the depth. From all that, scientists assume that the Earth must be solid to the core and that temperatures should gradually increase until you reach certain levels in the interior.

This is not science but pure presumption based on insufficient data. If we make an analogy, it would be the same as accepting that, in the human body, there is no blood, for the unique reason that an incision in the skin to the depth of 1mm did not show any trace of it. In the case of drilling in the Earth's crust, the holes that have been made are extremely superficial and few in number when compared to the magnitude of the planet. However, can official science answer the following questions with sufficient rigor?

Why are icebergs formed by fresh water? Why have stones, sand, tropical seeds, plants and trees been found in them?

What is the reason thousands of species of tropical birds migrate to the north in winter?

How can we explain the finding of butterflies and bees beyond the barriers of the arctic ice? How could they have resisted the low temperatures if they originated from the south?

How was the great ice barrier of Antarctica formed, that extends more than 400 miles long and 50 miles wide with a height from 60 to 200 feet above the water? Does anyone dare to suggest that such a mass is the product of rain and snow?

Why, according to all the Arctic explorers, after crossing 70° latitude, does the wind coming from the North, and the water, become warmer as they get closer to the North Pole?

I will try to shed some light on these questions. Science tells us that there are two cardinal points: the North Pole and the South Pole, which are the places where the meridians intersect, however, no expedition has ever succeeded in reaching these points. What we know is that there have been expeditions which came close to the poles, though they were often lost, not knowing their precise position. In 1906, William Reed published *The Phantom of the Poles*, which summarizes the theory of the hollow Earth: The Earth is hollow. The Poles, so long sought, are phantoms. There are openings at the northern and southern extremities. In the interior are vast continents, oceans, mountains and rivers. Vegetable and animal life are evident in this New World and it is probably peopled by races unknown to dwellers on the Earth's surface.

Reed points out that the Earth is not a true sphere, but that it is flattened at the poles, which in reality do not exist because there are openings to the interior of the Earth. As such, the geographic poles would be in the air and not on the surface. This comment seems reasonable in terms of new Russian research and discoveries on the Magnetic North Pole, which have led to the conclusion that the difficulty in determining a stable and fixed point at the Magnetic North Pole might be because it is not a fixed point, but infinite points that form a circular line at least 1000 miles long.

According to this, one might call any point in the circle the Magnetic North Pole because, in those places, the needle of the compass would point down and, in this way, when explorers or pilots believe they have reached the point furthest north, it is because their compasses confuse them with their strange behavior; in reality they are at the edge of the polar concavities, which is where the circle is located that makes up the true Magnetic North Pole. It would be interesting to organize an expedition to travel in a straight line to the north and continue traveling in that direction once the compass signals that one has reached the Magnetic North Pole.

It is an undeniable fact that icebergs are formed by fresh water. The conditions of the Arctic Ocean in the north and the Southern Ocean in the south show the impossibility that they were made from fresh water, so we must conclude that these icebergs must be formed by water from another source, that is to say, water not from the seas. The difference between the water of the sea and that from rivers is that the first is salty, while the latter is fresh. At this point, no rivers have been found in the polar regions. In fact, it seems a little crazy to consider it, but everything would make sense if there really were entrances to the interior of the planet in the polar regions, from which flowed the warm waters of underground rivers that, when they reached the outside of the planet and the freezing temperatures of the area, would solidify in the form of icebergs. In this regard, the discovery of the underground Lake Vostok beneath the surface of the Antarctic, with all its tropical ecosystem and hydrothermal vents that reach 382° C, represents indisputable evidence in support of this.

In defense of the thesis which postulates that icebergs of fresh water are not formed on the outside of the Earth but come from freshwater rivers in its interior, Reed quotes the words of the Antarctic explorer Louis Bernnachi: *"There was less than two inches of rainfall in eleven and one-half months, and while it snowed quite frequently, it never fell to any great depth."* Under similar conditions… How could an iceberg be formed?

However, the largest iceberg on the planet is there: the Great Ice Barrier, more than 400 miles long by 50 wide and extending from 60 to 200 feet above sea level. So there are icebergs composed of fresh water in the middle of an ocean of salt water, where precipitation is rather scarce. What a mystery. Where does the fresh water that produces large quantities of icebergs come from?

What can be said of the discovery of frozen tropical seeds in these icebergs? Official science solves the mystery by arguing that these seeds come from the Paleozoic Era, when the area of the poles had a tropical climate. This happened 290 million years ago, and since then there have been hundreds of glaciations and thaws. Thinking that this is the reason to continue finding seeds and tree trunks in the icebergs of the current poles is to omit with the stroke of a pen all of these glaciations occurring over millions of years, rather like trying to explain the origin of babies due to the existence of storks.

Another significant phenomenon is the finding in these icebergs of sand and rocks as well as the phenomenon of colored snow. It must be said that this phenomenon is not unique to the polar regions; the study of some events in other places can help to understand what happens at the poles. On March 2, 2007, the inhabitants of approximately 50 villages south of the Siberian region of Omsk, on the border with the Republic of Kazakhstan, were perplexed by the phenomenon occurring in front of their eyes. The snow that had fallen during the previous night was not the usual color, but yellow, in some places even orange, and a few miles further to the north, in the region of Tomsk, was even blue. It was quickly noted that the snow had a viscous consistency and an unpleasant odor of rotten eggs.

Alexei Kisilov, Greenpeace representative in the area, thought it was obvious that the smell and color acquired by the snow reflected the presence of sulfur, pointing to the possibility of a failure in an oil refinery in the area producing an emission of pollutant gas with these effects. According to Civil Protection, the analysis carried out on the snow samples collected showed the existence of a high concentration of iron, which focused attention on the metallurgical plants in the region. Particles of sand had also been found in places where the snow was orange. The relative proximity of the Baikonur Cosmodrome caused some to argue that the launching of rockets could be related to the colorful atmospheric phenomenon, although *Roscosmos*, the Russian space agency, was quick to deny such a possibility.

This incident, in which dirty snow was detected in Russia, was not unique, as it was observed in previous years in the neighboring region of Altai and on Sakhalin Island, in the Pacific. In the latter case, according to witnesses, at the places where the snow melted there were yellow colored spots and a distinct odor of rotten eggs. The experts thought that the mystery of the colored snow was a consequence of the activity of Ebeko volcano on the island of Paramushir, near Sakhalin, as, in the two weeks prior to the phenomenon, the volcano threw smoke, ash and gases more than a mile into the atmosphere, and could have caused the colored snow that fell in the Russian village. The yellow color and the smell, possibly caused by particles of sulfur in the snow, are a characteristic element of volcanic activity.

The phenomenon of colored snow in these cases seems to be linked to the emission of gases or materials from the Earth's interior, something that has to make us think when we see this phenomenon in the polar regions, where there are no known volcanoes in close proximity. Arctic explorers talk constantly of annoying and irritating dust in the air, something typical of volcanic eruptions. Being extremely light, the wind carries it and it falls on ships, causing great inconvenience to sailors. When this dust falls in snow, it produces the phenomenon of so called black snow. Analysis shows the existence of coal and iron in it. Where do these materials from the interior of the Earth come from? From a non-existent volcano in the polar regions?

Another disturbing phenomenon for orthodox science is the fact that, as you move further north from latitude 70°, the temperature becomes warmer, vegetation has more life, and fauna is more abundant. How can we explain that the temperature goes steadily down until this latitude and, from this point, begins to increase? How can it be explained that the source of that heat does not come from the south, but from a series of winds and currents from the north, the area made up of ice? Why is there a temperate sea in the place where scientists expect to find large masses of eternal ice? Where does that unusually warm water come from?

When you read these lines you may think, well this is all right and even makes me think of it as a possibility, but let us not be naive, it is very strange that no one has discovered large entrances to the interior of the Earth if they really exist. To respond to this natural argument some other questions must be answered. Why were we so sure for centuries that the Earth was flat? Why did we not discover, simply by looking around, that the Earth was round and that we lived on the surface of a large sphere?

The answer to these questions and, therefore, also to the mystery with which we are dealing, is that man is so tiny in relation to the dimensions of the area he inhabits, that due to an optical effect he is unable to perceive the curve of the planet. Something similar may be happening with these expeditions in which polar explorers never reach the North Pole. They reach the outer edge of the polar opening, but the opening is of such dimensions that the descending curve inwards is not noticeable. Its diameter is so broad that it is not visible.

Ban Ki-moon, Secretary-General of the UN, stated in September 2009 that "*the Arctic could be nearly ice-free by 2030.*" According to data provided by NASA, until a few years ago, the perennial ice covered between 50% and 60% of the Arctic; in 2010 the surface cover was reduced to less than 30%. This decline reflects the trend of global warming, according to the American space agency. In this simple manner and with subsequent statements, the vast majority of political and scientifi authorities echo the politically correct theory in vogue, but devoid of scientific basis, the so-called climate change and global warming produced by the emission of polluting gases into the atmosphere.

Please don't misunderstand me; I do not mean the emission of gases due to human activity should not be regulated, something that would be beneficial to the Earth's ecosystem, both for present and future inhabitants of the blue planet. This is one thing but it is very different to state, based on flimsy computer climate models, that the main cause of climate change and the melting of Arctic ice is the emission of these gases.

Nowadays, there is probably no greater heresy than questioning the role of CO_2 in rising temperatures. However, Henrik Svensmark, director of the Center for Sun-Climate Research in Copenhagen, proposes solar activity and cosmic radiation as the two fundamental factors that are influencing the heating of the Earth, far more than the gases produced by human activity. Based on Henrik Svensmark's research, *The Chilling Stars: A New Theory of Climate Change* outlines a brilliant and daring new theory that has already provoked fresh thinking on global warming. Nigel Calder and Svensmark explain that an interplay of the Sun and cosmic rays, subatomic particles from exploded stars, seem to have more effect on the climate than man-made carbon dioxide. I am glad that some scientists have begun to wake up from their placid sleep and hope that this will lead to a total comprehension of the role that the Sun plays in this whole story. My advice to those interested in learning about the role of the Sun from a different perspective than the official is to read, at the end of this work, Appendix B, entitled *Final station: the Sun*.

In fact, it is not scientific to assert that the cause of the melting of Arctic ice is global warming produced by the action of man, when neither one thing nor the other is correct. You only have to go a few pages back and look at the Mercator map of the Arctic, made in the seventeenth century. Anyone can observe that the Arctic polar cap, this pipe dream that some scientists say has disappeared in recent years by action of global warming, did not exist at the time the map was made. That was 400 years ago, when the emission of pollutants by man were virtually non-existent. Mercator had already illustrated the Arctic area with no perpetual ice but a huge ocean surrounded by ice, which indicates that things do not seem to have changed so much since then. How can it be explained that Mercator drew that map four centuries ago?

Each year, a great number of tourists visit the far north of Scandinavia, in the vicinity of the Arctic, seeking to observe a fantastic phenomenon of nature. It is a natural light display in the sky, predominantly seen in places north of the Arctic Circle or south of the Antarctic Circle in the latitudes near the poles. The variety of shades of blue, green and red, as well as the dizzying speed at which they develop makes for a genuinely amazing and compelling spectacle. The best time to see it is between September and March in the northern hemisphere, and between March and September in the southern hemisphere.

In the northern hemisphere it is called the *Aurora Borealis*. The etymology of the name comes from "Aurora", the Roman goddess of the dawn, and the Greek word *boreas*, meaning north, since in Europe it usually appears on the horizon with a reddish tone, as if the Sun emerged from an unusual place. In the southern hemisphere it is called the *Aurora Australis*. Science explains that this phenomenon occurs when an ejection of solar wind charged with ions collides with the poles of the Earth's magnetic field, producing a collision with molecules of oxygen and nitrogen in the upper layers of the atmosphere, releasing its energy in the form of visible light in the skies over the poles.

The North American author, Marshall B. Gardner, spent more than twenty years studying the reports of the Arctic explorers, as well as different astronomical aspects, before publishing his book, *A Journey to the Earth's Interior*. He observed many strange phenomena and explained them with new theories. Gardner argues the existence of a central sun in the Earth's interior, which would explain the origin of the high temperatures in the area, as well as the phenomenon of the *Aurora Borealis*. He also claims that, not only the Earth but all the planets in the solar system, are hollow and have central suns. He argues that the original formation of the planets was due to a spinning nebula and that, as a result of the centrifugal force of its rotation, the constituent elements were thrown out, forming in this way a solid crust on the outside surface of every planet, leaving an empty interior. Following the same argument, due to the force of rotation and movement through space, openings in the polar extremities were made.

For someone who understands the ancient hermetic laws, this is not at all surprising, and at the same time is very much in line with modern scientific theories on fractals that are recovering that ancestral wisdom in current times. The term "fractal" was proposed by the mathematician Benoit Mandelbrot in 1975 and derives from the Latin *fractus, which* means broken or split. Fractals can be defined as complex geometric objects whose constituent parts are similar to the whole. Fractals are never-ending patterns that are similar across different scales. Another way to explain it would be like a geometric shape that remains unchanged regardless of the size. Fractal patterns are extremely familiar, since nature is full of them. For example: trees, rivers, clouds, coastlines, mountains, hurricanes, cells etc.

Figure 12.6 Example of a fractal structure

At present, physics is developing a principle called "Scale Relativity". It is a geometrical and fractal space-time theory that covers not only the Cosmos but the quantum level. Laurent Nottale proposed to combine fractal space-time theory with relativity principles and this is the way he defined the principle in his own words

The laws of nature must be valid in every system of coordinates, whatever their state of motion and scale.

According to Nottale, quantum theory, applied to molecules, atoms and subatomic particles, is relativistic; and it is possible to deduce the most probable stellar structures depending on the conditions of its environment. With this model, which defines the Universe as a great wave function, the astrophysicist has been able to determine the positions of all the planets in the solar system and predict their new positions, without correspondence with any identified object. The discovery of other exoplanets around other stars, as well as objects that are located in the Kuiper Belt, beyond Pluto, have confirmed the peaks of probability of the theoretical predictions of the principle of Scale relativity.

You can guess the profound implications on the physical and philosophical levels, derived from the possibility of verifying the hypothesis of a Fractal Universe and the principle of Scale Relativity with new experimental observations. When looking back to the distant past, it is dizzying to see that what science is doing is to rediscover something that was already known in antiquity, giving other names and expressing with another language something that was already defined with the simplicity of true wisdom. It is one of the seven hermetic principles included in the *Kybalion,* one of the best written summaries of hermetic philosophy. The similarity between Nottale's statement and the millenarian aphorism that defines the hermetic principle of Correspondence should be noted.

The laws of nature must be valid in every system of coordinates, whatever their state of motion and scale.

Laurent Nottale

As above, so below; as below, so above.

The Kybalion

The fractal nature of space-time underlies the fact that the birth and structuring of all the entities of the physical world and living matter seem to develop and be constructed following the fractal model, in which the constituent parts are similar to the whole or, in other words, that tiny things are similar to larger ones.

In this regard, for the benefit of the hypothesis of Gardner, I have to say that planetary nebulae generally have an external shell, hollow, with a central star and open at the poles. It is widely recognized that the origin of the solar system was in a nebula that condensed as it cooled and the effect of the centrifugal force was to form the planets and the central sun. What conclusions can be drawn from this?

We can use both the principle of Correspondence and Scale Relativity to state that, knowing the structure and origin of a nebula, it is possible to know the structure and origin of a planet. In this way, we can reach the conclusion that, just as happened in the formation of our solar system, part of the original fire remained in the center like a sun; the same process would have happened with the formation of each planet. In the formation of the solar system, the mechanism of rotary motion threw the heaviest masses toward the periphery, giving rise to the formation of planets. The same process would happen with each planet, on a different scale; the heavier masses would be pushed toward the outside, so forming the solid layer of Earth's crust, the consequence being a less dense interior or even an empty space.

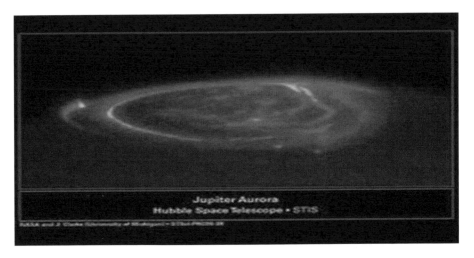

Figure 12.7 Aurora on Jupiter as observed by the Hubble Space Telescope

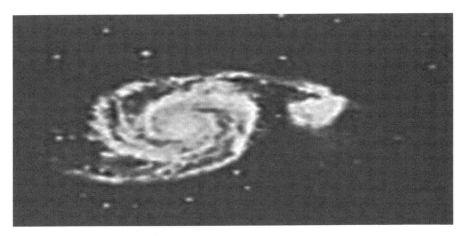

Figure 12.8 Image of a Spiral Nebula

Figure 12.9 *Aurora Borealis* **on Jupiter**

To complicate matters further, and a source of even more controversy, are alleged pictures taken by a NASA satellite. The image below was taken in 1968 by the North American satellite *Essa 7*, on the vertical axis of the South Pole. It should be noted that there is a large black circle, which seems to hide or conceal something. The second image is a photo mosaic by Dr. David S Johnson, of the National Environment Satellite Center, of photos taken by *Essa*. It is also notable that the area which coincides with the South Pole has been removed without explanation.

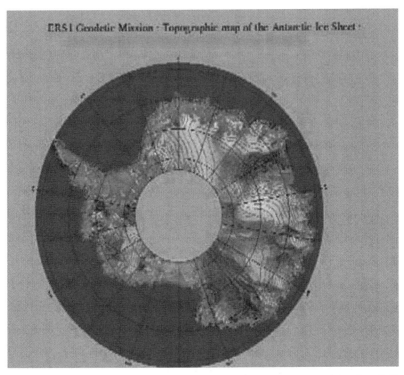

Figure 12.10 Photo-mosaic of images taken by *Essa* satellite of the South Pole

The controversy over possible counterfeiting by NASA reaches the other planets of the solar system. The photo below, taken by the *Cassini* spacecraft in 2001, is of the planet Jupiter.

Figure 12.11 Image of Jupiter taken by *Cassini*.

Is it possible that NASA has falsified the photographs taken from satellites? If so, for what purpose?

There are many questions that cannot be answered satisfactorily by official explanations and wait for answers

After this brief exposition on the mysteries of the Earth's interior, you are ready to interpret certain Bible verses from a different perspective to the orthodox point of view. In light of this new data, the apparent contradictions of the story of how long the Deluge lasted disappear. Contrary to the widespread popular opinion that the Flood was caused by torrential rains, the Mesopotamian sources make it clear that, although it rained, the catastrophe began as a result of one or several monumental waves which came from the south. Thus, *Genesis* explains the Flood, giving valuable information on how it began, where the waters came from and where they went after it was over.

In the six hundredth year of Noah's life,
in the second month, on the seventeenth day of the month,
on the same day were all the fountains of the great deep broken
up, and the windows of heaven were opened.

Genesis 7:11

The *Book of Genesis* speaks of two sources for the waters of the Flood: the great deep and the rain. The rain fell for forty days.

And the rain was upon the earth forty days and forty nights.

Genesis 7:12

However, the water from the great deep flowed for 150 days

And God made a wind to pass over the earth,
and the waters assuaged;
and the fountains of the deep,
and the windows of heaven were stopped,
and the rain from heaven was restrained;
and the waters receded steadily from the earth:
and at the end of one hundred and fifty days the waters decreased.

Genesis 8: 1-2

Let's have a look at the original words used in Hebrew for "the fountains of the deep". In the original Hebrew, the expression used for the fountains is the *ma'ayanot*, which literally means springs. A spring is any natural source where water flows from an aquifer to the Earth's surface. The term used for the deep is *Tehom*. When the Bible says that the fountains of the deep were broken, it refers to the large masses of water that had been maintained until that time under pressure in the interior of the Earth and that, through the action of God, in the Sumerian case by the action of the gods, the pressure was released, bringing disastrous consequences for humanity. The Sumerian version says that the cataclysm was caused by Enlil and his Assembly of gods and that the water came from the *Apsu*, the abyss of the deep. The mysterious words used in the biblical version that have been interpreted in a self-interested manner by theologians, regain their full meaning when we understand their provenance from a previous story. The biblical version speaks of springs that emanate from "the deep of the sea" or from the *Tehom*, these words being translations of the Chaldean word *Apsu,* meaning the abyss, and the more distant seas located south of Mesopotamia.

It is a fact that ancient Mesopotamians and Greeks believed in the existence of a subterranean ocean that was the source of all the world's rivers and springs, as the *Iliad* says: *"from which all rivers and all the seas and all the springs and deep wells take their flow."* The Greeks called this ocean *Okeanos* and applied it to all of the waters on the planet, a huge river that surrounded the world and that was the father of all the rivers and springs. This implied groundwater as well as a network of channels under the surface of the planet. As Martin West writes in his book *The East Face of Helicon*:

> *Although* Okeanos *is normally mentioned only in connection with the ends of the Earth, as the stream that encircles the Earth, it also appears as the father of all the world's rivers and springs... This implies a mass of water, or at least of water channels, below the Earth, and it makes* Okeanos *into something not altogether unlike the Hebrew Tehom... or the Mesopotamian Apsu.*

Let's see what modern scientific discoveries reveal about the ancient concept of Okeanos. On March 12, 2014 the scientific journal *Nature* covered a study undertaken by Graham Pearson, a mantle geochemist at the University of Alberta in Edmonton, Canada, and his team. Pearson used data obtained from the USArray, which is part of the EarthScope experiment, a 15-year program to place a dense network of permanent and portable seismographs across the USA to study the mantle and core of the earth. The discovery at the heart of Pearson's study came through an ultradeep diamond weighing less than one-tenth of a gram, found in Brazil. *"Most diamonds form at depths of about 150 to 200 kilometers, but ultradeep diamonds come from a region of the mantle known as the transition zone, 410 to 660 kilometers below the surface,"* says Pearson.

Impurities in ultradeep diamonds can be used as probes to study the regions in which the stones formed. Thus, in this case a worthless-looking diamond that survived a trip from hell enclosed a tiny piece of an olivine mineral called ringwoodite, a mineral that makes up much of the upper mantle, This microscopic crystal of a mineral, never before seen in a terrestrial rock, holds clues to the presence of vast quantities of water deep in Earth's mantle. *"These high-pressure diamonds give you a window into the deep Earth."* says Pearson.

Unlike better-studied forms of olivine, ringwoodite can hold a substantial amount of water. Using infrared spectroscopy, Pearson's team found that this tiny fleck of ringwoodite contained about 1% water by weight. *"That may not sound like much,"* Pearson says, *"but when you realize how much ringwoodite there is, the transition zone could hold as much water as all the Earth's oceans put together."*

These amazing words, coming from a respected scientific source, may provide evidence of a vast wet zone deep inside the Earth's transition zone; a zone that could hold as much water as all the world's oceans put together... Scientists are learning more and more about the interior of the Earth, and this particularly striking discovery suggests that the water of the planet's surface could be connected with that of the interior and indeed, could proceed from it. This completely contradicts the dominant paradigm, that the water of the Earth had its precedence in outer space, in frozen comets that passed by a million years ago. It seems that modern scientific discoveries are giving credence once again to ancient concepts.

From the point of view of an observer located at the mouth of the Tigris and the Euphrates, the *Apsu*, the springs located "at the deep of the sea", beyond the Indian Ocean, are the Antarctic Ocean and its icy continent. I would also suggest that the only way life could be swept from the Earth in such a short space of time through the action of water was by a *tsunami* of enormous proportions, not due to excessive rainfall, which also existed as a result of the ecological imbalance created by the rising levels of the waters. The *tsunami* was produced by water coming from the interior of the Earth, from where it poured violently onto the outside of the planet through the Antarctic polar opening. The *tsunami* was from the south and caused a gigantic tidal wave that moved north, sweeping across all the coastlines in its path until it reached Mesopotamia.

> *On the first day the tempest from the south rose up,*
> *Blew swiftly and brought the flood,*
> *Like a battle force the destructive* **kashushu** *passed over the people.*
>
> Epic of Gilgamesh. Babylonian old version

The Bible, later, makes it clear that it was a phenomenon of ocean tides, using terms such as ebb and flo , closely linked to this phenomenon. The waters descended, not by the action of evaporation or filtering, but by a phenomenon similar to the movement of a wave on the beach, but on a vastly greater scale:

> *And the waters returned from off the earth continually:*
> *and after the end of the hundred and fifty days the waters were abated.*
>
> Genesis 8:3

The water level gradually dropped and, after ten and a half months, had returned to its previous level. The water slowly returned to its place of origin, disappearing from the Earth's surface:

> *And it came to pass in the six hundredth and first year,*
> *in the first month, the first day of the month,*
> *the waters were dried up from off the earth.*
>
> Genesis 8:13

Although it took almost another two months to dry:

> *And in the second month,*
> *on the seven and twentieth day of the month, was the earth dried.*
>
> Genesis 8:14

Another Mesopotamian source that casts light on this subject is *The Epic of Erra*. It dates from the first third of the first century BC and is a Babylonian poem inspired by older sources. The protagonist, Erra, is the god of plague, pestilence and Hades, the underworld;, that is, the subterranean world... the world that exists below the surface of the planet. Erra feels restless in his dwelling, the underground world, and breaks into a soliloquy. He is anxious to fight and campaign, but hesitates through natural inertia.

Finally, he is convinced to make war by the pressure from his armies and troops, in particular from his Military Command, the *Sebitti*, the seven terrible warriors marching by his side. Erra urges his vizier Ishum, who is not yet convinced, to attack Marduk. For this reason, he visits the temple of his rival, criticizing him and telling him that his appearance is not appropriate for the ruler of the gods. Marduk is convinced, and travels to the underground world of the sweet waters so that the artisans who live there will help him to change his appearance.

In Marduk's absence, Erra plans to devastate Babylon although Ishum tries to change his mind. Finally, Erra, at his third attempt, ravages Babylon and kills without remorse. In this poem it must be noted that Erra embodies, among others, the fresh groundwater of the planet.

> *O Lord Erra, why have you plotted evil against the gods?*
> *To lay waste the lands and decimate the people.*
> *Oh, warrior Erra, thou hast brought the face of death to the fair,*
> *thou hast brought death to the unjust,*
> *thou hast put to death the man who had offended you,*
> *thou hast put to death the man who had not offended you...*

Ishum tells Era that the entire world is overwhelmed by his landslide victory. Erra (the groundwater), victorious, challenges the other gods before returning to his temple in the underground world. Ishum reassures him:

> *Oh, warrior, calm down and listen to my words!*
> *What if you were now to rest and we took care of you?*

We all know that no one can face you in a day of wrath!
Appeased, Erra retires to his temple in Khuta.

The Mesopotamian narrative points out that the floodwaters that produced this great wave came from the south, a result of the transfer to the surface of the underground freshwater. Waters produced from an opening in the Antarctic area, which somehow remains open today, as the facts show that icebergs are formed by fresh water. The poem adds Marduk's complaint and explains what happened:

...the Erakallum quaked and its covering was diminished,
and the measures could no longer be taken.

Erakallum is a term that is usually translated as "lower world", although today the academics leave it untranslated. In the present work I suggest that its meaning refers to the underground world.

In this way, the story is told of one particular aspect of Enki's third attempt to destroy the race of humans who had been created by the Anunnaki aliens, coming from Heaven, 450,000 years ago. Humans had begun to disturb Enki with their behavior and their irreverent and exponential reproductive growth. After two failed attempts, Enki made the definitive plan to place explosive charges of great magnitude in the Earth gates that contained the fresh waters of the Earth's interior. These gates were located in the Antarctic area.

When the explosions occurred and the cover was broken, the fresh waters of the planet's interior sprang up in abundance, causing a rise in sea levels as well as a *tsunami* of gigantic proportions that advanced from the south, inexorably, toward the north until it reached the Persian Gulf. The results are well known.

The detailed reading shows that biblical and Mesopotamian sources agree on the later succession of facts. After the giant wave subsided, the water level began to decline gradually. They also agree on the episodes of sending doves to explore the field in search of solid ground, the arrival on the Mount Ararat, the construction of an altar and the offering of a sacrifice to a divinity, followed by the blessing of Yahweh or Enlil on Noah/Ziusudra.

The Mesopotamian sources describe in greater detail the rapprochement of the hungry gods to the last human survivors, since there was nothing left to eat in all the Earth. Utnapishtim describes how he offered a sacrifice to the gods and how, when they smelled the sweet aroma, they were attracted like flies. Ninmah immediately realized what had happened and solemnly swore by the jewels that Anu had gifted her that she would never forget what had happened. They then invited the rest of the Anunnaki to share the food offering, excluding Enlil, who was responsible for the extermination of humans because of the Flood.

When Enlil came and saw the boat, he was filled with wrath and turned it on the *Iggigi*, accusing them of having helped man to escape from destruction. However, Ninurta quickly suspected that the one responsible for the escape of some men from the deluge was another, and so he said to Enlil:

> *Who is there of the gods that can devise without Ea?*
> *It is Ea alone who knows all things.*
>
> Epic of Gilgamesh

By joining the meeting, Ea/Enki acknowledged his responsibility; at the same time he made clear that he had not violated his oath to keep secret Enlil's plans. All that he had done was to bring a premonitory dream to Atra-Hasis; it was the intelligence of this human that had allowed him to unravel the secret of the gods. Then Enki began to remonstrate with Enlil, asking whether he now repented of what had happened:

> *Wisest of gods, hero Enlil,*
> *how could you so senselessly bring down the flood?*
>
> Epic of Gilgamesh

The text does not make clear what motivated Enlil to change his mind, but it leaves no doubt that he did. So say Utnapishtim/Atra-Hasis:

Then Enlil went up into the boat,
he took me by the hand and my wife
and made us enter the boat and kneel down on either side,
he standing between us.
He touched our foreheads to bless us.

Epic of Gilgamesh

The blessing of Utnapishtim/Atra-Hasis and his wife had a deep meaning, beyond simple religious connotations. Enlil gave the human couple who had escaped from the Deluge the immortality which the Anunnaki gods enjoyed.

In time past Utnapishtim was a mortal man;
henceforth Utnapishtim and his wife shall be lofty like unto the gods
he and his wife shall live in the distance at the mouth of the rivers.

Epic of Gilgamesh

The final outcome of this drama is, according to the biblical sources, a commitment on the part of Yahweh before the survivors, that such a cataclysm as this would never be repeated. Something that has only relative value coming from one of the Mesopotamian gods like Enlil, who had demonstrated a highly unstable personality.

CHAPTER XIII

THE MYSTERY OF ATLANTIS UNVEILED

Captain Nemo came over and stopped me with a gesture. Then, picking up a piece of chalky stone, he advanced to a black basaltic rock and scrawled one single word: ATLANTIS. What lightning flashed through my mind! Atlantis, that ancient land of Meropis mentioned by the historian Theopompus; Plato's Atlantis.

Twenty Thousand Leagues Under the Sea, Jules Verne

Much has been written about Atlantis, the fabulous and mysterious lost continent. The legend emerged almost 2,400 years ago, from a single written source: *The Dialogues* of Plato, the Greek philosopher, who has had so much influence on Western thinking. The fact that Plato promoted Atlantis as a true story has led to various theories searching for its location, and its popularity has served as inspiration for many literary works and films of fantasy and science fiction. The story is contained in two dialogs: the *Timaeus* and *Critias*. Critias begins by saying that the story had been told to Solon, one of the great sages of antiquity, by his great-grandfather:

Then listen, Socrates, to a tale which, though strange, is certainly true, having been attested by Solon, who was the wisest of the seven sages. He was a relative and a dear friend of my great-grandfather, Dropides, as he himself says in many passages of

240

his poems; and he told the story to Critias, my grandfather, who remembered and repeated it to us. There were of old, he said, great and marvelous actions of the Athenian city, which have passed into oblivion through lapse of time and the destruction of mankind, and one in particular, greater than all the rest. This we will now rehearse. It will be a fitting monument of our gratitude to you, and a hymn of praise true and worthy of the goddess, on this her day of festival.

Timaeus

Socrates responds that he has never heard anything about this wonderful bravery performed by the inhabitants of Athens. Critias continues to explain that this knowledge had been transmitted through four generations of his family, and that Solon, in turn, had picked up this knowledge during his stay in Egypt amongst former priests of the city of Sais. When he was a child, Critias had heard the story from the lips of his grandfather, who had recited it from memory during the Apaturia festival.

Critias continues with the story of Solon's stay in Egypt and tells how the conversation that Solon had with the priests reached a climax when he spoke about the age of the Greeks. This provoked one of the more elderly priests to mock Solon, joking about the Greeks' lack of knowledge of the past:

O Solon, Solon, you Hellenes are never anything but children, and there is not an old man among you.

Timaeus

Solon, in return, asks the priest what he means. The priest continues with his explanation:

I mean to say, he replied, that in mind you are all young; there is no old opinion handed down among you by ancient tradition, nor any science which is hoary with age. And I will tell you why. There have been, and will be again, many destructions of mankind arising out of many causes; the greatest have been brought about by the agencies of fire and water, and other lesser ones by innumerable other causes.

Timaeus

The old priest asserts that the land of the pharaohs is the depository of a knowledge that is lacking in the lands of the Greeks:

And whatever happened either in your country or in ours, or in any other region of which we are informed, if there were any actions noble or great or in any other way remarkable, they have all been written down by us of old, and are preserved in our temples.

Timaeus

He continues, saying that before the largest of all the floods occurred, there lived, in Athens, a race of superior men from whom the Greeks were descended:

And there you dwelt, having such laws as these and still better ones, and excelled all mankind in all virtue, as became the children and disciples of the gods.

Timaeus

From here, the priest narrates the story that has since become popularized as "Atlantis", a large island located beyond the Pillars of Hercules, where there lived a civilization that waged a war against the mythical inhabitants of Athens in remote prehistoric times, and from whom the Athenians of Solon's time were descended:

The records speak of a vast power that your city once brought to a halt in its insolent march against the whole of Europe and Asia at once, a power that sprang forth from beyond, from the Atlantic Ocean. For at that time this ocean was passable, since it had an island in it, beyond the strait that you people call the Pillars of Heracles. This island was larger than Libya and Asia combined and it provided passage to the other islands... From those islands one could then travel to the entire continent on the other side, which surrounds the real sea beyond...

Timaeus

This Atlantean civilization, according to Plato, had tried to conquer the world but disappeared overnight when the island sank into the depths of the sea:

But afterwards there occurred violent earthquakes and floods; and in a single day and night of misfortune all your warlike men in a body sank into the earth, and the island of Atlantis in like manner disappeared in the depths of the sea.

Timaeus

The influence of oriental themes, in the literature and the other arts of Greece, has received increased attention from scholars in the last few decades. As I have already explained in previous chapters, everything began in Sumer and was disseminated from there. But, the argument has been proposed, and defended in different circles – possibly because of an arrogant inner wish of the Western world, which considers itself as original and independent of any other outside influence – that Greek civilization, likewise, originated independently. However, when speaking of early Greek civilization, we have to understand that it did not emerge from nowhere; foreign influences have formed part of Greek civilization since Minoan and Mycenaean times.

In the area of arts, it can be seen that Eastern motifs appear in the graphic and plastic arts of early Greece. The metal working and the proto-geometric decoration on ceramics, the ivory carvings, the artworks of gold and crafting of objects from silver show the direct influence of the east (albeit modified through domestic experiments with them in the early centuries of Greek civilization).

Improved reconstruction of the myths, religious tales and writings of the Ancient Near East from Sumerian, Akkadian, Hittite or Ugaritic sources all support this view. The evidence shows that the Greeks borrowed, from previous civilizations of the Mesopotamian Middle East and Egypt, their myths and their stories, in this way forming their own prehistory or mythical stage. These myths, with the well-known pantheon of gods, were built and adapted as their own, but the truth is that these myths are talking about events that happened in geographical locations other than Athens, although they expressly mention Athens and Greek civilization. They are talking about earlier civilizations than the Greek.

Pythagoras was a mathematician, astronomer, musician, scientist and one of the most important pre-Socratic philosophers of ancient Greece. He is known, among other things, for his theory of metempsychosis, which stated that souls are immortal and transmigrant. This theory is nothing more than a restatement, with slight variations, of the ancient belief in the doctrine of reincarnation. Pythagoras had drunk from this knowledge, and others, during his trips to Chaldea. On his death, in 500 BC, his teachings about man and the Universe were continued by the Pythagorean school in southern Italy and Sicily.

Plato visited the Pythagorean school in the year 388 BC, where he formed important ties with the community. The following year, Plato returned to Athens and founded his "Academy of Philosophy", where he taught this knowledge. It is important not to lose sight of this point in order to correctly interpret the writings of Plato, since all of his cosmogony is rooted in Pythagorean beliefs that had, in turn, been imported from the Middle East.

Who were, then, these Athenians who fought with such vigor and virtue against the omnipotent power of the Atlantean civilization? Was there an Athenian state in the year 9600 BC? When Plato refers to Athens and its settlers in prehistoric times, he is incarnating in this city events that were lost in the mists of the prehistory of mankind, when the gods came down from Heaven to the Earth. To give you a modern-day analogy, imagine a country like the USA, with such a short history in comparison with Europe. Suppose that a North American intellectual of the twenty-first century wrote a book which describes a pre-existing New York population in the fourteenth century, from which the present inhabitants of New York are descended, when everyone knows that New York was not founded until centuries later. The imaginary writer would be referring to the Irish, English or Dutch people, who were still in Europe in the fourteenth century and had not yet come to Manhattan. The writer is allowing himself a literary license, calling them New Yorkers of the fourteenth century. Similarly, Plato, when talking about these mythical Athenians, would be referring to people and events in a much earlier time. This is an important point, if we are to correctly interpret Plato's text.

The search for Atlantis has led different investigators, psychics and mystics of the New Age to locate it in places as diverse as the Caribbean, the Mediterranean, the Aegean Sea, the Black Sea or the Canary Islands. However, according to Plato, it is well established that Atlantis was located in the Atlantic Ocean, so searching for its location in other seas ignores what has been written. In *Critias*, it is explained that the names "Atlantis" and "Atlantic Ocean" had their etymological origin in the god Atlas:

And he named them all; the eldest, who was the first king, he named Atlas, and after him the whole island and the ocean were called Atlantic.

Critias

Nevertheless, researchers have mapped and swept the floors of the Atlantic Ocean using the most advanced methods: acoustic sensors, radar by geodetic satellite (GEOSAT), cameras, lights and sonars, without finding even the slightest trace of the lost continent. Could an island of the dimensions with which Atlantis is described sink and disappear, without leaving traces of its existence verifiable by current technological capabilities? Certainly, no trace of evidence has been found.

The explanations for the lack of findings are diverse. Scholars say that Plato's writing is a fable without factual foundations; others say that he was simply wrong on its geographical location. This draws attention to the manner in which Plato asserted the veracity of his account. Some people seek to prove that Atlantis was just a myth by using the argument that Aristotle, a disciple of Plato, did not believe in Atlantis.

Many quote Aristotle as saying that "he who invented the island also sank it", with Strabo given as the source of this quote; however, such a statement does not appear directly in the work of Strabo. Instead, the quote is a conflation of different passages of Strabo's *Geography* and Homer's *Iliad*, an inference drawn by attributing the quotation to Aristotle in multiple secondary sources, based on the repetition of similar phrases. This may be justifiable but is not certain, so to present the idea of Aristotle denying Atlantis as evidence of its non-existence is a very feeble argument.

Let's consider the passages that have contributed to the quote being attributed to Aristotle. In this passage of *Geography*, Strabo makes his only mention of Atlantis, talking about the earlier and lost work of the philosopher Posidonius:

> *However, he [Posidonius] is right in attributing to earthquakes and other similar causes, which we also have enumerated, the risings, slips, and changes which at various periods come over the earth. He did well, too, in citing the opinion of Plato, "that the tradition concerning the Island of Atlantis might be received as something more than a mere fiction, it having been related by Solon on the authority of the Egyptian priests, that this island, almost as large as a continent, was formerly in existence, although now it had disappeared". Posidonius thinks it better to quote this than to say, "He who brought it into existence can also cause it to disappear, as the poet did the wall of the Achivi [Achaeans]".*
>
> Geography

As you can see, there is no denial of the existence of Atlantis in this text at all, either on the part of Poseidonius or from Strabo himself. At the same time, note the similarity of the above quotation, referring to the wall of the Achivi, with the one that is later attributed to Aristotle about Atlantis. The wall of the Achivi (Achaeans), mentioned above, was a large construction built to protect Greek ships, described in Homer's *Iliad* (12.5) as:

...the wall that they had built as a defense for their ships and had drawn a trench about it.

The Classical Greeks could find no trace of the wall, leading Aristotle to the conclusion that Homer had invented and disposed of a fictitious construction. Later, Strabo states, in *Geography* (13.1.36):

...perhaps no wall was built and the erection and destruction of it, as Aristotle says, are due to the invention of the poet.

Strabo mentions Aristotle's quotation as referring to the non-existence of the Achaean wall, and never to the non-existence of Atlantis; as you can see, a statement from Aristotle denying Atlantis' existence does not appear anywhere.

The indisputable fact is that the story of Plato deals with recurring mythological themes of earlier civilizations, such as the wars between the gods, the distribution of the lands on the Earth between the gods, the Golden Age of humanity or the wonderful islands located at the ends of the Earth. All of this corroborates the fact that Greek culture did not arise in isolation and without external influence. The key, again, is in the proper decoding of the myths. And yet, the vast majority of scholars, when addressing the myths, do not wonder what they mean or try to find out what is behind them, but rather rely on the interpretations made by the so-called authorities in this matter, accepting them without any criticism as their own, with closed eyes. And what do the authorities say about this matter? Effectively, they say that these myths are incomprehensible, or that they reflect the archetypes of the collective unconscious of humanity; they are all very ethereal and ambiguous, and lack tangible and concrete bases to enable us to locate a lost continent.

Added to the lack of unprejudiced research is the current problem represented by the many different translations of texts written in ancient languages. The meanings and connotations of some words and linguistic concerns have varied over the centuries, to the point where the meaning of the original message may have been drastically changed, depending on the translation that a person chooses to use. For instance, the meaning of one translation of Plato's text says that "Atlantis was located in front of the Pillars of Hercules", which is very different to another translation that says that "Atlantis was located beyond the Pillars of Hercules".

What were the Pillars of Hercules and where were they located? The Phoenicians called them "Pillars of Melkart", in honor of a deity to whom a sanctuary was consecrated in Gades, modern Cadiz, on the islet of San Fernando, near the Strait of Gibraltar. This temple had two huge pillars at the entrance and was a consecrated place for making sacrifices to propitiate a safe voyage. Later, the Greeks termed it the "Pillars of Heracles" and the Romans the "Pillars of Hercules". The Pillars of Heracles, in Homer's writings, were the two pillars that Heracles pushed to split the Atlas Mountains, separating Europe from Africa, and that are today associated with the two mountains at the mouth of the Mediterranean, where it meets the Atlantic Ocean.

The one on this side they call Abila (Jabal Musa), the one on the far side Calpe (Gibraltar), they call them together the Pillars of Hercules. Oral tradition goes on to give the story of the name: Hercules himself separated the mountains, and the water was let into those places that it now inundates. On this side of the Strait, the sea pours in over a rather broad area and with its great rush it pushes back the lands it has cleared from its path.
Pomponius Mela's 'Description of the World'

In Greek Antiquity, these columns indicated the limit of the known world, and the Strait of Gibraltar was the last frontier for the navigators who dared exit the Mediterranean and delve into dangerous seas. Beyond that point, there were only chaos and darkness; it was the end of the navigable sea.

There are different translations of Plato's original text. Some researchers, based on a mistranslation, say that "Atlantis was located in front of the Pillars of Hercules", meaning in the vicinity. The expression "in front" connotes a certain proximity, and in this context would indicate that Atlantis would be located in front of the Strait of Gibraltar. For this reason, searches have been carried out for its remains in the vicinity of the Iberian Peninsula. In the second version, the expression "beyond" does not imply the same notion of proximity, but rather suggests passing or crossing a certain point. From this point of view, Argentina, for example, is "beyond" the Strait of Gibraltar, but not "in front" of it. Depending on the translation that we choose, we can see that the meaning changes. Plato's text originally said that "Atlantis was located beyond the Pillars of Hercules" and this is the meaning that I have taken in this research.

What is the real meaning of an uncharted island in the Atlantic Ocean, and of a continent on the other side that, in the words of Plato, *"was surrounded by the real ocean"*? Despite *Timaeus* and *Critias* being the only written sources to speak explicitly of Atlantis as such, there are other writings and Greco-Roman traditions that speak of territories or fantastic islands located beyond the known world (once more we find the expression "beyond").

The Elysian Fields, according to Greek mythology, was a sacred place located in the western confines, in the remote west. This paradisiacal place was located in the underground world, and there the souls of virtuous men and heroes enjoyed a happy life after death, surrounded by green and flowery landscapes in an eternally pleasant environment. Both Homer and Hesiod refer to it as a distant isle in the ocean at the world's end. To reach these fields it was necessary to cross the waters of the river Acheron in the underworld. Homer describes it in Book IV of his famous *Odyssey*:

Elysium shall be thine; the blissful plains
Of utmost earth, where Rhadamanthus reigns.
Joys ever young, unmix'd with pain of fear,
Fill the wide circle of the eternal year:
Stern winter smiles on that auspicious clime:
The fields are florid with unfading prime:
From the bleak pole no winds inclement blow,
Mould the round hail, or flake the fleecy snow.

Odyssey

Pindar refers to them as "the islands of the Blessed" or "islands of the gods", a land of happiness. And Fray Bartolomé de Las Casas, the Spanish writer, in Volume I of *La Historia De Las Indias* (*History of the Indies*) described them with these words.

It is always summer in the Elysian Fields; there are all kinds of fruits; cheerful water springs with soft, smooth sounds; green fields painted with various colors. There is no cold winter nor hot summer, but perfection and temperance in the sky, because the equilibrium of the air and the heat of the sun contemplates all things and make them enjoyable.

There is a curious resemblance between the Spanish expressions *Campos Elíseos* (Elysian Fields), where there is a never-ending summer, and *Vientos Alisios* (Trade Winds), known in meteorology as places with no snow, no long winter and no rain. Where does this phonetic similarity in the Spanish language come from?

Greek mythology also speaks of the Garden of the Hesperides, a beautiful orchard property of the goddess Hera, located in a far west corner of the world. In the garden there was a tree of golden apples that gave immortality. The tree had been a wedding gift from Gaea (the Earth) to Hera. She, in turn, entrusted its custody to the Hesperides. It must be emphasized that the nymphs, the Hesperides, are daughters of Atlas and also receive the name of Atlantides, and that Heracles was the only one capable of stealing the golden apples. In this myth, in particular, there are mixed elements of diverse origin that reference the Garden of Eden on the one hand and Atlantis on the other.

We find in this myth of the Garden of Hesperides three linguistic elements (Atlas, Atlantides, Heracles) related to the history of Plato. So who was Atlas? He was the son of the Titan, Japetos, and the nymph, Climene or Asia, depending on which version you choose. His kingdom stretched across the west, beyond the Pillars of Hercules, at the ends of the Earth, as Hesiod says in his *Theogony*. It is told by the legends that the daughters of the night, the Hesperides or Atlantides, lived on the slopes of the Atlas Mountains and had the mission to guard the golden apples beyond the ocean, which gave immortality. However, the term "Atlas" should not be confused with the mountains that currently carry that name in North Africa. Rather, Atlas was, according to tradition, the mountain of the Universe that was located in the west, at the ends of the Earth.

It is important to point out that, when writing about the Underworld, the Greeks described the location of these legendary territories by interchangeably using the expressions "beneath the earth" and "beyond the western horizon" (the west). The explanation given by academic authorities for this is that in ancient times, the geographic west was identified in a symbolic way with death, and therefore with the underground world or the world of the dead, since the Sun died when it got to the west at dusk.

For this reason, always following the academic argument, it should be understood that it was perfectly normal, from a symbolic or archetypal point of view, that Hades or the underground world could be located in two different places at the same time, both in the underground world and in the west. This is one more example of what I call a "dance of words", a process by which researchers use a mere hypothesis that has not been confirmed as the cornerstone of all the following deductive approach: that people in early times identified the underground world with the geographic west because the Sun died in the west every day. So the words involved in various translations and writings (west, western, underground world) lose their original meaning and become synonyms that have no real or precise meaning, leading to ambiguous and incorrect interpretations.

The common denominator in all these mythological traditions is that these dream lands were located within the confines of the known world. But where were the ends of the world? In the west, that is in the Atlantic Ocean? In the Elysian Fields, the Blessed Islands, the Garden of the Hesperides or Atlantis in the west? Were they located in the underground world? Or, if we turn to the original meaning of each word, were they located in the underground world, so that in order to access them the

Pillars of Hercules had to be crossed in a direction that leads towards the geographic west?

For Hesiod, in his *Theogony*, there is no doubt that the ends of the Earth were found in the underground world, and Atlas was in it:

> *Down there, in Tartarus, the Titan gods are hidden away down in the misty gloom... at the end of the vast Earth... Next to that, the son of Iapeto (Atlas) stands holding the broad Heaven firmly upon his head and untiring hands...*

From the perspective of an ancient Greek, experienced in navigating the known seas of the Mediterranean and the Middle East, crossing the Strait of Gibraltar had a very special meaning. An unprejudiced analysis of several mythical traditions, seemingly unrelated among themselves, reveals that the Pillars of Hercules were the entrance gate for the voyage that had these wonderful lands as a final destination; but departure from the Pillars of Hercules merely marked the beginning of a long journey. A journey towards the west. A journey through uncharted waters. A journey in the direction of the underworld. A journey to the interior of the Earth... Were, then, the Pillars of Hercules the first entrance gate to the underground world? Hercules, in the famous "twelve labors", also had the aim of finding the ends of the Earth, as the poet Pindar describes in the fifth century BC

> *The uncomfortable task,*
> *navigate the unknown ocean,*
> *beyond the pillars of Heracles,*
> *which that hero and god set up,*
> *as famous witnesses to the furthest limits of seafaring.*
> *He subdued the monstrous beasts in the sea,*
> *and tracked to the very end the streams of the shallows,*
> *where he reached the goal that sent him back home again,*
> *and he made the land known.*
>
> Nemean Odes, Pindar

A careful analysis of *The Twelve Labors of Hercules* suggests that the pillars that carry Hercules' name were, without doubt, the first departure point to entering the underworld; with total security his last three labors were carried out in the underground world, and it is likely that the others also took place there. In *The Twelve Labors of Hercules*, there are several keys to interpretation, one of which is astrological. There is a correlation of each labor with the path of the Zodiac, the astrological signs. Hercules represents each of us and the labors represent the difficulties that we face in the journey of life in the material world, a journey in which man, through different labors, must develop his potential for finally reaching mastery of himself. However, I am going to abandon this astrological interpretation, to focus on the main subject that occupies this chapter.

In the eleventh labor, Eurystheus commanded Hercules to steal the golden apples of the Garden of the Hesperides, or Atlantides. One version of the labor tells us that Hercules, after overcoming several dangers, arrived at the garden, killed the dragon with three heads and took away the apples that confer immortality. When he gave them to Eurystheus, he rejected them, so as not to cause the wrath of the gods. Hercules then gave them to Athena, who returned them to their place of origin. In the twelfth and final labor, Hercules had to capture the dog Cerberus (Can Cerberus), a three-headed monster with a serpent's tail that was the guardian of the entrance to Hell in the Underworld. Hercules overcame Cerberus with his own hands, slung the beast over his back and carried him out of the Underworld through a cavern entrance in the Peloponnese.

I would like to make a small digression here to reiterate the importance of this type of research into the origin and evolution of the linguistic terms used in ancient tales. Here is an example of how the words, their meanings and connotations evolve with time, so that it becomes very difficult to interpret ancient texts when applying the meanings that the words have in the present. Nowadays, it is common in the Spanish-speaking world that the goalkeeper of a football team receives the name of Cancerberus. Would anyone try to find some nexus of union between a soccer goalkeeper and the Greek guardian of the underworld? Would anyone in their right mind interpret that Hercules, in his twelfth labor, had to fight with a soccer goalie?

Returning to the main subject and to summarize, the labors of the hero were carried out in the Underworld and the Pillars of Hercules were the entrance to an ocean that should somehow take the hero to the confines of the world... to the Netherworld. At this point, it is important to remember that in Greek Antiquity the concept of the ocean (Okeanos):

> *...although identified with the western sea (the Atlantic Ocean) – was that the totality of the water on the planet formed a huge river that encircled the world. This great river was the father of all the rivers and fountains, implying a network of underground aqueous channels abutting surface waters...*
>
> The State of Hellicon, Martin L. West

So we can see that the meaning of the Pillars of Hercules, the Atlantic Ocean and the Underworld seem to be interconnected in this story...

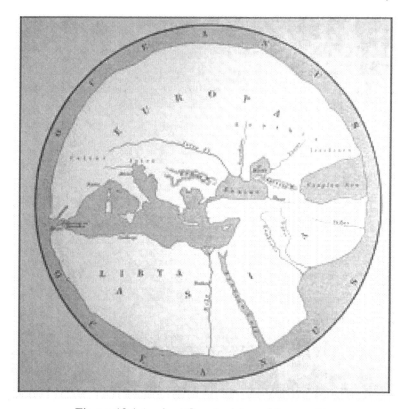

Figure 13.1 Ancient Greek vision of the world

Homer is universally accepted as the author of *The Odyssey*, an epic poem which is believed to have been written in the eighth century BC. It narrates the adventures of King Odysseus (*Ulysses* in Latin) on his journey back home to the island of Ithaca. It takes Odysseus ten years to return home, and during his absence his wife, Penelope, and their son, Telemachus, must endure a crowd of young men who enter the palace to compete for Penelope's hand in marriage, in order to obtain the throne of Odysseus, whom they believe is dead. After leaving Troy, during his adventures over unknown seas, Odysseus visits the islands of the Cicones, the Lotus-Eaters and the Cyclops, where he is captured by the giant Polyphemus, to finally arrive at the island of Eea, the home of the sorceress Circe. It is there that the poem tells the story of an amazingly significant fact; the hero was beside his men all day long on the island, savoring various delicacies, and when the Sun set and darkness ensued, all of them slept on the beach, but the next morning Odysseus gathered all his men urgently to say the following words:

We are utterly lost. We do not know where east or west is;
Where the light giving Sun rises or where it sets.

The Odyssey, Edge X

Let's shed some light on these mysterious words. A sailor, especially in antiquity, was guided by the position of the stars at night and the Sun during the day, which marked with its rising the east and with its setting the west. Odysseus, however, declared himself to be lost and his words indicate the movement of the Sun as the cause of his confusion. To understand the magnitude and scope of these declarations of Odysseus, they must be viewed in the proper context. Odysseus is on the island of Eea where the witch, Circe, will indicate, in brief, the path that he should follow to reach the underground world; the reason for this, it can be deduced, is that the island should not be very far from the entrance of the Underworld.

In the previous chapter, I made a suggestion about possible entrances to the interior of the Earth, located in the planet's poles. Imagine, therefore, that someone was located on an island at latitude 70N, for example, very near the hypothetical entrance to the interior of the Earth at the poles. How would this person observe the apparent movement of the Sun during the day? How would he see the sunrise and the sunset? In the countries of northern latitudes there is a phenomenon that has been called "the midnight sun", which has become an important tourist attraction, with thousands of people travelling to the Arctic latitudes to view it. Around the summer solstice (approximately June 21 in the north and December 22 in the south), the Sun is visible for a full 24 hours. This phenomenon, completely natural, occurs to the north of the Arctic Circle (also to the south of the Antarctic Circle) between the spring equinox (March 21) and the fall equinox (October 21), the summer solstice being the culminant point. During the summer solstice, the Sun, in its lowest position on the horizon, never hides, and so, at least when there is no cloud cover, it is visible at all hours of the day and night. The sun is only truly visible (or invisible as the case may be) for 24 hours on the actual Solstice, but during the surrounding time it still presents a very strange spectacle.

The geographical line that denotes the Arctic Circle is the line from where one day a year the Sun never goes down and, also, where one day a year the Sun never rises. From this line, the number of days per year with a potential midnight sun increases the further towards either pole one goes, depending on the latitude. From the line of the Arctic Circle to North Cape, considered to be the point of highest latitude in Europe, is a distance of approximately 530 kilometers.

An observer, for example, located in the north of Norway will see the Sun, at dusk, descend close to the horizon… only to rise again without setting. Dusk is immediately followed by dawn, without a night in between. This is very strange and disconcerting, even in modern times, for anyone who thinks that night and day are fixed phenomena. When we arrive at certain latitudes near the pole, whether we crossed the Arctic Circle or not, the apparent movements of the Sun are far away from what we consider to be its usual paths and movements at the mid-latitudes of the planet.

At this point it is important to remember that in the book *A Journey to the Interior of the Earth* – at the moment when Professor Lidenbrock arrives, around the summer solstice, before the *calendas* of July (the first day in July), in the place where the shade of Scartaris will signal the exact way to the interior of the Earth, the author, Jules Verne, also speaks about the midnight sun:

> *Finally, at eleven at night, very much in darkness, we reached the summit of Snaefells. Before going to shelter inside the crater, I caught sight of the midnight sun at the lowest point in its life's course, sending its pale rays over the island sleeping at my feet.*
> A Journey to the Interior of the Earth, Jules Verne

Is it mere coincidence that Verne was choosing as an entrance to the interior of the Earth a place and a time where the midnight sun phenomenon was occurring? Or is there a hidden message in it?

It seems indisputable that Odysseus was not used to seeing what was happening in the movements of the Sun; hence, his bewilderment and amazement. Odysseus, like Heracles, is located in the unknown ocean (Atlantic Ocean) and is on his way to the Underworld. Was Odysseus at that moment, described in Canto X of *The Odyssey*, located in latitudes near the Arctic Circle? The strange movements of the Sun seem to indicate this, and the subsequent entry of the hero into the Underworld would also suggest both his proximity to one of the poles and the theory that there are entrances to the interior of the Earth there. The witch, Circe, later on, said to Odysseus that he had to go down to the underworld:

> *Odysseus, man of many resources, scion of Zeus, son of Laertes, don't stay here a moment longer against your will, but before you head for home you must make another journey. You must seek the House of Hades and dread Persephone…*
> The Odyssey, Book X

And she also indicates to him the path to follow, with plenty of detail:

> *Don't think of finding a pilot to guide your vessel, but raise your mast and spread your white sail, and take your seat aboard, and the North Wind's breath will send her on her way. When you*

have crossed the Ocean stream, beach your ship by the deep swirling waters on a level shore, where tall poplars, and willows that shed seed, fill the Groves of Persephone. Then go to the moist House of Hades. There is a rock where two roaring rivers join the Acheron, Cocytus, which is a tributary of the Styx, and Pyriphegethon.

The Odyssey, Book X

Following the directions from Circe, the witch, Odysseus finally docks his vessel on the shore and goes, with his men, into the underground world. *The Odyssey's* Canto XI narrates:

All day long with straining sail she glided over the sea, till the sun set and all the waves grew dark.
So she came to the deep flowing Ocean that surrounds the earth, and the city and country of the Cimmerians, wrapped in cloud and mist. The bright sun never shines down on them with his rays.

An attentive reading of the instructions given to Odysseus reveals a very specific description of the path to follow to enter the Underworld, as if it were a new continent or land, and also that, just as with the Elysian Fields or the Garden of the Hesperides, it was located in a westerly direction, at the ends of the Earth… thus Atlantis.

Having arrived at this point, it is time to put the geographer, Abraham Ortelius, on stage, and to remember some very old legends that speak about a mythic and almost forgotten civilization that was located near the frozen regions of the North Pole. Abraham Ortelius was, with Mercator, one of the fathers of Flemish cartography and he was recognized as the creator of the first modern atlas. One of the ingenious ideas of the Flemish cartographer was that, as early as 1596, he speculated that the continents were originally joined together before drifting to their present positions. This theory was later developed by Alfred Wegener in the twentieth century. However, with regards to the issue we are dealing with, Ortelius, in one of his maps, illustrated on the top right corner a continent that occupied the whole polar region and called it

258

Hyper Boreas. It calls to attention the fact that Greenland, one of the biggest islands in the world, is situated between the Atlantic Ocean and the Arctic Ocean and 80% of its surface is covered by ice; whilst, at the same time, its name, quite clearly, means 'green land'.

Figure 13.2 Abraham Ortelius map

The Greeks speak about *Hyperboreans* as the inhabitants of a wonderful place. They lived in the homeland of Apollo (the god of the Sun), situated at the ends of the ocean, beyond the region of the North Wind, Boreas. *Hyperborea* was a region placed in unknown lands. Its name, in Greek, Υπερ βορεία (Hyper Boreas), means "beyond the North Wind". In this land, the Sun was supposed to rise and set only once a year, shining twenty-four hours a day; its inhabitants could live a thousand years, free of the decrepitude of aging and sickness. And it was almost impossible to get there because it was protected by huge walls of ice and powerful demigods. Hercules went to the country of the Hyperboreans to capture the Hind of Ceryneia in his third labor.

There are a lot of written references about it in antiquity. In the Greek tradition, Thule was the island on which was situated the capital of Hyperborea, and Ptolemy, in his *Geography*, and Marcian of Heraclea, in his *Periplus*, both placed Hyperborea in the North Sea, which they called the Hyperborean Ocean. The Greek poet Pindar, in his *Pythian Odes*, also spoke of it:

Neither by ship nor on foot could you find the marvelous road to the meeting-place of the Hyperboreans.

Pythian X, 29, 30

What did the poet mean by referring to a road so difficult to find? Also, what did Ortelius mean with his map, where he wrote Hyper Boreas? The Elysian Fields, the Blessed Islands, the Garden of the Hesperides or Atlantides and the Atlantis of Plato are all situated somewhere in the Atlantic Ocean to the west of the Pillars of Hercules. The mythic Hyperborea was also located beyond the Pillars of Hercules, in the Atlantic Ocean, and we also know that both Greek mythology and the cartographer Abraham Ortelius placed it in the North Pole region. It is also significant that ancient traditions speak about a place where the Sun rose and set only once in a year, shining for twenty-four hours, therefore suggesting a possible location within the Arctic Circle, especially if you remember all that has been said about the apparent movement of the Sun in these latitudes. Did Plato collect all these ancestral traditions and incorporate them into his writings with a unique and new name? Everything points towards this, and so this is probably what happened.

Atlantis belonged to a chain of islands, similar to the Blessed Islands of Pindar. Both the Elysian Fields and the Garden of the Hesperides were in the underworld, the place where Odysseus docks his boat after having entered into an area where the Sun moves in a strange manner, as it does in the polar regions of the planet. Was Atlantis located in the Underworld? Was Atlantis the lost continent located in the interior of the Earth? Was Hyperborea the continent of Atlantis? Were the islands of Thule and Atlantis the same thing?

Atlantis could be reached via a long journey that began by crossing the Pillars of Hercules, in the Strait of Gibraltar, and then sailing west across the Atlantic Ocean towards the Arctic Polar Circle – an area where, through a route only known by a few initiates, it was possible to enter into the interior of the Earth. Plato collected the old traditions and put them together in Atlantis, a word whose meaning is the daughter of Atlas, from which it takes its name (in the same way as the Hesperides or Atlantides were the daughters of Atlas).

There are three aspects in Plato's story that raise several questions: the *orichalcum*, the size of Atlantis and the reference to a sea of mud. I will discuss each of them in the following paragraphs. One of the big questions for those searching for Atlantis is the mysterious *orichalcum*. This legendary metal is mentioned by Plato in *Critias*. According to some specialists, *orichalcum* may have been a type of bronze or brass, or possibly some other metal alloy. However, in *Critias*, Plato eliminates the possibility of it being a metal alloy, because the metal was available in great abundance and mined in many parts of Atlantis. In antiquity, this metal would have been second in value only to gold, but by Critias' own time *orichalcum* was known only by name:

...and also that kind which is now known only by name but was more than a name then, there being mines of it in many places of the island, I mean orichalcum which was the most precious of the metals then known, except gold.

Critias

Orichalcum was the reason why the city of Atlantis was especially bright, because of the red glare of the metal. This characteristic brightness of the metal may provide support for its identification

And the wall surrounding the acropolis itself they invested with oreichalkos, which glittered like darting fire.

Critias

The name derives from the Greek ὀρείχαλκος, *oreikhalkos* (from ὄρος, *oros,* mountain and χαλκός, *chalkos,* copper or bronze). Its literal meaning is "mountain copper", although it is also sometimes translated as "mountain bronze". Nevertheless, it was not ordinary copper or bronze. It is worth noting that in this word the terms "bronze" and "copper" can be mixed, maybe because both have been interconnected throughout the history of humanity. Copper is a metal, a chemical element with the symbol Cu (from Latin *cuprum*) and an atomic number of 29. Bronze, however, is an alloy that is fundamentally made of copper, commonly with tin, often with the addition of other metals (such as aluminum, manganese, nickel or zinc) and sometimes non-metals or metalloids. Bronze can also be found as a naturally occurring alloy.

Copper is a metallic element that came from the depths of the Earth, millions of years ago, through the geological processes that created the planet. When it got near the surface at the Earth's crust, it was then that man was able to mine it. It is frequently found alongside other metals, such as gold, silver, bismuth and plumb. Copper is found all around the world in basalt lava. So, as you can see, we are again talking about something that is very closely related with the interior of the Earth, lava. If Atlantis is located, as I have suggested, in the Earth's interior, it is easy to understand that copper, bronze or any other kind of unknown metal would be abundant and easy to find and mine

Another bizarre aspect of Plato's story about Atlantis is the reference to a sea of mud:

> *...But now because of earthquakes it has subsided into the great Ocean and has produced a vast sea of mud that blocks the passage of mariners who would sail into the great Ocean from Greek waters, and for this reason it is no longer navigable.*
>
> Critias

In the Greek myths, mud was associated with the Underworld, so it makes sense that a sea of mud would mean a specific area situated in the Underworld. If we have a look at the sixth labor of Hercules, we can find some possible candidates for this sea of mud.

After Hercules returned from his success in the Augean stables, Eurystheus came up with an even more difficult task. For the sixth labor, Hercules was to drive away an enormous flock of supernatural birds that had gathered at a swamp near the town of Stymphalos. Initially, Hercules assumed that the labor would be easy; however, when he arrived at the marsh he realized that the swampy ground would not take his weight, nor was it liquid enough to use a boat. This is a good definition of a sea of mud.

The names of the place and of the birds are derived from the word *stymphallos*, meaning "phallic member". In this respect, it is very interesting to remember a moment from Verne's *A Journey to the Center of the Earth*, when the protagonists are traveling inside the Earth and find a forest of gigantic mushrooms. Have you ever noticed the similarity between a mushroom and a phallic member?

My uncle named them immediately: "It is just a forest of mushrooms." He was right. It may be imagined how big these plants grew in their preferred hot, humid environment. I knew that the Lycoperdon giganteum reached, according to Bulliard, eight or nine feet in circumference; but here we had white mushrooms thirty or forty feet high, with caps of the same width. There were thousands of them. No light could pierce their dense cover, and complete darkness reigned beneath those domes, crowded together like the round roofs of an African city.

A Journey to the Interior of the Earth, Jules Verne

Figure 13.3 Cover Illustration from A Journey to the Center of the Earth

And finall , I return to something I have already spoken about: the size of Atlantis. Plato, when speaking about it, says that it was extremely large:

> *This island was larger than Libya and Asia combined, and it provided passage to the other islands...*
>
> Timaeus

> *This island, as we are saying, was at one time greater than both Libya and Asia combined.*
>
> Critias

It has to be admitted that it is incredible that hundreds of Atlantis hunters, who have searched in many different places around the world, especially in the Atlantic Ocean, have not ever found a single trace of it, despite advances in oceanography and ocean floor mapping in the past decades. Although many mysteries remain at the depths of the world's oceans, it is difficult to accept that oceanographers, submarines and deep-sea probes have somehow missed a landmass that is larger than Libya and Asia combined. Something of that size does not get lost easily! Maybe, for that reason, they prefer not to talk about it. On top of that, modern plate tectonics confirms that over time continents have drifted and the seafloor has spread, not contracted. Therefore, it does not seem possible that a continent with such dimensions can exist at the bottom of the ocean; there is simply no space for Atlantis to have sunk into. As Ken Feder, a well-known skeptic and professor of archaeology at Central Connecticut State University in New Britain, said:

> *The geology is clear; there could have been no large land surface that then sank in the area where Plato places Atlantis.*

Until now no theory of Atlantis has been able to explain its enormous dimensions. Is it possible that Atlantis could have been as big as Plato described and still not found? The answer is clear; there is only one explanation for Atlantis' remarkable size that may also explain the total absence of findings. Atlantis was in the underground world. Only by being located in the interior of the Earth could the enormous size of the island be managed, because the only constraint on its size would be the dimensions of the underworld, the dimensions of the Earth's interior. At the same time, an Atlantis that is located in the underground world could be a continent that is geographically placed under the waters of the Atlantic Ocean. Then, the words of Plato would make sense; Atlantis would be both a sunken (located under the Atlantic Ocean, but at the other side) and a lost continent.

Let's go deeper in Plato's words. The philosopher speaks of a huge continent of such dimensions that it could only be lost without leaving a trace if it had originally been located in the interior of the Earth. However, at the same time, he makes a statement about Atlantis having a total diameter of 127 *stades* (15 miles), containing a central island of 5 *stades*, a city of land and sea rings of 27 *stades* and a grand canal of 50 *stades* that connected to the ocean:

> *...The greatest of the circles into which a boring was made for the sea was three stades in breadth, and the circle of land next to it was of equal breadth; and of the second pair of circles that of water was two stades in breadth and that of dry land equal again to the preceding one of water; and the circle which ran round the central island itself was of a stade's breadth...*
>
> Critias

How can all this be understood? Is Plato's description of Atlantis' measurements incoherent? No, not at all if we understand that Plato, when talking about Atlantis, according to a much older tradition, was really talking about the interior of the Earth, saying that it was enormous and at the same time relating it in scale to the structure of the interior of the Earth. If we put together all the facts about the findings in the interior of the Earth that I have been relating in both this chapter and the last, it will be easier to understand and unveil what Plato was talking about in his writings, which were the reminiscence of an anterior knowledge.

Atlantis was not a city or a continent, but it represented the complete interior of the Earth. Plato adapted the idea of an underground continent, located in the west and surrounded by the subterranean true Oceanus, to the mythical idea of the underworld. The subterranean continent was within a sphere: that of the Earth's crust itself.

In *Critias*, how Poseidon created the city is explained:

> *...Poseidon conceived a desire for her and slept with her. To make the hill on which she lived a strong enclosure, he broke it to form a circle and he created alternating rings of sea and land around it...he made two rings of land and three of sea as round as if he had laid them out with compass and lathe...*

Critias

Figure 13.4 Recreation of Atlantis.

The result, including the central zone and the continental lands of the planet's surface, are seven rings of land and water. Many rivers of ink have been spilled on the subject of the concentric rings of land and water surrounding Atlantis. The idea that Atlantis was included in an area with a bridge or channel that allowed passage from the first ring of sea makes sense only if we understand that what Plato describes is the planet Earth, which is spherical, and its measurements are thus measures of the interior of the Earth, to scale.

Let's look to the more distant past. One of the elements of Greek literature with amazing resemblances to ancient near Eastern traditions is the representation of the Netherworld. In Mesopotamian mythology, there are a lot of texts that deal with the Netherworld, like *Nergal and Ereskigal*, which have no Sumerian version. It is only known from a Middle Babylonian tablet found in Amarna, in Egypt, or the Neo-Assyrian *Erra Epic*. A comparable aim may be discerned in a badly preserved text from Assur, known as *The Underworld Vision of an Assyrian Prince*. Or the famous story which has been incorporated as Tablet *12* into the Nineveh-recension of *The Epic of Gilgamesh*. It is evident that this text was not an original part of this epic, but belonged to the Sumerian composition *Gilgamesh, Enkidu and the Netherworld*, of which it formed the second part.

A prominent place holds *Inanna's Descent to the Netherworld*, a Sumerian composition, which is a part of the Inanna-Dumuzi cycle. The story describes the unsuccessful attempt of Inanna/Ishtar to add the Netherworld to her zone of influence, to become the queen of all of the regions of the universe. On the way to the palace of the goddess of the Netherworld, Ereskigal (whose name means "mistress of the great Earth"), Ishtar has to cross seven gates and divest herself of all her divine symbols:

> *Neti, the chief doorman of the underworld,*
> *paid attention to the instructions of his mistress.*
> *He bolted the seven gates of the underworld.*
> *Then he opened each of the*
> *doors of the palace Ganzer separately.*
> *He said to holy Inanna: "Come on, Inanna, and enter".*
>
> Inanna's Descent to the Netherworld

If we review the information on the Netherworld which comes from these texts, we get the following picture: This region, called *ki* (Earth) or *kur* (foreign land) in Sumerian and *erset la tari* (The Land without Return) in Akkadian, is situated in the depths of the Earth and is antithetical to Heaven, but there is a ladder that connects Heaven and the Netherworld, on which messengers can go up and down. Access to the Netherworld is through seven gates, with a gate-keeper who takes care that nobody enters with the signs of his or her earthly power. Sometimes, but not in the epics, a river is named, Hubur, which surrounds the Netherworld and has to be crossed by ship.

The similarities of Greek mythology to the Ancient Oriental mythology are obvious. Sappho, Alcaeus and Aeschylos speak of the Acheron River, which has to be crossed in order to reach the land of the dead. In relation to the way to find Hades, the underground world, it is amazing the concrete description that can be found in another well-known Plato dialogue: *Phaedo*. Below is part of the text in which can be seen many of the aspects I have dealt with in the preceding chapters about the interior of the Earth.

Such is the nature of the whole Earth, and of the things which are around the earth; and there are divers regions in the hollows on the face of the globe everywhere, some of them deeper and more extended than that which we inhabit, others deeper but with a narrower opening than ours, and some are shallower and also wider. All have numerous perforations, and there are passages broad and narrow in the interior of the earth, connecting them with one another; and there flows out of and into them, as into basins, a vast tide of water, and huge subterranean streams of perennial rivers, and springs hot and cold, and a great fire, and great rivers of fire, and streams of liquid mud, thin or thick (like the rivers of mud in Sicily, and the lava streams which follow them), and the regions about which they happen to flow are filled up with them. And there is a swinging or see-saw in the interior of the earth which moves all this up and down, and is due to the following cause: There is a chasm which is the vastest of them all, and pierces right through the whole earth; this is that chasm which Homer describes in the words, 'Far off, where is the inmost depth beneath the earth;' and which he in other places, and many other poets, have called Tartaros. And the see-saw is caused by the streams flowing into and out of this chasm, and they each have the nature of the soil through which they flow. And the reason why the streams are always flowing in and out, is that the watery element has no bed or bottom, but is swinging and surging up and down, and the surrounding wind and air do the same; they follow the water up and down, hither and thither, over the earth—just as in the act of respiration the air is always in process of inhalation and exhalation;—and the wind swinging with the water in and out produces fearful and irresistible blasts: when the waters retire with a rush into the lower parts of the earth, as they are called, they flow through the earth in those regions, and fill them up like water raised by a pump, and then when they leave those regions and rush back hither, they again fill the hollows here, and when these are filled, flow through subterranean channels and find their way to their several places, forming seas, and lakes, and rivers, and springs. Thence they again enter the earth, some of them making a long circuit into many lands, others going to a few places and not so distant; and again fall into Tartaros, some at a point a good deal lower than that at which they rose, and others not much lower, but all in some degree lower than the point from which they came. And some burst forth again on the opposite side, and some on the same side, and some wind round the earth with one or many folds like the coils of a serpent, and descend as far as they can, but always return and fall into the chasm. The rivers flowing in either direction can descend only to the center and no further, for opposite to the rivers is a precipice.

Now these rivers are many, and mighty, and diverse, and there are four principal ones, of which the greatest and outermost is that called Okeanos, which flows round the earth in a circle; and in the opposite direction flows Akheron, which passes under the earth through desert places into the Akherousian lake: this is the lake to the shores of which the souls of the many go when they are dead, and after waiting an appointed time, which is to some a longer and to some a shorter time, they are sent back to be born again as animals. The third river passes out between the two, and near the place of outlet pours into a vast region of fire, and forms a lake larger than the Mediterranean sea, boiling with water and mud; and proceeding muddy and turbid, and winding about the earth, comes, among other places, to the extremities of the Akherousian Lake, but mingles not with the waters of the lake, and after making many coils about the earth plunges into Tartaros at a deeper level. This is that Pyriphlegethon, as the stream is called, which throws up jets of fire in different parts of the earth. The fourth river goes out on the opposite side, and falls first of all into a wild and savage region, which is all of a dark-blue color, like lapis lazuli; and this is that river which is called the Stygian river, and falls into and forms the Lake Styx, and after falling into the lake and receiving strange powers in the waters, passes under the earth, winding round in the opposite direction, and comes near the Akherousian lake from the opposite side to Pyriphlegethon. And the water of this river too mingles with no other, but flows round in a circle and falls into Tartaros over against Pyriphlegethon; and the name of the river, as the poets say, is Kokytos. Such is the nature of these things.

Phaedo, Plato

The Sumerologist, Thorkild Jacobsen, stated in his work *The Treasures of Darkness: A History of Mesopotamian Religion*:

The Underworld was of old imagined as a city ringed securely around by seven walks, and so entered through successive gates.

So, from the first water ring that represents the *true Greek Oceanus*, through some sort of channel in the opening of the Earth's crust (the second ring of spherical Earth), it would go through in the direction of the continent located in the inner world, moving through a succession of lands and seas in the interior of the Earth. This would be a great channel tunnel linking the Earth's surface with the interior of the planet, and the channel was situated at the poles.

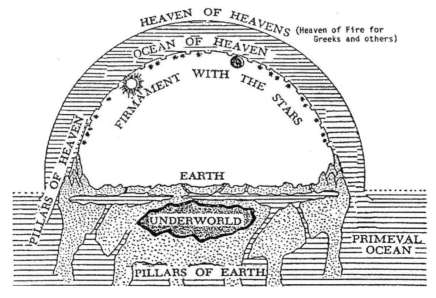

Figure 13.5 Ancient Greek vision of the world

I know that this idea that places the lost continent of Atlantis within the interior of the Earth will produce a few smiles, both for choosing a subject that is in itself controversial and fantasist, such as Atlantis, and also for placing it somewhere in the interior of the Earth. Nevertheless, there are enough arguments to move in that direction. Is it absolutely crazy? Did Jules Verne, a visionary writer, know something about this? What have Jules Verne and Plato got in common? This is something that you will have to judge for yourself, on the basis of the arguments used in this and previous chapters.

Jules Verne knew many more things about this subject, without any doubt. But the time has come for us to stop, for now. Dear reader, you can be sure that there is more to come about this, but for now we are finished. As the psychedelic vision that I narrated in the preface revealed to me, I have to warn you that, after this book is published, there will be opportunistic people who will develop this subject with ulterior motives…but without any foundations. Be alert to that.

CHAPTER XIV

IN SEARCH OF IMMORTALITY

There is nothing more powerful than an idea whose time has come.

Victor Hugo, French writer (1802-1885)

A t number 11, Magnolia Avenue in the city of St Augustine, Florida, is Ponce de Leon's Fountain of Youth Archaeological Park, built on the site of, and to commemorate, the founding of the oldest city in the USA. The park is in an area first explored by Juan Ponce de Leon in 1513, and colonized by Pedro Menendez de Aviles in 1565, the year in which he founded the city. The park is, without doubt, a wonderful place to spend a day with the family, enjoying many entertaining and educational activities related to the history of North America, archeology and evocative local legends; all in a colorful and unique setting.

On Easter Sunday, 1513, three ships, each flying the Spanish flag, skirted the coast of a land that was until then unknown. They had sailed a few weeks previously from the newly-colonized island of Puerto Rico, in search of a mysterious land known as Bimini, where the local legends had it they would find the fountain of eternal youth. In command of the expedition was Juan Ponce de Leon, a tough 53-year-old adventurer from Valladolid, who had just discovered the territory which in the following centuries was to generate a nation that would become the most powerful on Earth. Progress had been made, 117 years before the puritan pilgrims arrived in Massachusetts aboard the Mayflowe , in 1630.

Ponce de Leon believed that he had discovered an island, and since the event took place during Holy Week, he baptized it the Land of the Passover, naming it after the Spanish "Flowering Easter" or *Florida*. The biography of this Spanish conqueror is fraught with light and shadow, amidst which is found a mixture of courage and heroism, tyranny and cruelty. But perhaps the most significant of Ponce de Leon's traits was his obsession with specific myths and legends, an obsession that would drive him to become a tireless seeker of the so-called fountain of eternal youth.

Formally, history declares that Ponce de Leon's motivation to explore and adventure was his eagerness to find new wealth; thus official versions of his story deride as fallacy what was, in reality, his main objective, to find the so-called fountain of youth, which could restore youth to the old. The fact is that, according to numerous sources, he genuinely looked for the fountain, and everything points to the fact that he did so, although in vain.

The historian Robert H. Fuson, in his work *Juan Ponce de Leon and the Spanish Discovery of Puerto Rico and Florida*, explains that the adventurer was looking for Bimini, a place ambiguously described by the Arahuaco or Taino of the islands of Hispaniola, Cuba and Puerto Rico as a paradise located in the northwest, in the area of the Bahamas. They told him that Sequene, Arahuaco chief of Cuba, had set out, long ago, in search of a spring with healing powers, but the warlord never returned. The legends surrounding the healing waters of Bimini were frequently repeated in the Caribbean, to the point that even the Italian chronicler, Pietro Martire d'Anghiera, although he claimed not to believe in them, spoke of the legends in an epistle to the Pope in 1513.

The existence of a spring that heals and returns youth to whoever drinks or bathes in its waters is a symbol of the human race's eternal quest for immortality. Ever since man has existed, and known himself to be so, he has perceived that the essential difference between himself and the gods resides in his own mortality and loss of youth, in contrast with the deities' longevity or immortality.

The Epic of Gilgamesh, written several centuries before the Greek *Iliad* and the Hindu *Mahabharata*, constitutes the first known literary work, whose greatness, inspiration, strength and style have been acknowledged as possessing an epic quality. It recounts the adventures of a man, a Sumerian king, who did not want to die. The epic presents Gilgamesh as king of Uruk, a city-state whose ruins are located in the middle of the desert, in what is now Iraq, halfway between Baghdad and Basra.

An ancient manuscript, *The Sumerian King List*, describes Gilgamesh as the fifth ruler of the first dynasty that would have ruled in Uruk after the Deluge. His name is sometimes written with the prefix *dingir*, to denote his divine character, because even though his father was a simple high priest, Lugalbanda, his mother was the goddess Ninsun, which made Gilgamesh two-thirds divine. The monarch ruled for 126 years, in which time he strengthened the city of Uruk and even expanded its borders, through various military campaigns. But towards the end of his reign he began to worry about old age, and became obsessed with immortality.

The Epic of Gilgamesh narrates the adventures of Gilgamesh and his friend Enkidu, with whom he lives through various vicissitudes, until the latter's death. Tablet IX of the epic begins with the desperate and bitter cry of the hero for his friend Enkidu, who has died from a disease as decreed by the gods. Now Gilgamesh recognizes that in the face of death, heroism and courage are powerless and for the first time he asks himself the questions that plague him.

> *He wandered over barren hills, mumbling to his own spirit:*
> *Will you too die as Enkidu did?*
> *Will grief become your food?*
> *Will we both fear the lonely hills, so vacant?*
> *I fear death, and now roam the wilderness.*
>
> Epic of Gilgamesh

As he roams the steppe, terrorized by thoughts of his own mortality and that of the people he loves, Gilgamesh has an intuition and decides to go in search of Utnapishtim (the Sumerian Ziusudra and the Biblical Noah). According to the Babylonian tradition, Utnapishtim and his wife were the only humans spared from the Deluge, and the gods granted them immortality as a prize. The intention of Gilgamesh, in his visit, is to unveil the secret of that eternal life. However, the journey to Utnapishtim's dwelling-place is long, and Gilgamesh must travel a path fraught with dangers and populated by extraordinary mythical characters.

One such character is Siduri, the tavern-keeper of the Underworld. Siduri listens to Gilgamesh speaking of his desperate search for immortality, advises him and explains the destiny decreed by the gods for mankind:

She answered,
Gilgamesh, where are you hurrying to?
You will never find that life for which you are looking.
When the gods created man they allotted to him death,
but life they retained in their own keeping.
As for you, Gilgamesh, fill your belly with good things;
day and night, night and day,
dance and be merry, feast and rejoice.
Let your clothes be fresh, bathe yourself in water,
cherish the little child that holds your hand,
and make your wife happy in your embrace;
for this too is the lot of man.

Epic of Gilgamesh

The words of Siduri do not convince Gilgamesh, and he continues on his path until he finally reaches the home of Utnapishtim. This man also explains to him just what the status of mankind is, by virtue of the expressed will of the gods:

There they issue lengths of lives;
then they issue times of death.

But the last, last matter
is always veiled from human beings.
The length of lives can only be guessed.

Epic of Gilgamesh

In Tablet X, Gilgamesh expresses his desire to know how, that is to say through what events and procedures, Utnapishtim became immortal.

Then Gilgamesh said to Utnapishtim the Faraway,
"I look at you now, Utnapishtim,
and your appearance is no different from mine;
there is nothing strange in your features.
I thought I should find you like a hero prepared for battle,
but you lie here taking your ease on your back.
Tell me truly, how was it that you came to enter the company of
the gods and to possess everlasting life?"

Epic of Gilgamesh

Then, Utnapishtim tells the fantastic story of the Deluge, and how he was saved thanks to his construction of an ark. He explains that when the land emerged from the waters they were found by the gods, and were granted immortality, as a reward, by the own god Enlil in a solemn assembly.

Then Enlil went up into the boat,
he took me by the hand and my wife
and made us enter the boat and kneel down on either side,
he standing between us.
He touched our foreheads to bless us, saying
"In time past Utnapishtim was a mortal man;
henceforth he and his wife shall live in the distance at the mouth
of the rivers".

Epic of Gilgamesh

Utnapishtim adds that this gift was only once granted to humans, and it would never happen again.

As for you, Gilgamesh,
who will assemble the gods for your sake,
so that you may find that life for which you are searching?

Epic of Gilgamesh

Stating that the gods will never take a decision on the immortality of Gilgamesh, Utnapishtim puts Gilgamesh to the test and challenges him to go without sleep for seven nights. In doing this, Utnapishtim seeks to demonstrate the fragility of human nature and persuade Gilgamesh to abandon his quest for immortality. Gilgamesh does not pass the test and is ready to go home. However, Utnapishtim's wife feels compassion for the king of Uruk, and asks her husband to grant him a gift before he leaves their country. Utnapishtim addresses him:

Gilgamesh, you came here a man wearied out,
you have worn yourself out;
what shall I give you to carry you back to your own country?
Gilgamesh, I shall reveal a secret thing,
it is a mystery of the gods that I am telling you.
There is a plant that grows under the water,
it has a prickle like a thorn, like a rose;
it will wound your hands,
but if you succeed in taking it,
then your hands will hold that which restores his lost youth to a
man.

Epic of Gilgamesh

Then, the story goes on to tell how, somewhat unexpectedly, Gilgamesh "opened the sluices so that a sweet water current might carry him out to the deepest channel; he tied heavy stones to his feet and they dragged him down to the water-bed. There he saw the plant growing; although it pricked him he took it in his hands; then he cut the heavy stones from his feet, and the sea carried him and threw him on to the shore". Utnapishtim had not specified the location of the plant, and it seems obvious that we are faced with a short speech taken from another, more explicit source. Gilgamesh himself explains the use that can be made of this plant when he speaks to the ferryman:

Come here, and see this marvelous plant.
By its virtue a man may win back all his former strength.
I will take it to Uruk of the strong walls;
there I will give it to the old men to eat.
Its name shall be "The Old Men Are Young Again";
and at last I shall eat it myself and have back all my lost youth.

Epic of Gilgamesh

However, Utnapishtim's gift is only a substitute for immortality, a remedy for old age. Far from finding what he was looking for, immortality, Gilgamesh had merely secured a plant that allowed him to prolong the most vigorous period of human life, a plant of youth. References to this miraculous plant have a long tradition in eastern literature, for example in one of the most popular tales from the *Thousand and One Nights*.

Nowadays, stories frequently appear in the media that seem to herald, for the first time in the history of mankind, real progress in the bid to extend life beyond what has so far been seen as its normal limits. On May 4th 2014, the prestigious scientific journal *Science* published the results of research undertaken by Amy Wagers and her team at Harvard University, which once again seems to link modern scientific understanding with ancestral knowledge.

Wagers' work has been described under headlines such as "Young Blood Rejuvenates", a phrase that evokes the famous novel, *Dracula*, by Bram Stoker, or any of the vampire-themed literary sagas that are all the rage among today's youngsters.

Wagers is not the first person to suggest that the answers to the problem of ageing might lie in human blood. In 1615, Andreas Libavius, a German doctor and alchemist, proposed the use of blood transfusions to rejuvenate older people. He suggested connecting the arteries of an old man to those of a young man, and had high hopes for the procedure. *"The hot and spirituous blood of the young man will pour into the old one as if it were from a fountain of youth, and all of his weakness will be dispelled,"* Libavius claimed, in a chronicle described by Sally Rudmann in her *Textbook of Blood Banking and Transfusion Medicine*.

While this sounds like the dark plot of a vampire movie, it nonetheless resembles the conclusions drawn in several scientific research studies, including those by Wagers and her team.

Wagers believes that something present in the blood of younger mice (those aged 2 months) can rejuvenate the muscles and the brains of mice older than 22 months, which by mouse standards means they are in the latter stages of life. Conversely, Wagers and her team found, blood from the elderly mice damaged the health of the younger ones. This concept is not new; indeed it was observed more than a century and half ago, using techniques whereby two living organisms are joined together surgically and develop single, shared physiological systems, such as a shared circulatory system (parabiosis). However, what it is new in Wagers' work is the identification by researchers of a blood-borne protein that can enhance or optimize all those processes. The Harvard team called it Growth Differentiation Factor 11 (GDF 11).

Wagers and her colleagues found that GDF11 boosted the growth of new blood vessels and neurons in the brain of elderly mice, and prompted stem cells to regenerate skeletal muscle at injury sites. Furthermore, it improved the cerebral circulatory and the cardio-vascular system in general, as well as boosting muscular strength.

Obviously, it is not yet known whether GDF11 is the only factor that influences these processes of rejuvenation; it seems unlikely, but we are at least now seeing cutting-edge research, and are likely to see more arising from the many relevant studies that have been developed over the last few years. These will lead to the next technological revolution: extension of the life span of the human being to new extremes.

In the first human trial on the effects of young blood, Dr. Tony Wyss-Coray of Stanford University, California, took blood plasma from young people aged less than 30. He infused this plasma into older adults suffering with mild to moderate Alzheimer's disease. The research team was somewhat surprised to find that the process led to marked improvement in the recipients. The same research team has declared that the research with mice has shown that blood infusion from young mice seems to improve cognitive health in the older mice. It could even be said that the animals looked younger. The study was published in *Nature Medicine* in 2014, and Wyss-Coray received a flurry of e-mails in response. It seemed that many individuals, from those with Alzheimer's to wealthy older people, felt they too might benefit from infusions of youthful blood.

In time, there were even plans to monetize the findings through a commercial company. One Stanford neuroscientist and entrepreneur, Karoly Nikolich, traveled to Hong Kong to meet the family of Chen Din-hwa, a Chinese billionaire who had died with Alzheimer's disease three years previously. Towards the end of his life, Chen had been unable easily to recognize members of his own family. Then, he received a plasma infusion for an entirely different health condition – and his mental and communicative faculties improved dramatically. Nickolich shared details of Wyss-Coray's work with Chen's family, who invested in the company that was subsequently formed.

That company, Alkahest, describes its mission as being to develop anti-aging therapies and, in particular, to identify key proteins in plasma that are linked to the human aging process. Once these proteins are identified, Alkahest intends to manufacture a product that uses them, but that could take more than a decade.

However, Alkahest also has a shorter-term plan. Working in collaboration with Spanish blood products firm Grigols, Alkahest will undertake further research on the effects of various elements of human plasma on brain function. Initial trials will be conducted on mice. Those proteins that are found to boost mouse brain function will then be rolled out for human trials and when these are successful, developed into products; assuming, of course, that relevant research outcomes can be replicated elsewhere to an extent sufficient to convince scientists. Thus, for those currently working in this field, the focus is not as much on extending life to 150 or beyond, as it is about improving the quality of life as people age.

Human beings have made numerous attempts throughout history to find the source of, or obtain the elixir that will maintain, eternal youth. This is not the place to present a detailed study of each and every one of these attempts, which can be found in places as diverse as ancient legends, myths, witchcraft, magic, alchemy and vampiric rituals, among others. However, this is the time and the place to see what the science of the twenty-first century has to say about the matte .

So, can the process of aging be slowed down and the life of a human being thereby extended to limits we would now consider amazing? Or is this pure fantasy? During the second half of the twentieth century, advances have been made in biochemistry, genetics, medicine, computing and other areas of knowledge, which are at last allowing us to fit the pieces of the puzzle together and answer the question categorically. Yes, it is possible to extend the life of the human being beyond the span currently considered normal, and to reverse the effects of aging. We are not there yet, but there is real scientific evidence to show that we can and will be, in time.

The process underway is a little like that of building a mansion, where for a while the project is only alive in the mind of the designer, or as a pile of sketches and mess of papers. Later, a bank grants a mortgage and with the financial resources obtained, a builder is contracted. He brings in an excavator, makes a hole in the ground and directs a group of workers who raise the foundations. The walls are built and the roof is raised. At this point, is the mansion a fantasy or is it real? The house is not yet ready to live in, but it will be soon. It is not mere imagination, only time is needed to complete it. This is where we are at the moment, when we talk about aging and extending human life beyond the usual limits.

It all started with Dr. Leonard Hayflick, at the beginning of the 1960s, and his research carried out at the Winstar Institute in Philadelphia, Pennsylvania. Until then it was accepted in academic circles that individual cells could live forever, *in vitro*, in a laboratory if they were cared for properly. Hayflick, however, found that no matter what he did with the cells that he carefully grew in the lab, they always ended up dying. He noted that the cells reproduced – that is to say, divided, a number of times – but then they stopped dividing, no matter what he did to prevent this.

Hayflick found that lung tissue cells died after having divided around 50 times. In a second experiment he let these cells divide 25 times and then froze them for a while. When the cells were thawed, they continued to divide until they reached the same limit as their predecessors, and then died. As the cells were approaching this upper age limit, they showed greater signs of aging and deterioration. Hayflick postulated that the number of times a normal human cell population will divide until cell division stops is limited; since then, this has been known as the "Hayflick limit". Hayflick published his results, which at first drew enormous criticism and mockery from many of his contemporaries. Ultimately, however, fame and recognition emerged and the work became a classic, proving that our cells age and die.

As early as the 1990s, scientists began to investigate the "clock" that determines the length of time over which cells age and die. And their exciting discovery was that cells do not have to grow old. Cells have "clocks" in their chromosomes that determine the extent of their lives, in such a way that a cell dies when its time is up according to its own internal clock. In contrast, cancer cells continuously reset their clocks, which allows them to live eternally. Thus, we can infer that if we reset the clock of any healthy tissue cell, it will have a renewed life span ahead, and conversely if we were to stop the clock of a cancer cell, it would die.

To put it another way, when science allow us to manipulate the internal clocks that control the life span of cells, in the same way that you change the time on the clock on your bedside table, then normal cells won´t age and cancer can be cured. And although it is obvious that a human being is something more than the sum of all its cells, this will allow the physical body, formed by tissues, not to age, or at least to do so but at a very different pace to that seen currently.

Such biological technology is currently developing, but it is only a matter of time before such goals are reached, as the fundamentals are already clear. Therefore, I am not talking about fantasies, but rather something that is going to revolutionize the way we live on this planet, in the coming decades. This technological advancement will, in common with everything that exists in this phenomenological world, have both good and bad aspects, depending on how it is used, but there is no doubt that it will happen, sooner or later.

Why is this scientific event taking place now, at this particular time in the history of mankind? As I have repeated throughout this work, the key to the advancement of science is in the investigators' abilities to transcend dogmatic beliefs that have been anchored in societies over generations. For example, a belief in the impossibility of flying impeded the creation of airplanes, and the belief that certain diseases were incurable impeded or even prevented searches for their cure. It has been accepted for centuries that the maximum span of human life is dependent solely on a higher law, which mankind cannot change and with which humanity should not interfere, since it is a divine prerogative. But in the last few decades, open-minded scientists, who have never believed these dogmas of faith, have been leading what will ultimately become the greatest revolution in human existence since its origins.

Please do not think that I am talking about immortality… at least for the moment. It is one thing to extend the present limits placed upon life span, and delay or prevent the signs of aging, and quite another to talk of avoiding physical death. Humankind will, in the coming decades, establish greater control over its own life and biology, but will continue to be mortal. No matter what genetic changes are made, no matter how healthy or young we can be, despite all this we will continue to die. But even though we are mortal, we will be able to escape aging as it is understood today.

All of our cells get older, with the exception of our germ cells, that is to say the sperm and egg. Interestingly, these cells never grow old, although they are not immortal. They have not done so since Life began, and have carried the genetic information from generation to generation, until the present day. This is the tiny part of you that has never aged. So why do the germ cells not age, while the rest of the cells that make up the human body, carrying the same genes, supporting the same dangers and with the same cellular metabolism, do?

In the answer to this question is the key, both to slowing down the aging process and to eliminating the constant threat of cancer. The solution is inside our cells, where there are clock-like mechanisms that mark their life span. The good news is that they can be reset. But let us not get ahead of ourselves here.

Orthodox science is based on the belief that matter is the essential foundation of everything. Life, mind and consciousness are secondary phenomena emanating from matter, although we do, unfortunately, lack models to clearly explain the appearance of life, mind and consciousness. However, all these paradoxes can be clarified if we exchange the fundamental premise on which science is currently based for another, in which mind and consciousness, and not matter, are the essential source of all things.

I should pause at this stage to point out that there is an ancient body of wisdom that has been transmitted by word of mouth, from master to disciple, from generation to generation, until the present day. This knowledge, which rests in hands of just a few people, has recently been popularized to a certain extent, and it provides answers to many of the toughest questions that are now posed by science.

The first of the so-called seven hermetic principles, which are collected in a work entitled *The Kybalion*, is "*The All is mind; the Universe is mental.*" In other words, this principle explains that the entire Universe is a mental creation of the All, in whose mind we live and act. Furthermore, it can be said that the human being, just like everything that make up the Universe, is basically, in its foundations, information that through a quantum leap has been energized, condensed and finally crystallized into forms and actions in the material and phenomenological world in which we live.

This idea explains how, from the union of two simple germ cells, may be developed a human being consisting of millions of cells and possessing complex features: because the information or data (mind) that carried the germ cells is subsequently energized and made material. This, and not the contrary, is the process, despite what may be said elsewhere.

The physical body of a person is made of cells. Together, these cells constitute a universe that is now extremely overpopulated. Nobody has ever determined the precise number of cells in an organism, but it will be somewhere in the trillions, perhaps as many as 100 trillion. Each cell is different, although some, depending on their functions, are almost identical, and are grouped into tissues: muscle, brain, lung, bone, etc.

Modern science knows that all the cells of an organism have within them a library of information, with "instructions for use". As in any library, there are equivalents to books, phrases, words and letters. The information written in these books tells the cell how to organize itself, carry out maintenance work, reproduce, differentiate itself from others, and so forth. In biomedical terms, these books are referred to as chromosomes, long molecular chains in which are written phrases; these are called genes. Thus, chromosomes are made up of genes.

The sum of all the chromosomes (books) makes up the human genome (which in this example, might be compared to a library). In this way, each cell contains a complete collection of all the genes. In the case of the human being this library consists of 46 books of which half, 23, were donated by the father and the other half, 23, by the mother. The instructions written in these books (chromosomes), the phrases (genes) on each page, will describe our skills and define, to a large extent, our existence. Each sentence has precise and detailed information, directing not only the way in which our body will be transformed from fetus to adult, but also providing the resources needed to rebuild it second by second in response to the challenges of daily life.

Chromosomes are organized structures, located in the nucleus of the cell, composed of DNA, RNA and proteins that contain most of the individual's genetic information. Science divides the chromosome into different parts: chromatid, centromere, short arm, long arm, secondary constriction, satellite, and telomere, of which the latter plays a vital role in the aging process.

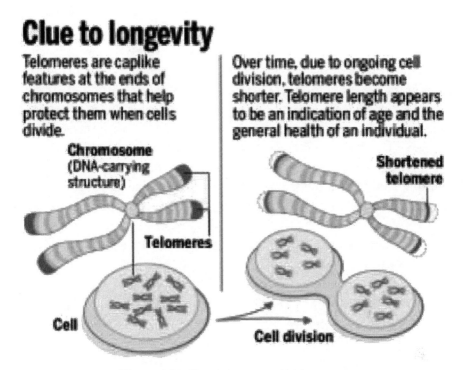

Figure 14.1 Chromosome and Telomeres

The telomeres (the word comes from the Greek *telos,* "end" and *meros,* "part") are protective caps, found at the end of each chromosome. The telomere's shape is similar to that of the plastic that covers the ends of shoe laces. Telomeres were discovered by Hermann Joseph Muller in the 1930s, and since then science has discovered a great deal more about them, thanks to the techniques of molecular genetics.

James Watson observed, in 1972, that every time a chromosome is replicated, it shortens, and he dubbed this the "end replication problem". In cellular terms, this means that each time cells divide and the chromosome is duplicated, it loses part of the telomere. However, even before Watson noticed the fact, Alexei Olovnikov, a Russian biologist, had already begun to question whether this shortening in the length of the telomeres acted as a clock for cellular aging. His idea was brilliant and completely correct. Some years later, Harley, Greider and Futcher published in *Nature* the results of their research, which was along the same lines as Olovnikov's. Initially, the publication was delayed because one of the journal's editors rejected the article, due to the fact he did not understand how the data could be so unquestionable. This echoes a phenomenon that I have identified throughout this work, namely that the vast majority of scientists sometimes find it difficult to accept simple ideas based on indisputable data, when these are contrary to the dominant paradigm or to those scientists' own beliefs. Finally, the paper by Harley and colleagues was published, probably due to the support of James Watson. This was the beginning of a series of exciting research studies that have led to a fairly good understanding of the role that the telomere (and telomerase) plays in the process of cellular aging.

In 1984, Greider and Blackburn identified the substance that helped telomeres to resist shortening. The telomere is composed of an enzyme called telomerase. Unlike other enzymes, telomerase is not a simple protein. Telomerase is a "ribonucleoprotein complex" made up of a protein component and an RNA primer sequence, a kind of molecular fossil species with few parallels in biology, which acts to protect the terminal ends of chromosomes. Some time after Grieder and Blackburn's study was published, some scientists began to claim, *"We can stop the cell clock by using an enzyme called telomerase. Its presence prevents telomere shortening after each cell division."*

In humans, as in all vertebrates, the telomere is a repetitive sequence of thousands of bases of DNA, in the following order: thiamine, thiamine, adenine, guanine, guanine, guanine (TTAGGG). With each cell replication process, the end of the DNA is not copied, which is why the length of telomeres reduces with the passage of time. This means that the telomere's length depends on age. Cells get older because telomeres shorten, and the degree of shortening seen in telomeres is related to the number of cell divisions. The greater the number of cell generations occurring, the shorter will be the telomeres, and the shorter the telomeres, the more signs of aging will be seen in the behavior of the cells.

How accurate is the telomere as a predictor of cellular aging? Currently, it is the best method we have. It is even more accurate than the actual biological age, although there is usually a pretty good correlation between the age of a person and the biological behavior of their cells. However, this is not always the case. It is easy to find people who seem to look younger or older than their years, to the extent that it would be fair to say that a person exhibits the age of his or her telomeres' length.

Dr. Michael Fossell, in his 1996 book, *Reversing Human Aging,* gives a detailed explanation of telomeres and the process of cellular aging, and of possible medium-term solutions to the ravages of old age and its ailments. Over the next three decades these emerging anti-aging technologies will mature, and it is more than likely that they will lead science to identify new weapons and solutions for use in the fight against cancer. In this process of developing what undoubtedly is going to become the world of antiaging therapies, different avenues of research will be opened by various scientists, of which I will outline just a few. In time these different therapies will converge and snap into place one to another in a harmonious way, just as the pieces of a puzzle integrate to finally create a sharp and precise image. It is only a matter of time

Geron Corporation, located in Menlo Park, California, USA, is a bio-technology company. Geron was founded in 1990 by the gerontologist Michael West and has for some time been traded on NASDAQ. Geron's primary focus is on the study of telomerase and stem cells. It is known that some cells, such as germ cells and carcinogenic cells, do not shorten their telomeres, and it is also known that telomerase plays a key role in this. Geron seeks to implement applications that regulate telomerase, and to find treatments for cancer and aging

Geron has already manufactured some products to activate telomerase and protect telomeres. Although this is only a first step, the result of millions in investments, the company has developed a fairly expensive product that claims to activate the hTERT gene that in turn, activates telomerase. This product is TA-65, a pure molecule extracted from the root of astragalus and able to activate telomerase.

Astragalus has been used in traditional Chinese medicine for centuries, being credited with anti-aging properties and the ability to extend life. It has often been given in combination with other herbs to strengthen the body against disease. Astragalus is an adaptogen, that is, a non-specific remedy that helps protect the body against various stresses, including physical, mental, or emotional stress. The *astragalus membranaceus* or root of astragalus, was employed primarily to replenish the body's *chi* (vital energy) and to increase the *yang* energy, while simultaneously eliminating toxins. It is a powerful adaptogenic herb with amazing qualities to strengthen the immune system. The product TA-65, like ascorbic acid, is considered a *nutraceutical*. Nutraceutical is a word that joins the meanings of nutrient and pharmaceutical, that is to say it refers to a food with medicinal properties and not a drug.

According to Geron, TA-65 is not the same extract of astragalus that can be bought from herbalists and health stores. The difference lies in the purity and concentration of the extract, achieved as a result of a method established by Geron, which explains its elevated price. However, I believe you can achieve the same results in a more cost-effective manner, if you follow, at home, the traditional Chinese herbal recipes. Thus, we note for the umpteenth time, that modern science returns to rediscover and glorify ancient knowledge.

On a different note, a team of researchers from Harvard Medical School in the USA seems to have identified one of the causes of the aging process in mammals; and they have found that its effects may be reversed. At the cellular level, a number of molecular processes facilitate optimal communication between the core and the mitochondria, the latter being the energy factories for cellular activity. When this communication ceases to be fluid, the aging process accelerates. According to Professor David Sinclair at Harvard, studies have revealed that the aging process resembles a marriage. When the relationship is young, the couple communicates well, but with the passage of time that communication breaks down. In both cases, better communication can resolve problems.

In experiments with mice, researchers found that restoring the communication between nucleus and mitochondria had a rejuvenating effect on the body. To investigate this, they increased in the animals the level of a naturally-occurring molecule called NAD (nicotinamide adenine dinucleotide). Usually, NAD levels in the body decline with age. The results of this experiment were that some of the signs of aging were reversed in the rodents given extra NAD. When the mice were examined for indicators related to aging (insulin resistance, inflammation, and loss of muscle mass) it was found that the muscle tissue of two-year-old animals who had received the compound, was similar to that of six-month-old mice in their natural state. In human terms, this is the equivalent to a twenty-year-old age.

Sinclair's team research has been for some years focused on the aging process, and in 2008 they published a paper in the journal *Cell*. In that paper the team claimed to have found a universal mechanism of aging in which a protein called sirtuin played a key role in gene expression. Sirtuins are NAD-dependent, i.e. they respond to NAD activity, so there is overlap between this and the study described immediately above. Mouse experiments showed that by restoring levels of sirtuins with resveratrol, an activator of the protein, DNA repair was more efficient and rodents retained the genetic expression of youth. It was also found that the resveratrol increased their life expectancy by between 25% and 45%.

Why is the NAD molecule so important? Without it, sirtuin (SIRT1), being dependent on NAD, loses its ability to control another molecule, HIF, which in turn interferes negatively with the communication between the nucleus and mitochondria. This has been observed in many types of cancer; therefore, the greatest value of the NAD molecule could lie in its ability to decrease levels of HIF. Later on, we will look in more detail at the role of sirtuins throughout this process.

From analysis of previous investigations, we can draw a clear conclusion: that there is a very close relationship between metabolic activity and the extension of life. We also know of a place where people live the longest… Okinawa is part of Japan, and comprises the largest island of the Ryukyu

Archipelago, in the Pacific Ocean. Okinawa is known to be home to one of the most long-lived populations in the world, and probably the greatest concentration of centenarians. In particular, the area has a lower than usual rate of mortality from cancer and cardiovascular disease.

What is the reason for all this? Have the people of Okinawa managed to delay the aging process? Have their diet and way of life something to do with it? The fact is that residents of Okinawa do consume many fewer calories than most Japanese people (in fact, around 30% less) and their diet is distinctive.

In 1935, American researchers McCay, Crowell and Maynard published a study they conducted on a population of rats, to explore the relationship between growth retardation and the maximum duration of life. To do this, they restricted the total number of calories in the animals' diet, although they maintained a proper balance of nutrients (proteins, fats, carbohydrates, minerals and vitamins). Various physiological features were analyzed, but no reference was made to the brain. Little did these scientists know, at this early stage, that the brain was going to experience major changes, and that this would influence activity in the rest of the body and the longevity of the animals.

The study results showed that the rats subjected to caloric restriction lived longer. Furthermore, the effect on the extension of the life was dependent on the degree of caloric restriction, being truly effective when it stood at around 30-40% of what the animal consumed daily when fed without restriction. The extension of the life span of the rats reached a maximum of 40%. Several researchers have since conducted similar studies, trying to clarify which are the molecular and cellular bases for such surprising results.

Nowadays we can say that caloric restriction is the only proven method, apparently universal, by which to delay organic aging, both in mammals and invertebrates, increasing the maximum life span of the species while improving health and vitality. This work shows that the pathologies associated with aging decrease in such a situation, and the older animals have a more vigorous aspect than would otherwise be the case, undertaking more activity than their abundantly-fed peers.

What happens in the bodies of these longer-lived rats? What slows down their aging processes? Investigations suggest that the calorie restriction generates a more efficient metabolism. It is thought that the food eaten is converted with greater efficiency into the chemicals that the cells of an organism consume, and therefore the digestion process generates fewer toxic free radicals. This is indicated by the experiments of Sohal and Weindruch, which show a decrease in the generation of free radicals of the mitochondria (the powerhouse of the cell).

Calorie restriction produces a broad spectrum of genetic changes in studied animals, both biochemical and physiological. Approximately 90% of these changes improve the process of aging. Such beneficial effects include the reduction of certain catabolic hormones and glucose levels, as well as an increase in insulin sensitivity.

However, can this effect of calorie restriction in rodents be extrapolated to human beings? It is well known that this type of experimentation with human beings entails enormous difficulties, being possible only if there is rigorous scientific monitoring of individuals that have freely chosen to live a Spartan life.

Meanwhile, animal studies continue. In 2014, the latest results were released from a 25-year study of diet and aging in monkeys. These showed a significant drop in mortality and age-related disease among those subjects subjected to caloric restriction. The study, which began in 1989, was started at the University of Wisconsin-Madison, and is one of two current, extended studies of its type to be undertaken in the USA. The study's aim is to clarify the effects of caloric restriction on (non-human) primates. I will focus on the Wisconsin-Madison study, in light of protocol issues with the other study, by the National Institute of Aging. The protocols used in the latter had basic deficiencies. For example, it included animals already caloric restricted in the control monkey group, so that study's results may not be useful here.

The Wisconsin-Madison study, published in *Nature Communications*, is of 76 rhesus monkeys. At ages between seven and 14 years, the monkeys were placed on a restricted calorie diet, whereby their caloric intake was reduced by 30%. The comparison group, of monkeys given an unrestricted diet, showed a disease risk 2.9 times greater than that of the restricted diet group, and a threefold increased risk of mortality.

"We think our study is important because it means the biology we have seen in lower organisms is germane to primates," said Richard Weindruch, a professor of medicine and one of the founders of the Wisconsin study. He added, *"We continue to believe that mechanisms that combat aging in caloric restriction will offer a lead into drugs or other treatments to slow the onset of disease and death."*

Caloric restriction, while continuing to supply essential nutrients, has been shown to extend the lifespan of flies, yeast and rodents by up to 40%. Many of the benefits of caloric restriction are linked to regulation of energy, affecting how fuel is utilized. Caloric restriction basically causes a reprogramming of the metabolism. *"In all species where it has been shown to delay aging and the diseases of aging, it affects the regulation of energy and the ability of cells and the organism to respond to changes in the environment as they age,"* says Anderson, one of the researchers. Scientists have sought for some time to understand the mechanisms involved and some are already exploring drugs that affect the relevant physiological mechanisms. These are of great interest to the private sector and likely to generate substantial revenue.

Another interesting finding from the study was that the scientists saw diabetes in some of the control animals (those allowed to eat as they wished) within six months of the study's start, whereas no diabetes was seen in the restricted animals until many years later. Diabetes is a common metabolic deficit, and signals an inability to respond properly to nutrition. It can cause many complications, and is a leading cause of death and disability in the USA. Thus, the Wisconsin study does seem to raise some hopes for humankind: particularly given that humans and the rhesus monkeys studied, are both primates.

According to Weindruch, the basic biology of caloric restriction in rodents, worms, flies and yeast seems to carry over to primates, so we have a real opportunity to dissect that mechanism, look at how we can work with that basic biology, and benefit all those human primates who are so closely related to our rhesus monkeys.

And yet, the question arises, could it be possible to obtain some of the benefits of a calorie restricted diet without having the discomfort of being hungry?

Metformin is not a new drug. The blood sugar-lowering chemical compound, galegine, that ultimately became metformin, was identified in the 1920s in the French lilac plant *(Galega officinalis)*. In 1958, England approved the use of metformin to treat type II diabetes, but it was not until 1995 that the FDA approved it to treat type II diabetes in the USA. In 2015, the FDA finally approved a clinical trial called *Targeting Aging with Metformin* (TAME), which aimed to test its performance as a geroprotectant. The lead researcher on the study is Nir Barzilai, MD, who is the director of the Institute for Aging Research at Albert Einstein College of Medicine in New York. As I write this, the results of the study are still unknown but there is a great deal of optimism. Dr. Robert Temple, Deputy Director at the FDA, has stated that the TAME study team is looking at metformin in the context of various age-related problems and that if the study's aims are realized its outcomes will be revolutionary:

> *Their hope is that a wide variety of age-related problems, loss of muscle tone, dizziness, falls, dementia, loss of eyesight, all of those things [sic]. That would be something never done before. If you really are doing something to alter aging, the population of interest is everybody. It surely would be revolutionary if they can bring it off.*

Metformin is an orally-administered diabetes medicine, used to improve blood sugar control in people with type 2 diabetes. But, dear reader, having arrived at this point, you already know that the aging process is very closely related to metabolic processes, and specially to sugar. So, could we use metformin to generate some of the beneficial effects that have been to result from caloric restriction?

Some scientists view metformin as the current best candidate for an anti-aging drug. As an anti-diabetic medicine, metformin suppresses glucose production in the liver and boosts insulin sensitivity. Positive benefits for patients include normalization of glucose levels, lowering of LDL and triglyceride levels and the facilitation of weight loss. Metformin is a relatively safe, and cheap, prescription drug, but some people do experience digestive distress while taking it.

This drug increases the number of oxygen molecules released into a cell, and this appears to boost robustness and longevity. Metformin enhances the activity of an enzyme found within our cells called adenosine monophosphate-activated protein kinase (AMPK). One of the benefits of caloric restriction is a substantial increase in AMPK activity, as cells go into a semi-starvation mode and increase their survival efficienc . People who practice sport in a regular and vigorous way also boost their AMPK levels, and this may be the mechanism by which exercise notably lowers cancer risk.

Could metformin really be an anti-aging drug? And, if science is right about it, are there natural ways to get the same results? Some people are already taking metformin daily, but there are natural supplements that boost AMPK activity. While humans must not ingest French lilac because of its toxicity, there are other plants that boost AMPK activity, including gynostemma and rose hips.

Gynostemma pentaphyllum, known as *jiaogulan*, literally "stranded blue plant", is an herb of the family Cucurbitaceae (cucumber or gourd family) indigenous to China, Vietnam, Korea and Japan. It has been used in Chinese herbal medicine and is reputed to have powerful antioxidant and adaptogenic effects. *Jiaogulan* is also known as the sweet tea vine, fairy herb or southern ginseng. In China, there is a valley called "The Valley of the Ancients" where *jiaogulan* tea is consumed, and there are many centenarians in this region. The leaves of the *jiaogulan* plant can be eaten raw, or boiled as a vegetable. They can also be used to make a delicious infusion, with a flavor reminiscent of licorice. An extract of *gynostemma pentaphyllum* has been used for centuries in traditional Chinese folk medicine to promote longevity.

There have been many studies of *jiaogulan*, showing a wide variety of benefits, but in 2010, researchers from several universities (Karolinska Institute, Stockholm, Sweden; Hanoi Medical University, Hanoi, Vietnam; National Institute of Gerontology, Hanoi, Vietnam), collaborated on a study called *Antidiabetic Effect of Gynostemma Pentaphyllum Tea in Randomly Assigned Type 2 Diabetic Patients*, and documented the antidiabetic effect of a *jiaogulan* infusion. Twenty-four participants, all with type 2 diabetes, who did not take medications to regulate their blood sugar, drank either *Gynostemma pentaphyllum* tea or tea with a placebo, for 12 weeks. There was a significant decrease in blood sugar and a significant decrease in insulin resistance in participants that took *gynostemma pentaphyllum* tea, compared to the group that took the placebo tea. None of the participants developed low levels of sugar or hypoglycemia, nor did any have negative outcomes affecting the kidneys, liver or digestive system. You can find *Gynostemma* leaf extract in shops that sell specialized nutritional supplements.

Trans-tiliroside, extracted from rose hips (*Rosa canina*) also boosts AMPK activity. Trans-tiliroside has been shown by researchers in preclinical studies to promote healthy blood glucose levels and lower body weight. In addition to lowering glucose, it also lowers LDL and triglycerides, raises HDL, and increases the antioxidant effects of superoxidase dismutase (SOD). Oral use of *Rosa canina* extract has been shown to improve skin moisture and elasticity, and to reduce facial wrinkling. Rose hip extract is considered safe and non-toxic, but gastrointestinal effects including loose stools and gas have been reported. However, it may also cause constipation. No contraindications or interactions with other drugs are documented.

However, we should ask, how new is this knowledge? Was some of it already known, earlier in our human history? The findings of some apparently avant-garde scientific research are beginning to justify one of the most ancient health-related practices used in the past: fasting.

Dr. Mark Mattson, Chief of the Laboratory of Neurosciences at the National Institute on Aging, undertook and published with his colleagues an impressive study: mice that achieved very low glucose levels by fasting, scored better on maze tests than did controls, and the fasting mice did better even than mice whose calorie intake was restricted. Blood tests helped to explain why: certain molecules, such as brain-derived neurotrophic factor, which promotes the formation of new neurons, were higher in the mice that fasted.

This was big news in the longevity world. It gave people who were already slim a way to get the benefits of calorie restriction without losing too much weight. While calorie restriction improves cognitive functions, the Mattson study indicated that fasting worked even better, but without limiting calories. Mattson explains the principle behind intermittent fasting:

> *If you challenge your cells bio-energetically through exercise or fasting, nerve cells respond adaptively, and pathways are activated that increase neuronal resistance to stress and age-related neurodegenerative disorders.*

Would the same thing work in humans? Glucose control is key, as we have seen. Studies have found that mice with very low glucose levels from fasting score better on tests than controls, and better even than mice whose calorie intake is restricted. Since early times in the history of mankind fasting has been known an essential tool for the conservation of health and for the development of the inner faculties of the disciple. It has been held to be the finest of the su geries of nature.

From a mystical point of view, the physical body and the spiritual body are two vibratory ends of the same element: the human being. Just as when brightness increases, darkness decreases, and when heat increases, cold decreases, if the physical body is deprived of its food and nutrients and thus in a relative manner it is weakened, the other end of the equation, the human being's more subtle and spiritual side, strengthens.

This is why, when you have been fasting for several days, thoughts begin to have a clarity that they lacked before. The mind begins to see things from another point of view, a perspective that is higher, less conditioned by matter and closer to those dimensions that we only fully cross when we die and peel off the physical vehicle. While fasting, a quantum leap is produced, through which the insight and speed of the intuitive mind infuses the rational mind. The result is a certain degree of enlightenment, or *satori*.

It is a memorable experience for those who are engaged in creative activities such as writing or painting, since at such times inspiration knocks at the door with unusual strength, it seems, in an almost tangible way. Something as trivial as walking in nature or watching a sunset becomes unforgettable, because of the special perception of colors, smells and sensations that fasting conveys. Perform a meditation after several days of fasting; it is something that cannot be explained in words, and that you are encouraged to experience, since only in this way you will be able to understand the before and after.

So, what is fasting? It is helpful to explore this concept by contrasting it with the everyday world. Each morning, upon waking up from a night's rest, most people take some form of food. Such meals may have different forms and quantities, depending on the country and customs in which the person lives. Such an act is called "breakfast". From a linguistic point of view, the prefix "break" means to end what has been done. In the case of the word breakfast, the meaning is "ending the fast", that is to say the period from dinner until the first meal of the day, during which food is not consumed.

Herein lies the true meaning of fasting: the total absence, not merely partial absence, of food during a certain period. I want to emphasize this concept, since today the popularity of some types of diet have caused the word "fast" or "fasting" to be used incorrectly. During the fast it is permissible to drink water, but not food in liquid form, such as fruit juices or syrups. The key is to stop the activity of the digestive system, and digestion happens when there is food to digest, even if the amounts are minimal. There is a kind of fasting that suspends fluid intake, too, but that is not something that will be explored in this book.

Why should a person fast? To answer this question, I will use a familiar analogy. The oil in your car has a purpose: to grease, lubricate and maintain the engine in perfect condition. However, when oil molecules come into contact with oxygen they begin to oxidize, and over time their ability to fulfil their role deteriorates, until it finally breaks down. This means that the oil can no longer perform its function, which is to lubricate, and this is dangerous for the engine, so we have to change the oil from time to time. When you change the oil in your car, the first thing you do, is to open the nut so that all the used oil runs off, and it is not until the tank has been emptied and cleaned that the new oil is poured in. With the human body, something similar happens; there is a process of oxidation and degradation, until at the end the body dies and decomposes.

Today, the dominant paradigm of health worldwide is the western prototype. This model emphasizes the physical and the intake of nutrients (yang principle) in the form of protein, carbohydrates, vitamins and mineral salts. In other words, the dominant model recognizes that we need to change the oil, but neglects the value of cleaning. In contrast, the eastern model works on the subtler energies, the elimination of toxins and the cleanliness of the body (yin principle).

To attain healthy process (the Tao) the body needs to be emptied before being filled up, or to put it another way, it should first be detoxified (yin) and only after that, nourished (yang). The hermetic equation is perfectly developed when the opposites are integrated in such a harmonious manner. In short, if we want to derive the maximum benefits from the nutrients in our food, we must first cleanse the body of the debris generated by the digestive process. Is it conceivable to fill your lungs with fresh air without having expelled the stale air within them? What would be the purpose of filling a glass with liquid, without having emptied it beforehand?

Fasting is used by animals and children in an instinctive way, to heal the body when they sense some imbalance. Wise Mother Nature, in certain situations, makes you lose your appetite, sometimes even vomiting in response to food, and it is only human stupidity that persists with feeding in the face of this, in blind accordance with cultural programming. When a person is close to death in this physical plane, they lose their appetite in a natural way, and if we strive to feed such a person, we will increase their suffering. We must learn to listen to our bodies, and not merely comply with cultural norms.

Fasting is a therapeutic method and means of spiritual growth. It was used by the oldest civilization in humanity, the Sumerians, from where it spread to other peoples and cultures. It was practiced regularly by Aristotle and Plato to improve physical and mental performance. Pythagoras fasted 40 days, recommending the practice in his school of mysteries, and in the Bible there are dozens of references to prolonged fasts on the part of Jesus and the apostles, as well as in the *Mahabharata* and the *Upanishad*, among many other ancient writings. Hippocrates, the father of medicine in the fifth century BC, declared

Everyone has a physician inside him or her.
We just have to help in its work.
The natural healing force within each one of us is the greatest
force in getting well.
Our food should be our medicine.
Our medicine should be our food.
But to eat when you are sick is to feed your sickness.

And Plutarch, the Greek philosopher, who had more than a casual interest in medicine, said:

Instead of using medicine, rather fast a day

What biological processes take place during fasting? Through fasting, a series of metabolic changes are generated in the body, which prompt the expression of certain genes that were previously inactive. This generates beneficial psychophysical effects. During the first phase of fasting, the body consumes the circulating glucose and glycogen stored in the liver and muscles. This phase lasts between 24 and 48 hours. After that, you enter into a state of lacking glycogen, or hypoglycemia, and although later the body automatically self-balances, and the blood glucose normalizes, some (harmless) symptoms such as dizziness and cold sweats can occur.

During this second phase, the mechanisms for the consumption of fat begin, acting on nerve endings, the hypothalamus, adrenal glands and pancreas. The hypothalamus begins to release growth hormone, among others, and the pancreas decreases its production of insulin. I point to these two factors because they are important, active elements identified in the cutting-edge research conducted in recent decades and still ongoing, on life extension.

During fasting, the main fuel used by the body is fat, and occasionally proteins that are not essential to life, which with their glucogenesis help the brain to adapt, until it is able to use ketone bodies as a source of energy. If all the fat in the body were to be consumed, it would begin to consume those proteins that are essential for life, so that at that point the appetite returns and eating must begin, because otherwise death would ensue.

There are many reasons for fasting. It normalizes sensitivity to insulin and leptin, helping to improve the operating energy efficiency of mitochondria (as has been seen to happen with caloric restriction in rats and primates). Although sugar is the source of energy used by the body, it promotes insulin resistance when consumed in the monstrous quantities present in our modern diet, thanks to processed foods. Resistance to insulin, in turn, is a key driver of chronic diseases, from heart disease to cancer.

Fasting increases the production of Human Growth Hormone (HGH). This is a hormone that humans barely produce from their third decade of life, but it plays an important role in health and sports performance, and can slow down the process of aging. HGH is also a fat-burning hormone, which helps to explain why fasting is so effective for weight loss.

Fasting also decreases levels of triglycerides and improves other biological markers of disease. It reduces the oxidative stress produced by the accumulation of free radicals in the cells, and therefore prevents oxidative damage to the cellular proteins, lipids and nucleic acids, associated with aging and disease.

The latest scientific research is corroborating ancient hermetic wisdom, giving clear evidence in this regard. A few years ago Leonard Guarente, biologist at the Massachusetts Institute of Technology (MIT) discovered that activating a protein called sirtuin, (SIRT1), was sufficient to prolong the life of brewer's yeast. Other researchers have proved that it produces the same effect in worms, flies and mice, extending their life by up to 50%. Pere Puigserver, at the Dana-Farber Cancer Institute, showed that the restriction of calories increases levels of NAD in the liver, which in turn stimulates the activity of SIRT1. As you can see, all of this establishes a clear connection between food supply and the expression of SIRT1, as well as with the mysterious effects attributed to caloric restriction and fasting.

So, what are sirtuins? They are a type of protein that activates the survival genes. When food is scarce they come into operation, allowing the organism to live longer and with better health. The SIRT1 activators confer, at first sight, the same beneficial effects as a low-calorie diet or fasting, and this has been demonstrated by Carles Canto from the Auwerx laboratory in Lausanne with the drug SRT1720. The drug completely prevented the fattening of mice after several weeks of a high-fat diet; at the same time the mice did not develop resistance to insulin, which generates diabetes and cardiovascular damage.

It is not my intention to provide a detailed guide on how to fast. If you decide to try it, you will have to prepare carefully and in detail, and look for medical supervision, although for a healthy person a short period of food abstinence should not present any problems. Grab it as a moment of special reconnection with yourself, and integration with the Cosmos, and you'll get the best results. It is an ideal time to meditate, walk, read, and pursue other creative endeavors. If you practice fasting in a scientific manner, you'll get amazing results at every level. It is not easy, but the reward is worth it. Remember that the science of alchemy is not for the lazy or the faint-hearted. You can receive payouts in proportion to your stake, to what you invest in the process. And the currency exchange is effort. However, you can be sure that the recompense will more than offset your investment.

Another option to consider for those who resonate with it, and something that science is beginning to discover, is "intermittent fasting" in the form of consuming a single meal over a period of 24 hours. Although it is generally accepted by schools of medicine and therefore by society that is healthier to eat several meals a day, everything you have read in this chapter suggests that once again the dominant scientific paradigm is questionable.

There are many people who say that an army cannot march on an empty stomach, but the implication is simply not true and there is no scientific basis for saying that. I invite you to reflect on what happens to you after eating. You feel sleepy and without energy, because the digestive process itself needs to use energy. What is more, a team of researchers led by Martin Wegman has carried out a study at the University of Florida College of Medicine and concluded that intermittent fasting produced a slight increase in SIRT3, with the implications this has for health and longevity. This study is particularly noteworthy if we take into account that participants alternated between a day in which they ate 175% of daily ingestion and another in which they ate 25%, which cannot be regarded exactly as fasting.

Personally, I take one meal per day, that meal being dinner, if you have no activity planned for later and can fully relax or even go to sleep. It is said that it is not good to sleep immediately after dinner, but this is another dogma of faith without any scientific basis. If dinner makes you feel sleepy, why not follow your natural instinct? Once again we see that the human being has ceased listening to himself and to the wisdom of his body, instead choosing to follow supposed medical truths. Those that are against going to sleep right after dinner, or who assert that the dinner must be very light, may nonetheless defend as very healthy a good nap after a good midday meal.

As you can see, this kind of advice and opinion is very inconsistent. And although each person must search for the type of diet and food that is best suited to their personal characteristics, I suggest that you do not discard or overlook an option that has stood the test of time and, given that we are entering the age of Aquarius, will in future receive the backing of the majority of researchers and scientists.

CHAPTER XV

THE AQUARIAN AGE: A MORE MYSTICAL SCIENCE AND A MORE SCIENTIFIC RELIGION

To know that we know what we know, and that we do not know what we do not know, that is true knowledge

Confucius, Chinese thinker (551 BC– 479BC) The search by humanity for knowledge has been constant throughout its history. However, that knowledge has been tempered by the cosmic cycles or rhythms of that great cosmic being in which we are immersed. And although knowledge is a singular phenomenon, there are very diverse ways of approaching it, which depend on where the observer is located.

Throughout this work I have given evidence that shows everything started in Sumer, and spread from there. The books of the Old Testament were written by Hebrew scribes during the era of Aries, the astrological time before the Christian era of Pisces. But they were compilations of much older Mesopotamian texts, written in the eras of Aries and Taurus, and even in earlier times than those. Each astrological era of 2,160 years is a new step in the evolution of mankind, and in each era the same knowledge is expressed from different points of view.

During the era of Gemini (approximately 6,480 BC – 4,320 BC) the first writing systems appeared. The invention of the wheel and other transport systems occurred under the influence of mercurial Gemini. It has been said that Sagittarius, the opposing constellation, signaled the beginning of philosophy and of the concept of ideals in mankind.

The Mediterranean cultures of the Taurus period (approximately 4,320 BC – 2,160 BC) have left behind numerous artistic remains and legends that focus on the sacred bull. In Crete it is the Minotaur. The practice of bullfighting in the Iberian Peninsula, which continues to this day, originated in those pre-Christian times and integrated the concept of the bull (Taurus) with the act of defying death (Scorpio). This is clearly seen when the bullfighter exposes his chest to the horns of the bull in order to lean over the animal´s head and plant his sword between the horns.

Egyptian art also shows the influence of Taurus in terms of strength and durability. This is seen in the pyramids. At the same time, the opposing constellation, Scorpio, has combined with these features a concern about, and reflection upon, physical death and the post-mortem life, in forms such as embalming, sepulchral chambers, etc.

Just as a special labyrinth was built in Crete for the Minotaur, a similar construction was made for the Apis Bull in Memphis. In Saqqara, clay bull-heads, complete with natural horns, were placed in recesses within the tomb of a Second Dynasty pharaoh, while a Third Dynasty ruler, the pharaoh Zoser, is known to have ceremonially honored the Bull of Heaven. These events all occurred during the period referred to as the Old Kingdom, which ended in around 2,180 BC

In Egipt the transition to the age of Aries (2,160 BC to the year 1 approx.) began after the Theban victory and the exaltation of the dynasties of the Middle Kingdom. In the course of celebrations of the New Year, coinciding with the rising of the Nile, hymns of praise were sung to Amun-Ra, for example:

Oh brilliant One
Who shines in the inundation waters.

I who raised his head and lifts his forehead:
I of the Ram, the greatest of heavenly creatures.

The Ram took pride of place in the New Kingdom, with temple avenues adorned with statues of the creature. In Karnak, the great temple of Amon-Ra, in a secret observation perch, instructions were left for the astronomer-priest whose job it was to open the perch on the day of the winter solstice:

One goes toward the hall called Horizon of the sky.
One climbs the Aha, "Lonesome place of the majestic soul",
The high room for watching the Ram who sails across the skies.

The people of Mesopotamia marked the opening of the age of Aries with a changed calendar, and adjusted their list of stars so that the list now began with Aries, rather than Taurus. The coins issued during the fourth century BC showed the head of Alexander wearing the horns of a ram.

The peoples of this era combined an aggressive tendency to engage in war with a refined cultural and artistic quality, the latter being a property of the constellation opposite to Aries, which is Libra. Also in this era, Moses banned worship of the golden calf (Taurus) and began the myth of the paschal lamb (Aries).

The biblical *Book of Exodus* tells the story of the enslavement of the Hebrews in ancient Egypt and their subsequent release by Moses, who guided them to the Promised Land. *Exodus* narrates the miracles that Moses generated in order to protect his people. In Cecil B. DeMille's epic film of 1956, *The Ten Commandments*, there is a masterly portrayal of the miraculous parting of the waters of the Red Sea that allowed the Jewish people to rid themselves of the yoke of the Egyptian army, and to begin their pilgrimage through the desert, always guided by the hand of a brutal and blood-thirsty god of war, Yahweh (Enlil).

The third month after their departure from Egypt, the Israelites came to the Sinai desert and camped in front of the mountain:

In the third month, on the same day of the month
that the Israelites had left the land of Egypt,
they entered the Wilderness of Sinai.
After they departed from Rephidim,
they entered the Wilderness of Sinai and camped in the wilderness,
and Israel camped there in front of the mountain.

Exodus 19: 1-2

The Exodus account states that in this place the alliance between Yahweh and the Hebrew people was sealed:

Then Moses went up to God, and the Lord called to him from the
mountain and said,
"This is what you are to say to the descendants of Jacob
and what you are to tell the people of Israel:
You yourselves have seen what I did to Egypt,
and how I carried you on eagles' wings and brought you to myself.
Now if you obey me fully and keep my covenant,
then out of all nations you will be my treasured possession.
Although the whole earth is mine,
you will be for me a kingdom of priests and a holy nation.
These are the words you are to speak to the Israelites."

Exodus 19, 3-6

With the Covenant came commandments, laws and restrictions, the price paid by the Israelites to become the chosen people.

So Moses came and called for the elders,
and set before them all these words
as Yahweh had commanded him.
So Moses brought their answer back to the Lord.
And all the people answered together and said,
all that Yahweh hath spoken we will do.
And Moses told the words of the people unto the Lord.
Yahweh said to Moses,
"I am going to come to you in a dense cloud,
so that the people will hear me speaking with you

and will always put their trust in you."
Then Moses told the Lord what the people had said.

Exodus 19, 8-9

Yahweh told Moses to prepare his people for the third day, when he would descend upon the mount for all the people to see him. Yahweh warned that such a landing would be a physical danger to any who got too close, so urged Moses to maintain a security zone:

Put limits for the people around the mountain and tell them,
"Be careful that you do not approach the mountain or touch the
foot of it. Whoever touches the mountain is to be put to death."

Exodus 19.12

All these instructions were followed precisely, and on the third day the promised landing of Yahweh on Mount Sinai took place. It was a fiery descent, and a noisy one:

On the morning of the third day
there was thunder and lightning,
with a thick cloud over the mountain,
and a very loud trumpet blast.
Everyone in the camp trembled.

Exodus 19, 16

This event, far from being ethereal and spiritual, is described as a very physical phenomenon, with all the dangers that this entails. So when the landing began, Moses placed his people within the limits that had been marked as security zone, at the foot of Mount Sinai:

Mount Sinai was covered with smoke,
because Yahweh descended on it in fire.
The smoke billowed up from it like smoke from a furnace,
and the whole mountain trembled violently.
As the sound of the trumpet grew louder and louder,
Moses spoke and the voice of God answered him.
The Lord descended to the top of Mount Sinai

and called Moses to the top of the mountain.
So Moses went up.

Exodus 19,18-20

It was then that *"Elohim spoke the following words"* thereby establishing the Ten Commandments, which constitute the essence of the Jewish faith, and the alliance between Yahweh and the Israeli people. The Ten Commandments, along with some more detailed ordinances to guide daily conduct, rules concerning the worship of Yahweh, and strict prohibition of the worship of other gods, were all written on stone tablets, as follows:

I *I am the Lord your God,*
   who brought you out of Egypt, out of the land of slavery.

II *You shall have no other gods before me. You shall not make*
    for yourself an image in the form of anything in heaven
    above or on the earth beneath or in the waters below. You
    shall not bow down to them or worship them; for I, the Lord
    your God, am a jealous God, punishing the children for the
    sin of the parents to the third and fourth generation of those
    who hate me, but showing love to a thousand generations
    of those who love me and keep my commandments.

III *You shall not misuse the name of the Lord your God, for the*
     Lord will not hold anyone guiltless who misuses his name.

IV *Remember the Sabbath day by keeping it holy. Six days*
    you shall labor and do all your work, but the seventh day
    is a Sabbath to the Lord your God. On it you shall not
    do any work, neither you, nor your son or daughter, nor
    your male or female servant, nor your animals, nor any
    foreigner residing in your towns. For in six days the Lord
    made the heavens and the earth, the sea, and all that is in
    them, but he rested on the seventh day. Therefore the Lord
    blessed the Sabbath day and made it holy.

V   *Honor your father and your mother, so that you may live long in the land the Lord your God is giving you.*

VI   *You shall not murder.*

VII   *You shall not commit adultery.*

VIII *You shall not steal.*

IX   *You shall not give false testimony against your neighbor.*

X   *You shall not covet your neighbor's house. You shall not covet your neighbor's wife, or his male or female servant, his ox or donkey, or anything that belongs to your neighbor.*

Many authors, among them Zecharia Sitchin, have claimed in their writings that never before these ten commandments had there been established so clearly and with such originality a code of ethics, arguing that the *Code of Hammurabi,* of around 1754 BC, was a code of justice but not a complete spiritual guide. But is this completely true?

The *Schoyen Collection* is currently the world's most extensive private collection of manuscripts, most of which are housed in Oslo and London. Martin Schoyen was an exceptional twentieth-century architect, and his unique collection includes more than 13,000 manuscripts from 134 countries or territories, comprising works in 120 different languages and covering 5000 years of mankind's history.

The Ten Commandments of Christianity, or to be more precise, those accepted by Christians as having been revealed by God, were granted by God to Moses on Mount Sinai, through the covenant between the people of Israel and the divinity, known as the Old Covenant. Israel undertook to fulfill the Commandments and God, in exchange, would help his people in all their endeavors, for as long as the chosen people went on fulfilling them. It is said that God himself wrote them on two tablets of stone. But the Commandments, as well as the biblical narrative of the Universal Deluge, have been shown to be based on earlier, Sumerian, texts. Thus, the Christian Ten Commandments are not original and exclusive to the religion that has dominated the west for the past two thousand years, even though the defenders of this claim are not happy when this is said. The evidence is to be found on the clay tablet MS 2788 of the Schoyen collection, known as *The Instructions of Shuruppak*. This is a very old Sumerian text, as is reflected in the words with which Ubar Tutu, the antediluvian king of Shuruppak addresses his son Ziusudra, the Flood hero:

> *In those days, in those far remote days, in those nights, in those faraway nights, in those years, in those far remote ...*

The Instructions of Shuruppak is, once again, a Sumerian text that both precedes and heralds Hebrew writings which have, for many years, been accepted as unique and original. *The Instructions of Shuruppak* takes the form of a book of proverbs, and has a clear intent to inculcate virtues and piety in the community. It contains precepts that were later included among the Ten Commandments of Moses, as well as in the biblical *Book of Proverbs*.

Thus, where the Sumerian text says, "*You will not blaspheme*", the tables of the Hebrew law say, "*You shall not take the name of the Lord your God in vain*"; where the Sumerian text says, "*You shall not laugh or sit in a room alone with a married woman*", the Mosaic law says, "*You shall not commit adultery*". Both texts agree that, "*You shall not steal*", "*You must not lie*" and "*Do not murder*", with exact translations of the Sumerian rules appearing in the Ten Commandments...

In the Biblical narrative, the compilers of the Ten Commandments, as their peers did when describing the earthly Paradise, have retained some details that support the Sumerian origin of the story, which allows it to be dated to a time long before the Israelites' exodus. According to the *Book of Exodus*, Moses was on Mount Sinai for forty days and forty nights, during which time God gave him the Ten Commandments written on two tablets of stone. When Moses walked down from the mountain, he saw people worshipping a golden calf, so he became angry and broke the tablets:

When Moses approached the camp
and saw the calf and the dancing,
his anger burned
and he threw the tablets out of his hands,
breaking them to pieces
at the foot of the mountain.

Exodus 32, 19

Thereafter Moses ascended the mountain once again and asked God to forgive the people and seal the Covenant with him. Then the Lord called Moses to take two stone tablets upon which he would write the Ten Commandments of the Covenant.

Yahweh said to Moses,
"Chisel out two stone tablets like the first ones,
and I will write on them the words that were on the first tablets,
which you broke."

Exodus 34.1

Can you imagine Moses coming down from Mount Sinai, along testing and dangerous tracks full of huge, rough rocks, carrying two heavy tablets of stone, one in each hand? It had to be a stressful and risky undertaking. If we believe the biblical version, rather than Moses breaking them when saw his people worshipping the golden calf, it would seem that the tablets may have slipped from his hands in a moment of such rough voyage, being so heavy and bulky. In addition, the Israelites had fled Egypt, where there was papyrus of excellent quality.

Don't you think it would have been more logical and less tiring to write the Ten Commandments on such a material? Papyrus, apart from being more lightweight, can remain very well preserved, more so even than stone, to the point that even today we can see 4000-year-old papyrus in a fairly good state of preservation.

So we see, once again, a reiteration of earlier texts, this time as elements of the *Book of Exodus*, in which the Hebrew scribe took no care over the details and forgot something as basic as the need to change the name of the original material on which were written the divine prescriptions, in this case on clay tablets used at the Sumerian times, thereby failing to adapt the narrative to the historical time in which the text was rewritten, that is to say, a time when the usual practice was to write on papyrus.

On the other hand, we do know with certainty that the Sumerians wrote on clay tablets with cuneiform writing, and we also know of the existence of the Sumerian text called *The Instructions of Shuruppak*, whose chronological dating is anterior to *Exodus*. In the Sumerian text are already collected, and written on a tablet of clay, the so-called Ten Commandments. It does not seem very difficult for an unprejudiced mind to realize what has happened.

Will it surprise historians in 4000 years' time if someone says that at the beginning of the twenty-first century, the US president, Mr. Trump, travelled from New York City to London in a steam boat to attend to an important meeting? As you know, it is quite obvious that the dominant transport system used at the beginning of the twenty-first century is not the steam-ship, so in the same way, it was not customary to write on tablets of stone at the time of the *Exodus*... but it was in Sumerian times. We can lay bare the facts before those who claim that the Ten Commandments were originally Jewish and engraved on stone, something unlikely to happen at the time of Moses.

The nuances of history are very important to research, and in previous pages I have provided data and evidence that what is written in the Bible has a background rooted in truth, but it is necessary to emphasize this authenticity is given because their writings originated from Mesopotamian texts, which were much older. If you extensively analyze biblical texts, without bearing this influence in mind, your conclusions will not be accurate, and this is something that happens frequently to the great biblical exegetes. We cannot afford to lose this general vision if we want to be accurate when it comes to the details.

With the birth of Jesus Christ, the time of Aries closed and the era of Pisces began. The New Testament appeared and the commandments of the Mosaic Law were interpreted and prioritized in a manner consistent with the sign of Pisces, through the Christian message that would come to dominate the entire era:

A new command I give you:
Love one another.
As I have loved you,
so you must love one another.

John 13:34

The first Christians used as a symbol two small fish placed in opposing directions, which represent the contradictions and oppositions between science and religion, man and woman, east and west, materialism and spiritualism. The multiplication of fishes and loaves symbolized the spread of the teaching of Pisces and Virgo. This last constellation is represented by a woman with an ear of wheat in her hand, hence, the bread, the elaboration of the fruits of the Virgin Mother, Nature.

On the other hand, the imagery of the virginity of the Mother of Christ, a symbol present in many religions, took on special importance in the cosmic period of Pisces. In contemporary times the separation of science and spirituality began when René Descartes decided to differentiate the knowledge of mind, which he reserved for the religious sphere, from the knowledge of matter, which he placed in the scope of science. Then, Newton laid the foundations of classical physics on which current scientific knowledge is based

During the twentieth century, quantum physics made its appearance and with it the possibility of a return to the harmonious integration of science and spirituality. At present, we are witnessing the harrowing confrontation of currents of antagonistic thought. In these very moments, the more materialistic movements face the free thought of those cutting-edge scientific precursors of the new paradigm that will prevail for the next 2,160 years. We are at the dawn of the new zodiacal era of Aquarius and watching the agonizing throes of the end of the era of Pisces.

The current scientific materialistic thought, heir to the Newtonian paradigm, seeks to explain the Cosmos in terms without the existence of a superior intelligence. However, the new Aquarian science will restore the role of a cosmic mind, a consciousness, as something that is a precursor of a "smart energy" from which emanates the known material universe, reversing the position that is currently postulated by materialistic science.

In the forthcoming era, the era of Aquarius, science will be more mystical and spiritual. Meanwhile, religion and the philosophies will become more scientific. The differences between religions, philosophical systems and schools of mysteries will disappear, allowing the emergence of a unique and authentic scientific knowledge that will collate the essence of objective knowledge, common to all the religious and philosophical systems of the past. The most important religions will be transformed: Christianity, Buddhism, Islam. The new mystic science will delete all the tricks and superstitions of the past. We are on the brink of a scientific-spiritual rebirth

Mankind will no longer be confronted by religions, faiths and philosophical systems, since the truth of knowledge will clear its own path, in the same way as do the rays of the rising Sun (symbol of the sign of Leo, which is opposed to Aquarius and that will operate in line with it). For the first time a universal language will appear. This will unify philosophical, hermetic and scientific concepts, in a way that has never yet been seen. Currently, depending on the school or creed to which one belongs, the meanings of words vary to such an extent that it is usually impossible to maintain a coherent conversation, and very often this is comical to an observer, to see two or more persons taking apparently irreconcilable positions, who in reality are saying the same thing with different words. Terms such as "soul", "spirit", "ego", "mind", "God", "cosmos", "energy" and others, will no longer challenge the seekers of truth. In this way, the human species will experience a scientific advance without precedent.

However, the birth of this new age will not be a quick and easy delivery; it will not be without pain. It will not be the work of just one day, and it will not be easy, because there are still many forces from the previous system to be overcome, the majority of them rooted in the depths of the subconscious of the people, in the form of religious beliefs, and therefore difficult to remove. It will require several generations until finally the new scientific-mystical paradigm, devoid of fantasies, is seated with authority within society. But I must also say that the change is inevitable, since the great cosmic cycles, the beats of that great being in which human beings enjoy their existence, are inexorably pushing us in this direction.

Dear friends, may you be attentive to the two signs that announce the new times. The water-bearer (Appendix A) who pours the water of knowledge with its jug into the glass, and the sunshine (Apendix B) that illuminates it. But you ought also to be prepared for your glass to be empty (Appendix C), so that in this way the water from the water-bearer can be poured into it; and clean, so that the sunlight can reflect without any distortion.

APPENDIX A

THE WATER-BEARER AND THE AWAKENING FROM MAYA

What Albert Einstein termed optical delusion, the Indians termed Maya or Illusion.

Mohit K. Misra

What is real? How do you define "real"? If you're talking about what you can feel, what you can smell, what you can taste and see, then "real" is simply electrical signals interpreted by your brain.

Morpheus, The Matrix

If you want to change reality, you only have to use your TV remote control and change the channel, while you are lying on your sofa, sipping your favorite beer. That wide-screen television *à la carte* will allow you to secrete endorphins and feel all kinds of sensations, just as if you were experiencing them in your real life. Sex, crime, speed, trips to paradise, sports; all of these can be yours.

Similarly, you can have information without limit and theoretically without censorship, although the nature of such information without censorship will differ substantially, depending on the channel. The ability of the media to create reality has reached such a point that now, only events that have been recorded on camera are acknowledged as having happened, and the form and order in which they are narrated, is dictated by the media.

However, things are not merely what they appear to be, at first sight. The ancient oriental philosophies explained this, thousands of years ago with a simple sentence: "the world is maya". "Maya" means trickery, fraud, unreality, illusion. Illusion is what seems to be real but is not; and a great illusionist makes the audience believe that he can produce a white dove from nothing.

Most things that happen in this world are mere illusion ... and those who believe in the great illusion of this world, who believe that certain things are real when they are not, are dreamers. From a dreamer's perspective, a dream is real when the dreamer is in the dream state. But what happens when you wake up from your sleep and the dream comes to an end? The world is full of dreamers, people who accept the illusory (what it seems to be) as something real (what it really is).

Mankind is tangled in a spider's web, a network of illusions (a matrix) that makes you feel free, with room for maneuver. But the actual situation is the opposite, people are in a state of total slavery, with very little room or scope for action. That scope is in fact almost negligible. This is because the first illusion or belief that this network of illusions generates in the individual, is a mental assimilation of the belief that you are free to decide and act. Once this belief has been thoroughly assimilated in the deepest part of your subconscious mind, which is the part of the mind that is not aware, you have become unable to grasp and enjoy freedom. How can you reach for freedom if you are not aware of your slavery? How can you think freely if you do not realize that your thought processes are automatic?

This hidden network offers endless custom-made illusions to its "intelligent audience", and it is powered or fed by the human state of "sleep", which is to say, by the lack of consciousness in the individual. I will not explain in detail the nature and origins of the spider's web and network of illusions, but I would like to underline the fact that its survival is closely linked to the fact that the human species continues to exist in a state of automated thought, with a low degree of wakefulness that stops people thinking autonomously. Therefore, they cannot be free.

Although I could have used other terms, I have decided to use here the term "matrix", to honor the legendary film by the Wachowski brothers. Obviously, I do not know what the underlying motives of the Wachowski brothers were when they conceived *The Matrix*, but regardless, the premise of the movie can be used to explain certain aspects of the hermetic world. I must, however, make it clear that I speak at all times for myself and not for the movie's creators.

The plot of the film suggests that in a near future, almost all human beings are to be enslaved by machines and artifici l intelligence. In *The Matrix*, the machines raise humans for energy, and feed on them. However, seeing the film as a fight between men and technology is not the only possible interpretation. *The Matrix* can also be viewed from the perspective whereby each character and symbol in the film has an analogy within transcendental hermetic knowledge. From this perspective, *The Matrix* is about awakening, spiritual illumination and the search for the truth that is hidden behind appearances.

Let us look at some of the film s characters. Neo, as his name indicates, is "the new one", a neophyte, a student attracted by a mystery school. He wants to learn how to free himself from the network of mirages that catches people, feeding vampirically upon their energies through automated thoughts and acts.

All people are subjected to numerous incarnations throughout the cycle of birth, life and death in a phenomenon that Buddhists call "Samsara´s wheel". Ignorance must be replaced by the knowledge that will allow individuals to awaken from the semi-conscious state that has engulfed the human species. This too has parallels in *The Matrix*, where Morfeo, "the sleep", is a master of wisdom, guiding the neophyte on his journey from the sleep state to the awakening that will allow him to become an authentic initiate into the greater mysteries. To achieve this, Neo must perform specific (secret) practices that will expand his consciousness

What is the Matrix? In *The Matrix*, Morpheus states:

> *The Matrix is everywhere. It is all around us. Even now, in this very room. You can see it when you look out your window or when you turn on your television. You can feel it when you go to work... when you go to church... when you pay your taxes. It is the world that has been pulled over your eyes to blind you from the truth. ...The Matrix is a computer-generated dream world, built to keep us under control in order to change a human being into this* (at this point Morpheus holds up a copper-top D cell battery).

In the film, people are converted, while they sleep, into batteries of energy for use by the city of mechanical robots. People thus give up their vital force so that the web of artificial intelligence that was created by humans, but is alien to them, can function and survive. From a hermetic perspective, men become slaves and servants of their own mental and mechanical creations, of their automated thoughts. These creations have achieved self-awareness and can live independently, free of their creators, and in doing so feed upon people's energies and vital fluids. I know that this truth may seem extremely fantastical, but it is based on ancient knowledge that neuroscience has only very recently begun to understand.

Does mankind enjoy freedom or the illusion of freedom?

Morpheus says,

> *... you are a slave, Neo. Like everyone else you were born into bondage. Into a prison that you cannot taste or see or touch. A prison for your mind.*

Great thinkers have explained the same truth using other words and images, but their essential message is the same. Plato uses the allegory of a dark cave, in which are people who have been imprisoned since childhood, tied up. What they can see is the inner face of a wall, upon which are projected shadows from the fire that burns behind them. These people only see shadows and do not know that they are prisoners. They do not even consider that possibility, because this is the only word they have ever known. Plato describes this as a low level of reality. The life that these beings enjoy is of a vastly inferior nature to that they could have. If they could manage to break their invisible chains, they would see the world as it really is and not as it seems to be to them.

In the Wachowski brothers' film, Trinity (the trinity) and Morfeo look for Neo and offer him the chance to be disconnected from the network of illusions, to break free from his shackles and escape the karmic laws. However, it is difficult to escape the karmic laws that dominate our existence, and the Wheel of Samsara. What is more, the large majority of *homo sapiens* does not feel motivated to wake up from their comfortable sleep.

When an individual finally awakes and escapes from the network of illusions, he acquires powers until then unknown, which are considered miraculous by those who remain immersed in the system. This state has been given various names by different traditions, among them *nirvana*, *satori*, *samadhi*, *moksha* or "state of grace". Amongst these powers is a mental clarity sufficient to perceive reality from an objective point of view, undistorted by the matrix. Those who have reached this state find it extremely difficult to explain, given the limitations of verbal language, the scope of their lived experience.

It is necessary to say that this road towards the awakening of consciousness is an individual journey whereby certain individuals of the human species acquire the ability to rid themselves of the yoke of illusion. It is never an evolutionary process, affecting the species as a whole in the short term, but in the very long term, by measuring this time in cosmic values. This is because, if the human species as a whole were suddenly to be released from this multiform network of illusions, this would lead to such a huge cosmic imbalance in the cosmic ecosystem that it would endanger the very order of the Universe.

In *The Matrix*, Morpheus says:

> *Most of these people are not ready to be unplugged. And many of them are so inured, so hopelessly dependent on the system* [and the system upon them], *that they will fight to protect it.*

Note: The phrase written in parentheses is added to the original dialogue.

APPENDIX B

FINAL STATION: THE SUN

By making Samyama on the Sun, (comes) the knowledge of the world.

Yoga Sutras of Patanjali

In the previous chapter I used some aspects of the film *The Matrix* to illustrate the path of spiritual awakening. Now is the time to point out a very important fact of the movie's plot: that there is no sunlight left in the world. Dear reader, keep this in mind while reading this chapter! In this section I will look at a very controversial topic, and will likely produce a few smiles among academics. Let us explore the universe, the solar system and the planets from the point of view of consciousness, of the mind.

If you were suddenly to tell someone you came across in the street that the star that we call the Sun, thinks, that it is aware of itself and its place in the Universe and is a living being with the ability to communicate, it is more than likely that you would get some odd looks, maybe also a condescending smile. Your interlocutor may assume you to be a friendly fool, but surely someone who lacks the scientific knowledge needed to understand what the Sun is in reality. Everything seems so obvious at the dawn of the twenty-first century, that our imaginary pedestrian would surely reject such talk as ignorant and primitive. He would give you a warm pat on the back and tell you were right, in the way people often do with those they dismiss as 'crazy'.

However, in ancient times this train of thought was considered neither extravagant nor ignorant, and certainly far from crazy. On the contrary, it was knowledge accepted and shared among the greatest of wise men. In the course of this work I have presented a multitude of evidence to show that in the last five hundred years, science has been rediscovering knowledge that already existed in the remote past. Sumerians, Chaldeans, Assyrians, Greeks, Romans, Aztecs, Mayans, Incas, Hindus and Celts, among others, already knew so much. It is widely documented that ancient cultures gave greater prominence than we do to celestial activities and in particular to the Sun. In this appendix, I shall discuss the most transcendental knowledge of all times: that concerning the Sun, which, like the Earth and other celestial bodies, is a living being, with a consciousness of itself and a surprising intelligence that far exceeds that of any human being. The implications arising from the existence of a solar entity that is thus aware, explain many phenomena that modern astronomers simply cannot understand.

We all agree that in this small corner of the galaxy, nothing would be the same without the Sun. That star is the primary source of constant energy for all of the elements that make up the so-called solar system. Life on Earth would be a chimera, were it not for the actions of the Sun.

Our Sun has been in existence for approximately 4.5 billion years, that is to say a third of the Universe's lifetime. The opinions of modern astrophysicists coincide with those expressed in the old Sumerian texts, explaining that the planets of the solar system have their origins in the Sun, from which they emerged in the form of energy packets that later solidified as a result of their cooling, which occurred due to their moving away from the heat of the central star. After many millions of years, and not without traumatic events, as the *Enuma Elish* recounts, all planets of the system settled into stable orbits. This state of equilibrium allowed the planets not to be absorbed by the attraction of the central sun, at the same maintaining the degree of attraction at a level sufficient to keep a permanent link with their creator, and thus not to pull away from the solar system.

If you think carefully about it, this is a masterpiece of nature. And we cannot say that whoever thus acts lacks intelligence, whoever that may be. To further illustrate the magnitude and the scope of this achievement, you only have to ask a NASA engineer to describe the volume of work and mathematical calculations that are needed to put a satellite into orbit around the Earth. That NASA engineer would be the happiest of men if he could but get this satellite to sustain a stable orbit for one century, even though he would have to make constant corrections of calculation over the years. Human beings have the intelligence necessary to launch a satellite into orbit, but are we the only ones capable of doing this? The answer is that we are neither the only ones nor are we those who can do it with the greatest degree of perfection. The Earth and the other planets of the solar system have been orbiting the Sun for the last 4 billion years. What kind of intelligence uses such mechanisms to get similar, but infinitely superior, results to those sought by the intelligence of a NASA engineer?

Materialistic science does not consider that there may be any kind of conscious relationship between the Sun and the formation of planets, or with the stability of their orbits. The concept of an intelligent and aware Sun is in our time seen as being very far from scientifically correct. According to the scientific orthodoxy, everything that happens, in the Sun and around it, is nothing more than haphazard and a form of shuffle that occurs when a large number of atoms and particles move through space for long enough to generate events.

Although the activity of the Sun generates a very powerful electromagnetic field which envelopes the entire solar system, nobody seems willing to consider that this field could play a decisive role in the maintenance of the planets and their orbits. The Sun's role, venerated in ancient times, is for most people today that of a simple but gigantic bulb of light and heat. However, there are solar activities that are still far from being captured and understood by the current level of technological development, and phenomena that scientists are now observing and measuring are merely collateral side effects of something that is not well understood due to the unimaginable scale of its magnitude.

To use an accessible simile, this is like a group of researchers attaching sensors to different parts of the bodies of two people, a man and a woman. These sensors would receive data from the vital functions of the couple, heartbeat, hormonal and metabolic changes, temperature, etc. The researchers would know all of these variables yet they would remain ignorant of the main fact, that the man and the woman are having sex, an activity that has been generated as a consequence of a range of stimuli and contra-stimuli, left un-monitored by the team of researchers. The result is that the team of scientists gets lots of accurate data, but remains ignorant of the reality of the situation. Something similar applies to modern studies of the Sun by astrophysicists. They have an abundance of data but this is not equivalent to knowing what the Sun is, nor what in reality happens within it.

We are now going to make a small detour in order to extend our knowledge of the central star in our system. The Sun is not a solid body, nor does it have a defined surface like the Earth's. It is composed of what is called the fourth state of matter: plasma, or radiant matter. That state is not solid, liquid or gaseous. In the plasmatic state the harmonious equilibrium between positive and negative particles that is associated with the atoms that make up stable matter, does not exist. Plasma is a state in which gas supports a temperature so high that its atoms ionize. Therefore, the radiant matter state is loaded with electromagnetic energy, and the particles move as a fluid although they endure compressions higher than in more solid states of matter. This state of matter exists not only in the Sun, but also in the Earth's magnetosphere, most commonly when air in the atmosphere assumes the plasma state and generates electrical storms.

Solar energy is produced in the star's interior, in its nucleus. There, very high temperatures, reaching 15,000 million degrees Celsius, generate pressures sufficient to produce nuclear fusion reactions. Hydrogen cores are released that are melted in groups of four to form helium nuclei. Every second, 700 million tons of hydrogen are converted into helium ash. The energy generated takes a million years to reach the surface of the Sun. Those are cosmic magnitudes!

The energy produced in the core of the Sun begins its existence as photons, particles of pure energy in the form of gamma rays. Fortunately for all of us, when these photons leave the solar surface, they do so shaped by the form of light that is so beneficial to life on Earth and the solar system in general. Scientists claim that in just one second the Sun releases enough energy to supply Europe's energy needs for 4 million years. There is sufficient power in the interior of the Sun to destroy the whole solar system in the blink of an eye.

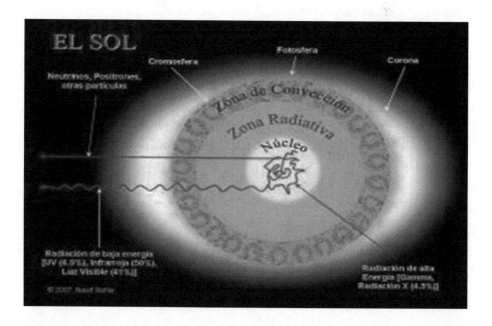

The Sun's energetic heart is surrounded by and contained within a belt approximately 315,000 kilometers thick, referred to as the "radiative zone". The energy generated by nuclear fusion in the core moves outward as electromagnetic radiation. In other words, the energy is conveyed by photons. Newborn photons have to cross this incredibly dense soup of energy and matter in their journey to the exterior. And though they travel at the speed of light and that journey should take just one second, "the time they spend in the journey is 1 million years." What happens during this long journey through the radiative zone remains a great mystery. When the photons finally graduate, they have already taken the form that we know and from which we benefit so much

At the next level, further away from the core, is the so-called "convection zone". At this point, turbulent convective motions occur, in a way that resembles a pot of boiling water. In this zone, the temperature and density are low enough to allow the plasma to move on to a more properly gaseous state. Can you imagine the wonderful spectacle of that huge ocean of hydrogen gas and helium, saturated with enormous quantities of energy in the form of photons ready to embark on their journey toward the exterior?

Photons take about a week to cross this area of turbulence and reach the surface of the Sun, "the photosphere". In this thin layer of some 300 kilometers, the temperature drops to 5,000 degrees Celsius and it is from here that light and heat is radiated to outer space in the form of photons. Most of the energy we receive from the Sun is the visible (white) light emitted from the photosphere. This zone looks somewhat boring at first glance, just a disc with some dark spots. Those sunspots are areas on the solar surface, each the size of a planet, where the temperature drops to 2,000 degrees Celsius. However, scientists have shown great interest in these sunspots because they are associated with strong magnetic fields. These produce changes in the solar activity that seem to correlate with various phenomena on Earth. Some astronomers believe that sunspots are related to certain meteorological events on Earth, including a brief glacial period that afflicted Europe at the end of the seventeenth century.

Even closer to the exterior it is "the chromosphere", a region with very low densities that extends for about 3,000 kilometers from the surface. To the human eye it appears as a thin reddish ring, visible only for the few seconds that precede and follow a total eclipse of the Sun.

As we get closer to the external borders of the chromosphere, a few thousand kilometers from the surface of the Sun, the temperature rises inexplicably, reaching 20,000 degrees Celsius. Finally, we arrive at the "transition region", a small area of some 150 kilometers between the chromosphere and the next zone, where the temperature increases even more dramatically to reach a million degrees Celsius. Very little is known of this region, which precedes "the corona". It remains a mystery and is the least understood of all the areas of the Sun.

The corona extends into space to cover an area larger than the Sun's own physical body, reaching 2 or 3 million kilometers beyond the photosphere, the 'skin' of the star. The temperature here increases even further, achieving a range between 1 and 5 million degrees Celsius. What drives such changes in the superlative heat that emanates from the core of the Sun at 15 million degrees Celsius, first descending to 5,000 degrees Celsius on the surface, later increasing as we move away from the solar surface, to finally reach 5 million degrees Celsius, at 2 or 3 million km from the Sun's core? This is apparently in conflict with the basic laws of thermodynamics. Where does it come from, this thermal increase in the vicinity of the Sun?

The corona is basically an invisible electromagnetic field which, like the chromosphere, can only be observed during a total eclipse of the Sun. This is because sunlight, from an optical point of view, makes the light of the corona invisible when viewed as part of the whole. However, during an eclipse the Moon covers the solar body and allows viewers to see the light of the corona.

What we see at that time is a changing crown that varies according to the sunspot cycles that occur in the photosphere. For scientists, the corona is a great unknown and they have serious difficulties explaining its existence. Nevertheless, modern parapsychology explains that people and living beings in general, have around them an energy field of multicolored light radiation that is invisible to the human eye, but that can be measured with special equipment such as a Kirlian camera.

Kirlian photography is a technique that was discovered by accident in 1939 and is used to capture the phenomenon of electrical coronal discharges. This electromagnetic field is known as the "Kirlian aura" or more frequently just "aura" and is said to reflect the mood of its possessor. I affirm that the corona is an aura of plasma that surrounds the Sun and other stars. Most modern scientists find this statement very difficult to accept because they do not accept the existence of the aura, nor the premise that the Sun is a living being with intelligence and awareness of itself.

Continuing with this descriptive analysis, we turn our attention to one of the most intriguing of phenomena produced in the coronal zone: solar wind. As the distance increases away from the solar surface, its magnetic field decreases. At this point gaseous material is ejected into outer space. This constant flow of material from the corona is the solar wind and is mainly constituted of charged particles, especially protons, electrons and alpha particles. The solar wind is released throughout our planetary system at speeds that exceed 3 million kilometers per hour. You might then ask, what are the effects of this solar wind on each and every one of the planets that make up the system and on the beings that inhabit them?

When the solar wind reaches us, it helps to constitute the terrestrial magnetic field with a pear-shaped configuration. The magnetosphere is formed by the interaction of the solar wind with the Earth's magnetic field. The shape and size of Earth's magnetic field is thus continually changing as it is buffeted by the solar wind.

We move now from astrophysics to quantum physics. This branch of physics describes the phenomena of the Universe from the perspective of probability amplitude. *Quantum* is the Latin word for amount and, in modern scientific understanding, means the smallest possible discrete unit that constitutes the light. Experiments carried out in the most advanced particle physics laboratories have shown that at the smallest level of matter, that of elementary particles, *"everything is energy"*, something that sounds extremely similar to the first hermetic principle: *"the All is mind"*.

To better understand this, we could say that *"matter is condensed energy"* and if you add a further twist you could say that *"matter is condensed light"*, light being both a wave and a particle. That is the dual nature of light and of the Universe. Matter and energy are two ends of the same universal essence: light. Man is made up of that same universal substance, pure radiant light. Recent scientific discoveries are ratifying something that was already known by the wise of earlier times: that "*the human being is in essence light*". With this scientific knowledge in hand, expressions such as "we are beings of light" and many others that have become popular in various religions and philosophies, no longer seem to be fantasies without foundation and thus acquire their true meaning.

The Universe, and everything within it, is a system of energies in continuous vibration; that is to say that the molecules that make up any object, even our bodies, are in constant vibration. Our bodies create electromagnetic energy bands with a defined wavelength, and this allows them to send and receive information simultaneously. In this way, you are in constant communication with a universal matrix of holographic character. This universal matrix is in essence light, and the way in which we communicate with it is a light code. The speed of light, a mathematic constant that reflects the relationship between spirit and matter, macrocosmos and microcosmos, the divine and the human.

Beyond what science is beginning to know about the central star of our planetary system, is the ancient knowledge of Hermeticism. This doctrine teaches that stars, suns, are equivalent to cosmic neurons that make up celestial neural networks. The Sun is a gate of entry through which the Infinite Cosmic Living Being, from whom all things come, transmits and receives information to and from all beings (including objects) that live in the Solar System. Among them is the human being. Each star or sun constitutes a cosmic nucleus whose mission is to transmit the light frequencies that determine the features of every astrological era: the average level of consciousness that the population reaches. The language code used to achieve this is that of the light, the biophoton.

The ancient secret traditions already knew that the Sun was a gateway, a means of access to a higher level of consciousness. In Egypt, Ra was the creator, being the quintessence of all manifestations. Shamas was the Sun god in ancient Mesopotamia. Helios in Greece and Apollo in

Rome represented the solar disk. The worship of Mithra in Iran and Persia was also a solar cult. Inti, of the Incas, Tonatiuh, god of the Sun for the Aztecs, and the North American Lakota Indians' dance of the Sun are just a few of the many examples that reflect the importance of Sun worship in all civilizations. The advent of Pisces and of Christianity formed a parenthesis, although Christianity itself is a religion based on the Sun cult.

This primordial knowledge has been hidden from the great majority of people, due to manipulation generated within Christianity, the human organization that has managed the West's dominant religion for the last two thousand years.

In the coming era of Aquarius, it will become public knowledge that Jesus Christ was the human recreation of a cosmic mystery. The myth of Christ was designed and created by men. That does not, however, diminish the value of his message of universal love and initiatory teachings. In the new age of Aquarius the hidden message of Christ will be disseminated: the preponderant role that the Sun has always played among the wise will be restored, with scientific foundations

In this section I have explained that the observer's point of view is decisive in the vision or perception of prevailing reality. The mystery of the Sun will be unveiled during the Aquarian Age, because the observers' point of view will change in relation to its position during the age of Pisces. In the year 1500, Europeans regarded Earth as the center of the Universe and held that the Sun revolved around the Earth. This geocentric model prevailed and the astronomical observation procedure (self-centered or egocentric) supported it. Nobody questioned its authenticity.

In time, however, the observer's perspective had to change, thanks to the use of the telescope, and ceased to be egocentric. Society realized the illusion in which it was immersed. The observer must be positioned outside the system to avoid this type of mistake. Today, analysts and Biblical exegetes are similarly immersed in an illusion, this time about the figure of Jesus, because their point of observation is located inside their own system, the very system they are observing.

In the Aquarian age it will be known that the story of Jesus of Nazareth, a man-made god, was an invention, a children's theatrical drama, a humanized version of Higher Cosmic Forces. Someone reading these lines may think that the writer has lost his mind when I say that the story and biography of Jesus originated from a human, self-centered point of view.

To understand it in its total magnitude I invite you to differentiate between the message and the messenger, or in other words to set different observation points on the same object, something that is quite difficult at the current state of evolution of human being. Was it not self-centered for humans to think that Earth was at the center of the Universe? And is it not self-centered to think that man is intelligent and the Sun is not?

Mankind has always needed to humanize all cosmic phenomena and place man at the center of the Universe, in order for certain knowledge to be understood by the infantile, dualistic and egocentric minds that prevail in society. However, Christianity, like religions that came before it and on which it is based, is a system of Sun worship and it gives the Sun the importance and recognition that deserves. It just happens that the original Christian texts have been manipulated or hidden.

Christian doctrine is apparently grounded on two aspects: the cross and the figure of Jesus Christ. Throughout the world, people regard the cross as the symbol of Christianity, as a place where the savior of Mankind died. Catholics and Protestants wear crosses on necklaces, bracelets, rings, keychains and other items of clothing. All this seems perfectly natural to most people. After all, Jesus was crucified on a cross...or was He?

What most people do not fully realize is that long before the coming of Christ, pagans used the cross as a religious symbol. The tau form of the cross was used as a pagan Egyptian symbol and later on adopted by Coptic Christians, in Egypt. What are the exact origins of the tau cross? The original form of the Babylonian letter T was †, identical to the crosses used today by Christians. This letter was the initial of Tammuz, a Babylonian god. That mystic Tau was marked in baptism on the foreheads of those initiated into the Hermetic Mysteries. . . The Vestal virgins of Pagan Rome wore it suspended from their necklaces, as nuns do now. . . and there is hardly a Pagan tribe where the cross has not been found.

And about Jesus Christ we should also say that December 25th in the old Roman Julian calendar was the day on which the pagan festivity of *Deus Sol Invictus* (Unconquered Sun) was celebrated. Later, in the times of the Roman Emperor Constantine (306-337) this festivity of the Sun was adopted as its own by Christianity, with the name of the feast of Christmas (from Latin *Nativitas*) referring with it to the date of the birth of Jesus Christ. After all, Jesus was born coinciding with the winter solstice... or was He not?

Nevertheless, Christianity has fulfilled its mission and its true message of love has become popular, but you have to keep in mind that it had a pagan origin and also that the story on which it was based has become a kind of Walt Disney fairy tale. However, to paraphrase Kipling, that is another story for another, later, piece of writing...

The scientific religion of the Aquarian age will teach that you have to get closer to the light, the heat and the life of the Sun, to find the wisdom that illuminates and resolves all problems. To awaken your conscience and turn to Christ means awakening consciousness of the Sun inside of you, something that exists in the ancient yogic path tradition, and thus is not new.

When you can observe your existence from the point of view of the Sun, the ego (the observer point of view is situated on the Earth) is reduced to its minimal expression and ends the illusions that previously imprisoned your inner self. In this way you get a clear and objective view of existence. You gain superior scientifi and spiritual knowledge. This art has been known ever since time began, by certain individuals who have carried the flame of this knowledge with security and discretion, depending on the times. In the Aquarian age comes the moment in which the Water Bearer (Aquarius) will reveal the true knowledge of the Sun (Leo).

By making Samyama on the Sun, (comes) the knowledge of the world.

Yoga Sutras of Patanjali.

In the solar system, the entirety of life depends on the Sun. Vegetables are nourished directly from it through the process known as photosynthesis, a process converting inorganic matter into organic matter used by plants and other organisms to convert light energy into chemical energy. Later, these vegetables are incorporated into the diet of animals higher in the food chain, among them mankind. When you eat, on an energy level you are incorporating solar energy within your organism in the shape of bread, wheat or any other food. Even when you eat meat, the result on an energy level, is that you incorporate into your organism, through the process of digestion, light energy that the animal had itself assimilated.

Can a human being directly feed off the light energy coming from the Sun? There is a technique or ritual called "sungazing", currently popularized by Hira Ratan Manek, that is rapidly gaining popularity. Sungazing is the act of looking directly into the Sun and its origins are lost in the mists of time. To sungaze, all you have to do is contemplate the Sun safely. When you look at the Sun, which is something that only should be carried out during sunrise or sunset to prevent damage, your body receives energy from the star. The human being possesses special organs in the eyes and elsewhere so that in this way you are able to assimilate the energy of the solar biophotons. With sungazing, you prompt your own photosynthesis. This practice of sungazing, during the age of Aquarius, will receive the recognition that it lacks today, and the genuine scientific basis on which it is based will become more widely appreciated.

APPENDIX C

KEYS TO SPIRITUAL AWAKENING

I'm trying to free your mind, Neo. But I can only show you the door. You're the one that has to walk through it.

Morpheus, The Matrix

When you wake up from the dream of the Matrix, then you can perceive the real world, the truth. But what is the truth? Is there an objective truth?

There is huge difference between what is true and what is false. It is falsehood to confuse what is not true with what is true; confuse what is apparent with the real thing; confuse the shape with the essence. If you are unable to distinguish objectively what is true from what is false, you will inevitably live an unreal existence, as a consequence of a fanciful interpretation motivated by a dangerous cultural and philosophic relativism.

In modern societies, an inappropriate cultural mantra has now been adopted, one that asserts that the truth is not objective and that you can only reach your own subjective truth, the apprehension of an objective truth being impossible. I know that way of thinking, where it originated and why... and you'd be surprised at what lies behind it.

Most people on Earth live in this situation, to a greater or lesser degree, without even realizing it. They direct their life in response to completely illusory visions and schemas that exist only in their own minds; that do not have objective existence in an unprejudiced reality. In this way, your vital emotional, cultural and religious responses are taking place on the basis of perceptions and conflicts that exist only in your imagination, that is to say on the basis of stimuli that have never existed as you believe or perceive them to have done.

Each person lives in a completely unique, individual world that corresponds to a particular vision and distorted perception of reality. However, and this is what matters, there is only one Universe in objective reality; all other versions of the Universe exist only in the minds of individuals. This process has been described by oriental wise men since the beginning of time. They thus described existence as Maya. But very few are those who truly understand what it means … because, I say again, the illusion that exists in their mind does not allow them to apprehend what is essential and objective.

Thus, most people are completely alienated from the time and environmental conditions in which they live. They are incapable of seeing, knowing and of course experiencing it … instead, they live in a similar world which is ultimately a copy, a fanciful microverse that is not related to reality. They are the living dead, existing in an imaginary world. As a result, their spiritual essence cannot be expressed in time and space, in the here and now. Existence is Maya and the man does not understand existence, what happens within himself or where he stands in this imaginary context. Surrounded by cobwebs and dreams… he sleeps … It is not strange that he feels lost.

However, it is crucial to understand that it is possible to awaken yourself and to experience the authentic existence that usually stays hidden behind external appearances, and in this way to know the objective truths of the Universe, human existence and indeed any specific situation. In most cases this process must be very gradual, because the experience can be traumatic. There are many opinions but only one truth. However each person thinks that their opinion is the genuine truth, but above those points of view is the objective truth: what is. This truth retains its validity in any spatial and temporal location.

To reach this truth, you have first of all to recognize its existence. We must overcome a false cultural dogma, one that alleges the absence of objective truth and the impossibility of this achievement. This limiting belief has been implanted in human minds with a clear purpose: to keep you away from knowing the truth. If you do not believe that something exists, you won't seek and thus find it

Once this first obstacle has been overcome, it is time to consider an essential element of the truth discovery process: the observer's mental perspective. The key here is your ability to put yourself in the right place as an observer, and in this way to transcend visions or points of view that have originated in your own ego. When I speak of mental perspective I am referring to the ideological, cultural and religious positioning of each person, this being the result of the education, constraints, experiences, beliefs and wishes. The cumulative result of this is a specific position in life and in relation to events. This means that, mentally speaking, each individual remains in a fixed place throughout his existence, and any change that occurs is only apparent. People prefer to stay in a permanent and familiar mental position, rather than live with change; it gives them a false sense of security. But change is the substantial reality of the Universe, as the hermetic Principle of Vibration states: *nothing rests; everything moves; everything vibrates.*

The inability to know the objective truth is a direct resulting of having an unshakeable point of view, since it is not possible to find something when you believe you already know it, or that it is non-existent. This is the main reason why oriental philosophies emphasize the need to empty the cup before you refill it. People are riveted to their beliefs, without being aware of the effects of this position. Indeed, they are often proud of it and even of believing that the inflexibility of their thoughts makes them stronger.

Believing, however, is the opposite of being conscious. Most people only recognize as truth those ideas that have already taken root in their minds. They do not realize that their own mental positioning is actually a firewall that shields them from the truth. Can anyone who lives in a dream distinguish what it is real from what is not? How can anyone who lives in the ego, an illusion, hope to understand what the ego is? How could people in the Middle Ages, living before the invention of the telescopes that allowed people to change their point of observation, be expected to realize that the Sun was not spinning around the Earth?

You should reflect on this to understand it. The truth has many faces, that is to say many viewing angles or perspectives. However, any single face does not encapsulate the whole objective truth. An opinion, generally, emanates from the position of the observer for a single viewing, thus one small part of the truth or rightness that the observer may obtain becomes an evident falsehood.

To understand the damage that is caused by the observer taking an immovable position in a single location (which is the authentic ego) you only have to listen to any discussion to realize how the participants get tangled in a web of semantics, of words and phrases, without getting near the objective, authentic meaning of them, and how the result is obvious miscommunication. If the truth has many viewing angles, it is obvious that you can only reach an objective knowledge of situations if you have the ability to drain your mind of your beliefs and established cultural knowledge, at the same time varying your point of view as an observer. Only by standing in many different mental and emotional locations you can observe the diamond of truth from countless angles.

If you observe a mountain by standing in front of that mountain, it will be impossible for you to see what is behind it. You could be contemplating a dry and arid hillside and behind it may be a fertile green landscape with plenty of trees. Imagine a mountain with 71 different slopes and you will understand how difficult it is to grasp reality. But what if you could carefully observe all sides of the mountain?

I affirm that this is possible! It is possible to get to know the absolute truth, which makes the knower authentically wise. But it is essential for you to understand that this ambition is impossible to achieve while you remain ideologically tied to a single viewing angle, that of your ego. You become rigid, because your thinking flows from an unshakeable mental position. Your own internal attitude makes it impossible for you to access all sides of the truth, to obtain a view of the whole.

Having arrived at this point, what follows is of the utmost importance. How can you get to this much-desired goal? You have to achieve what I will call *"splitting of consciousness"*. Few people will understand the concept. This notion is so challenging because even the idea of consciousness is not, generally, well understood. I hope that you, dear reader, are one of the lucky few who will. To successfully split or dissociate the consciousness (what you perceive consciously) is to perceive situations in a way that transcends association with a particular time and place, that is to say without the consciousness being anchored in a fixed place and time

Must you assume that each person has a fixed, defined character and personality, as well as unchanging behavioral patterns? Is it not possible to conceive the existence of someone de-programmed and therefore not subject to fixed patterns of conduct? Someone who does not exist in a particular way, who does not have a defined personality, but on the contrary, has transcended accepted behavioral, mental and emotional patterns and who thus expresses a higher reality? The splitting of the consciousness or ability to put one's position and perspective as an observer in an unlimited range of positions, at the same time, is vital if you are to apprehend the objective truth of things. In the authentic Initiatory Schools it is taught that all wise men have to become ubiquitous, that is to say, be nowhere and at the same time be everywhere.

I am not trying to kid anyone that this achievement is easy; it corresponds in spiritual alchemy to one of the highest levels of performance, and its achievement requires constant work and sustained sacrifice. Spiritual evolution and spiritual awakening cannot be separated from a process of understanding. Also required is the spiritual ferment that can only be received from someone who has already gone through the process, who has already walked the path: the master of wisdom, the water-bearer. At the same time, it is vital that the neophyte already has a minimum amount of that spiritual ferment, to be able to take advantage of what will be received, doing honor to the ancient texts of alchemy in which it is said that, "*to make gold you must already have gold*", in other words, one has to invest to make a profit

47470677R00190

Made in the USA
Lexington, KY
08 August 2019